SILENT

TOO
LONG

LILITH R. WHYTE, M.D.

Three Women And A Vision Publications

Three Women And A Vision Publications

Paperback ISBN: 979-8-218-96250-0
Hardback ISBN: 979-8-218-96251-7

Library of Congress Control Number: 2023916833

PRINTED IN THE UNITED STATES OF AMERICA

Use Your QR App
To Learn More Today

This book is dedicated to all the brokenhearted,
hopeless, unheard, overlooked, and exploited.

The Message: God sees, hears, and cares ....
and breakthrough is on the way.

Epigraph

"One day you will tell <u>your story</u> of how you overcame what you went through and it will be someone else's <u>survival guide</u>." - Brene Brown.

"And they overcame him (the devil) by the blood of the Lamb (Jesus) and by the <u>word of their testimony.</u>" - Revelation 12:11.

TABLE OF CONTENTS

ACKNOWLEDGEMENTS

Thanks to Chandra Tyler-Mountain, PhD - a special person and friend - for coediting this book with me and being a supportive friend in this venture with telling my story and being a voice to the voiceless and those wounded.

INTRODUCTION

THE TITLE OF this book says it all. This narrative that depicts the earth-shattering testimony the girls and I endured that commenced over ten years ago has been a long time coming, but is finally here. Interestingly, I wrote this book four years ago, but I found this window of time to be perfect for its release realizing that timing is everything. While I share a very difficult chapter in my life with you, I am encouraged and elated that through my transparency someone will be empowered, liberated, and transformed. This narrative depicts the many ways God miraculously intervened for the girls and me during this arduous journey and showed us favor in the inauspicious situations we encountered. We experienced firsthand how having His ever abiding presence makes all the difference. Without Him during this turbulent storm in my life, I realize that this story would be very different and not as inspiring and motivating. Picturing this journey without Him triggers shuddering thoughts. Thankfully, our story has a propitious outcome in spite of the vicious setbacks we braved because we were not alone.

In the following pages, my aim is to walk you through some of the major encounters I faced along the journey up close and personal. Through this narrative, you will vicariously experience our struggles, blessings, and miracles. The anecdotes shared are empowering, inspiring, and potentially life changing. Through my transparency, I pray that you are spiritually, emotionally, mentally, and physically unyoked, validated, and affirmed. In addition, I pray that you realize that partnering with God is a sure checkmate for your enemies or any opposition you meet because with Him you always win - no matter how it looks. I robustly declare this because I am a walking, living, and breathing testimony.

Chapter 1

A Rude Awakening

CONFUSION, SHOCK, BEWILDERMENT, and devastation were just a few of the emotions that bombarded my psyche that day as I grappled with trying to make sense of what had just happened. Was I dreaming or in a trance? I felt as if I were in a "twilight zone" momentarily just trying to awaken from a bad dream – a nightmare! Everything seemed so mysteriously surreal as I struggled with digesting this sudden disturbance and concomitantly answering the myriad of questions that flooded my mind surrounding this incident. What just happened? What went wrong? Who was this imposter? Surely not the love of my life, my soulmate, or my "True North" (borrowed from one of my favorite movies – *"Message in a Bottle"*). This couldn't be. I had never witnessed him like this before. What should I do? Well, for a moment, I had to step back into reality and snap out of my current state of shock as I faced the problem head-on. This was not a figment of my imagination, but a serious dilemma with life-threatening potential. The girls and I were in a precarious situation that demanded immediate attention, as well as a miracle. And that is just what happened that day.

Unbeknownst to me, my devotion time that morning was vital in preparing me for this unanticipated event. When the incident took place, I saw myself at a pivotal crossroad that would influence my future and that of the girls forever. There were no seconds to lose as I instantly sought divine guidance and help to catapult the girls and me to the next level that involved a detachment from the domestic unrest that had surfaced that morning. This separation was more than just removal from the present environment, but a farewell to the family bond we once cherished. It was a memorable day as emotions were unleashed and instability previously concealed was unveiled. The thickness of the hostility in the atmosphere was impenetrable, and my focus in this defining moment was for my girls and me to be liberated from this havoc and settled in a secure place.

As I recall that day in detail from the beginning to the end, I remember waking up early in the morning between the hours of four and five o'clock to start my day per my usual routine. My routine would usually begin before the crack of dawn where I would have devotion first, and then end with some form of exercise before going to the hospital to deliver a baby, round on a postoperative patient, or round on someone admitted for a gynecologic or obstetric problem. I would do this well before the household had awakened to optimize my quality time with the family later on in the evenings after office hours when everyone was awake and available. Having seen my patients at the top of the day, I could dedicate my time after office hours to my family instead of having to go see hospitalized patients then. This would prevent me from getting home late in the evening and trying to spend quality time when everyone was winding down and preparing for bed. Along with allowing me to optimize my time most efficiently, these early hours also afforded a "distraction-free zone" for me to quietly and pensively reflect and meditate. It was before daybreak and the stirring of the household, that I could experience Psalm 46:10, which says to "Be still and know that I am God". I would refuel spiritually during this "me time", which would equip and qualify me for any potential obstacle, threat, or challenge I would encounter that day.

So, as I was carrying out my normal routine that morning, I was suddenly interrupted abruptly by my husband, who I thought was fast asleep. He began hurling questions at me about what I was doing and where I was going this early in the morning as if this was out of my norm. Shockingly, he seemed to insinuate that he was suspicious of me waking up so early to start my day as if I had something to hide and as if this routine was foreign to him. I wondered briefly if he was experiencing temporary amnesia and forgot that I was a physician. To put it more explicitly, I was an obstetrician and gynecologist. So these hours were definitely not foreign to me. And because we had been married for twelve years at the time of this incident, they weren't foreign to him either. I didn't have a hospital obligation every morning, but often enough. So his behavior this morning was baffling, to say the least. In addition to the hospital obligations I mentioned above, I could also get a call from the ER (Emergency Room) for an obstetric or gynecologic emergency that would demand my immediate attention and potential surgery. So I found the inquiries and the accusatory tone he employed as he questioned me that day about my normal daily routine extremely perplexing. He acted as if my schedule and routine that morning were out of character. Initially, I was tempted to be sarcastic because I felt that this was ridiculous and insulting to me as his dedicated wife. I was not just bothered by his accusatory attitude, but hurt as well. However, my conscience dissuaded me from taking an apathetic attitude in jest and being sarcastic with this ridiculous insinuation because this would have only incited anger and fury that I needed to avoid. As I reflect on this incident, I am aware that it was God's voice I heard that day that discouraged me from being provocative during this dialogue. I was so thankful that I was not stubborn or uncooperative with that voice because things would have most likely been a lot worse that day. And I would have been tempted to believe that I triggered the turbulence witnessed later that morning.

My response to him was, "I'm going to the hospital" and he just grunted something under his breath and fell back asleep. So, I proceeded to go out of the room to have my devotion as usual and then get ready to go to the hospital. I was going to forgo exercising that day because I had a busy day ahead of me and wanted to get things started early. I had a full office schedule and surgery that afternoon leaving me no time to waste. While finishing my devotion, I heard my bedroom door open and then heard my husband saying something. He was requesting that I come back to the bedroom because he had something he wanted to talk to me about briefly. I said that I would come as soon as I finished my devotion, which was almost done. Shortly thereafter, I went to our bedroom only to find him fast asleep and unarousable. As I proceeded to close the door while exiting the bedroom, I heard him mumble something with disdain. He mumbled faintly under his breath for me to just forget about it. He sounded frustrated and angry all in the same breath, and I couldn't understand why. I had responded to his request but found him fast asleep, but now mysteriously awake. Upon leaving the room, I went to the kitchen and family room to get my purse and keys when I heard a thump and turned around. Right there in the doorway of our bedroom, I saw him standing there looking deranged. I attributed his appearance to his activity the night before when he was up late drinking, which also explained his behavior that day. As he stood there initially speechless, I realized that he was not fully conscious of what was going on in his current condition. In his inebriated state, I sought to arouse him out of this trance and direct him back to the bedroom and back to sleep so that he wouldn't hurt himself by falling or running into something. I attempted to do this by raising my voice and allowing him to snap out of his confusion and acclimate to his surroundings. It was then that I heard him say, "Why can't you be more compassionate?" I was taken aback. Surely he wasn't referring to me – his dutiful and faithful wife who did everything in her power to please him and make him happy. What an insult, I thought. And, where was all this emotionalism coming from? I chose to ignore the question to prevent triggering an argument and, therefore, I resumed preparing to go to the hospital with the goal to return in time to help the girls get ready for school. I trusted that he would just go back to sleep disgruntled for the moment and we could talk more sensibly later when he was more coherent.

As I went to the refrigerator to get one more thing before leaving, I heard him repeat the question, but with a very dark and frightening voice that seemed diabolical. I turned around to face him and that's when it happened. Without a warning, he lunged forward and began to charge me. While I was standing there paralyzed as if in a daze not believing that any of this was happening, I suddenly felt a strong grip encircle my neck firmly. That's when I snapped back into reality and immediately began to scream until his grip tightened and I felt myself choking to the point of suffocation. Being unable to scream any longer, I desperately struggled to free myself by removing his hand from my neck, but in vain. I faced the fact that I was hopeless - so I initially thought. This became my defining moment when I came in touch with the supernatural. Being forced into this speechless and breathless state of desperation, left me no other recourse but to look to a Source of help superior to all others. That Source is Jesus - the Omnipotent One Who can do the impossible. And that's just what He did that day. Even though my call was inaudible due to my circumstances, God heard my heartfelt cry and instantaneously responded not a moment too late. And miraculously I came out as the victor despite my seemingly powerless and defeated situation. And all because I put my trust solely in God. The Bible texts in 2 Corinthians 12:9 (His strength is sufficient in our weakness) and Isaiah 59:19 (When we're overwhelmed by the enemy, God will come to our rescue if we call on Him) became real and meaningful to me that day as I saw God show up and show out on my behalf at that nearly fatal moment.

As I recall seeing my oldest daughter witness this domestic turmoil at the height of its intensity, I gained strength and a reason to fight to live. The morbid thoughts that previously went through my head entertaining death in this moment of desperation, were all forgotten now. Seeing her internal struggle and fight to save me depicted by her body language at that moment, empowered and motivated me to survive – if only for her and my youngest daughter who were caught up in the mayhem that morning. In life, one's motivation to do something is strongest when someone else is totally dependent on this motivation for their well-being. That day my maternal instinct peaked to new levels when I saw my oldest baby girl – my flesh and blood - agonize as she watched her father almost end my life.

Feeling powerless to do anything, had to be concomitantly frustrating and terrifying for her. If I could turn back the tables of time, I would erase this horrific timeline in her life. But I can't, and I realize that the sorrows of this life will always be present until we inhabit the new earth where there will be no more sorrow, tears, dying, or injustice. Instead, there will always be love, peace, and joy always. However, for now, we have to be patient and persevere to that end. I remember hearing family members expressing how terrible they felt seeing Kelly and Haley going through this emotionally traumatizing ordeal at such young ages (10 and 7 years of age), and I recall telling them that there were children their ages and younger going through much worse unfortunately, so I refused to complain. Ironically, I was familiar with the upbringing of these family members saying these things and their situations weren't a bed of roses during their childhood either. So, I guess they had a momentary bout of amnesia. Nevertheless, I reminded them that in this sinful world, these misfortunes were inevitable, but God promised to comfort us and be with us (Hebrews 13:5,6) and not allow us to go through anything that we couldn't bear (1 Corinthians 10:13). So, we were encouraged with this promise to be strong and endure this test. I told family members that if God allowed this test, who would be bold enough to dare play God and suggest that our current trials were more than we could bear, and declare that we shouldn't have to endure them. I knew that they were just concerned about us, but I cautioned them to trust that God knew what He was doing because He allowed it and we would be stronger when everything was over. I was confident of that because I was determined to make it successfully through the struggles and tribulations before us as I leaned on God for His help and guidance in all the confusion around us. Nevertheless, looking at the face of my oldest daughter in that desperate moment and witnessing the fight in her spirit, gave me every reason to live. That empowering and inspiring vibe I received, awakened hope, courage, and purpose. I was reminded that my baby girls needed me. In the present fiasco that plagued our household that day, I was their sole source of stability and saving grace. I had to come through this victoriously. I had to win!

As I beheld my husband's ambiance of darkness that day and noted the demonic glare in his eyes, I discerned that I was dealing with "spiritual wickedness in high places" (Ephesians 6:12) and clearly understood that I needed to call on my Abba Father, my El Shaddai, and my El Elyon. From a little girl and up to my adulthood, my dad was my "go-to" guy, my hero, my mentor, and my best friend. However, this was one misfortune I had to weather without him as God allowed him to rest in peace on Memorial Day 2003 (nine years before this occurrence). But I was not alone during that vulnerable moment. God hand picked this time in my life to reveal Himself to me in an unforgettable and marvelous way.

Well, needless to say, He proved Himself to me that day and He didn't have to. I discovered Him to be my Father par excellence – my Abba Father on a different level that day. Although I cherish many fond memories of my earthly father responding to my urgencies and needs all throughout my life, this particular day my "heavenly Father" was my sole recourse and I wasn't disappointed. This day marked a very special and memorable moment in my life where He compensated in the absence of my usual paternal support and proved to be an "ever present help in trouble" (Psalm 46:1). He was right there by my side as He has always been all my life (Hebrews 13:5,6) and, consequently, He heard my despairing cry in the drama of things and delivered me not a second or nanosecond too late.

As I screamed when I snapped out of my astonishment, and then suddenly became silent when my husband's grip became suffocating, I sent up an inaudible plea for help and God responded. During the struggle for my life, I felt hopeless and defeated as I focused on my strength, which was obviously far inferior to my husband's. When I redirected my focus on the Most High as I mentioned earlier, it was then and only then that I realized that it's in my weakness that I'm made strong because His strength is activated in this instance and compensates for my lack (2 Corinthians 12:9,10). And because my God is the sole resource of all power as Matthew 28:18 states, His strength is more than sufficient for any problem I have as He proved to me that day. My reliance on God made all the difference. After connecting with the Supernatural One, I immediately felt no more sensation of choking. So, I looked up quickly only to meet the deranged glare of my husband at the time who appeared to still be choking me – only, now he had two hands encircling my neck instead of one and, mysteriously, I didn't feel a thing. The situation was so surreal that I almost failed to execute the phone call to alert the authorities for help due to my amazement. As I located the landline on the kitchen counter using my peripheral vision alone due to the inability to optimally turn my head in this situation, I dialed 911 and told them that my husband was trying to kill me. When he heard this, he suddenly snapped out of his state of confusion and slapped the phone out of my hand and it fell to the floor. Following this, he dashed to our bedroom in a frenzy and I took this time to head towards the girls' bedroom to see about them. I figured that my husband was going through his pretentious front of preparing for the police who were soon to arrive as he strategized to clean himself up, look sober, and appear calm while I looked disheveled and in a hysteric frenzy, which I assume he felt would discredit me to the police. I was fed up with his charades and dishonesty in our relationship concerning his intemperate habits that weighed heavily on the health of our marriage in the last few years before this incident, and I truly felt that we were now at a breaking point that revealed itself that day. Although putting on a facade appeared to be his modus operandi, I didn't waste time worrying about him or his motives. Instead, I chose to make the girls my priority and allow God to handle the rest. They were shaken up and they needed me to console and comfort them. I assured them that we were safe now that the police were on their way because I knew they could trace the call. It was then that the Emergency service called back to complete the call that was interrupted at the time he knocked the phone out of my hand earlier. I answered it and gave them the address just as he was entering the girls' bedroom, which would expedite their arrival now because they didn't have to trace the call.

Upon entry, he immediately hurled accusatory statements towards me claiming that I was villainizing him to the children. I discounted these accusations right away and concluded that the girls could make their own judgment of the situation just by what was apparent that day. He left abruptly and went into the family room. I confirmed that the girls were doing okay at the moment and then joined him in the family room where I planned to address this morning's drama. I noticed that he had changed into some slacks and a dress shirt to look as if he was headed for work at 6:30 in the morning, which was incongruent with his work schedule that normally started around 9:00 a.m. or later. His dress was also incompatible with the jumpsuit he frequently wore to protect himself while inspecting crawl spaces of homes during his inspections. As a residential and commercial inspector and entrepreneur, he rarely scheduled his first appointment before 9:00 a.m. He also was the practice manager for my medical practice and his hours were flexible there too. He would come to the office in the afternoon after his inspections. Therefore, I recognized his intentions to impress and persuade the police in his favor by his appearance, but I was trusting God to vindicate on my behalf. Because I was wrestling for my life earlier, I appeared disheveled and out of my mind, but I believed this would just validate my story of what happened. I discerned that his intention, however, was to make me look crazy in contrast to himself based on our appearances at the time and try to discredit me. But I decided to just trust God to work in my favor because I knew that it would have been apparent to the authorities what the real issue was had they been there to witness things in the height of the drama. In any event, counseling was definitely needed at this point, and would have been helpful before the situation had a chance to reach this level. Quite frankly, in this dysfunctional and broken world that we live in, it's not a bad idea for all of us to get some form of counseling on a routine basis. I am confident that we all have some form or degree of dysfunction and brokenness (some more than others) that could benefit from some counseling - whether it be with a pastor, psychiatrist, psychologist, licensed professional counselor, or a life coach. And then some situations may warrant some serious psychotherapy. Unfortunately, there are times when immediate intervention is mandated to prevent serious repercussions and precarious situations. So, I'm a firm advocate for counseling and believe that Christian counseling, in particular, would save this nation many of its woes.

Nevertheless, I capitalized on this time before the arrival of the authorities to say what was on my heart and mind. This window of opportunity was paramount for me because I didn't know when or if I would have another chance to express my thoughts concerning this memorable morning. I had already made up my mind to take the girls and separate indefinitely while he sought clinical help. I intended to be supportive from afar as much as possible until things calmed down while securing a safe environment for the girls and me. I envisioned him being receptive to rehabilitation, therapy, and anger management classes where I would be one hundred percent supportive of him. I also envisioned him making a complete turnaround allowing us to reconcile and reunite our family once again at some much later date when things had resolved and he had gotten the sufficient help that he needed. I was naive to this process of rehabilitation and in for a major disappointment because before this process could begin, he had to acknowledge his problem and want help for himself. Regrettably, he never acknowledged the problem and, consequently, never got help.

As I joined him in the family room and unloaded my concerns on him about our marriage and what had just happened, surprisingly, he sat there attentively with no opposition. I began by telling him that I was highly offended by his behavior towards me earlier and felt insulted when he insinuated that I was not compassionate with him. Later, when I had more time to reflect on the words exchanged that day, I felt that he was addressing someone else - like a family member - in all of the confusion. I also expressed my surprise and disappointment with him putting his hands on me to choke me in efforts to harm me when his role as my husband was just the opposite. I expressed how this made me feel unappreciated and unloved. I mentioned that from the day I said my wedding vows, I strove to be his soulmate and his "ride or die" wife who would be there for him physically, emotionally, and spiritually. Those were my intentions, although there were days I knew that I fell short. However, like we were informed in premarital counseling, prayer was the key to weather all marital storms and to get us safely through these turbulent times. This chaotic morning exposed the spiritual deficiency in the marriage that led to the discord and dissension we experienced that day. Interestingly, my husband was totally attentive while I vented my frustrations and disappointments and remained quiet and unresponsive the entire time. He appeared to be completely engaged and didn't offer an explanation or rebuttal. When I finally articulated all my concerns, there was a knock on the front door. It was a security guard in the neighborhood who stopped by to see what was going on. It was perfect timing as I was physically and emotionally exhausted and didn't know what to expect from my troubled husband now that I had finished passionately unloading my heart and mind on him.

Opening the door, I saw that it was the security guard of the apartment complex and not the police as I had called. The puzzled look on my face prompted him to explain his visit. He stated that because of all the commotion, he was notified by neighbors that there was a verbal altercation going on in our apartment that was concerning and he came to inquire. We realized then that the privacy we were previously afforded by living in a house, was lost when we temporarily relocated to our current apartment home during our plans to transition to the country. However, the close living arrangements that apartments offer, worked in my favor that day. Neighbors heard everything and alerted security. As we rewind time momentarily and digress for just a minute, I will take the time and update our residential plans that involved transitioning at that time.

My husband and I became interested in country living about two to three years before this incident when we were invited to a week-long training camp in California that taught gardening, food preservation, and survival off the grid. As natives of big cities (Chicago for me and Detroit for him), we were excited for the change and eager to learn the skills for independent living. Upon completion of the course, he and I resolved to transition to the country from our Georgia home in the next couple of years with the deadline being around the time of this incident (2012). Plans were made to get my OB/GYN practice ready to sell as we were almost ready to move into our country home. We had just sold our current city home and transitioned into the apartment that we were in at the time of this altercation. Our next move per our plans would be to our newly built home in the mountains, which was just about complete.

So, redirecting back to the security guard at the door, I let him in and he proceeded to ask me what happened. I explained how my husband almost choked me to death in his inebriated state. My husband responded that I was embellishing the facts and that my story was untrue. He denied that he touched me in a harmful way and accused me of making up the entire ordeal. As he began to give his spiel of what happened, I began to feel hopeless because it appeared that with all of our disputing back and forth, this issue would sadly end up unresolved leaving us to deal with our toxic home environment alone. Just when I thought all hope was gone and that my attempts for help were futile, an APD (Atlanta Police Department) officer walked in through the unlocked door. In a hurry to get things resolved, I had left the door unlocked when the security guard came in earlier which left the door unlocked for this police officer to enter almost unannounced. The Atlanta police officer came directly to me as if he and I were the only two in the room and asked me if my husband had put his hands on me. He completely ignored the security guard present and his futile efforts to resolve the matter. When my response was yes, the police officer asked if I felt threatened. My response was yes again. He then asked if there was anyone that could validate my story and this is when complete silence overtook the room. The silence was so thick that one could cut it with a knife. Of course, it seemed like forever as this awkward and prolonged silence lingered on momentarily, but my sister, who was visiting over the weekend, eventually confirmed my story and the police officer asked what I wanted to do at that point. Instantaneously, and without much thought, I said that I would like for us all to pray about this. This was my fail-safe and I felt that it was definitely needed now. I had never been in a situation like this before and realized that the decision made at that moment would strongly impact our family one way or the other – either negatively or positively. Needless to say, this was obviously not the answer the officer was looking for as he and the security guard had very confused looks on their faces when I made that suggestion as if I had said something insane. I knew at that point that my response would probably be the laugh for the day later when this police officer conveyed this scenario back at the police station. Nonetheless, the officer looked at me very respectfully and informed me that prayer at the moment was not an option as politely as he could. He also cautioned me not to prolong things as he needed to know right away so that he could tend to other things on his agenda that day requiring his prompt attention. I whispered a prayer as I felt the weight of the girls' and my future weighing heavily on my shoulders. My answer would either be courageous and lifesaving or timid with baleful consequences. I opted to have him arrested. This was one of the hardest things for me to do in my life, and because this experience was unknown to our household, it completely caught me off guard that morning. Severing a bond that I vowed and hoped to keep for the rest of my life was never on my marital purview as a wife, which made this moment even more difficult. As I considered the difficulty the girls would experience witnessing their dad get arrested, I also realized that it would be equally disconcerting for them to observe him get off the hook for nearly killing their mom. It was here in this pivotal moment that I realized that the quandary was real. Had they witnessed him get off the hook or go without penalty for his harmful actions that day, this would have been hard for them to process and would have weakened their faith in the justice system. But because of their love for him, it was equally difficult to see him apprehended. Thankfully and prayerfully, I came to a timely conclusion that he needed to be arrested not only for our safety but for his as well. I didn't want him to do something unwise in his present emotional instability and have major regrets later. While they handcuffed him, I chose not to watch so that my emotionalism would not cause me to interfere with the process and change my mind. He asked the policeman if he could say one last thing to me before they escorted him out of the apartment in handcuffs. His request was granted, and he turned to me and began ranting something that left me totally clueless. Later when I made out what he mumbled, I realized that he had concocted a flawed story in an attempt to excuse his aggressive behavior that morning and shift all blame and guilt to me. He alleged infidelity on my part, which I considered unthinkable. With my work schedule, the kids, the dog and him, there wasn't much space to breathe, let alone time to engage in an extramarital relationship even if I wanted to. And he was aware of this. Therefore, I recognized this for what it was - an attempt to shift blame. I must say that this rubbish gesture took me aback as it registered to me what he was doing - deflecting. Determined not to play into his strategy of deflection, I offered no rebuttal – just simply ignored the spurious accusations. But I recognized that he was preparing to concoct a bogus police report, which I learned later on that he did.

After he was escorted out of the door, I immediately embraced the girls and fell to my knees, and prayed for him. I prayed sincerely for his deliverance from his current troubled condition. It hurt me to see him in such a vulnerable and demoralized state. My love for him didn't wane immediately after this disgraceful episode, so I was very concerned about his behavior that day and his overall well-being. In fact, right after we prayed for him, along with everything that had transpired, I told the girls that I forgave him. I explained to them that forgiving him for everything was important for his healing as well as ours. Coincidentally, I had attended a "Forgiveness" seminar sponsored by the women's ministry department at one of the local churches two weeks before this occurrence and resolved not to let issues with forgiveness keep me out of heaven or deprive me of my quality of life. Fortunately, as I recollect on things, I see how God orchestrates everything perfectly, and how my attendance at that seminar wasn't a coincidence at all. God had prepared me for my test and trial, and now it was my responsibility to pass this test with the help of the Holy Spirit. Little did I know that I was entering "Forgiveness Course 101" and I had a lot to learn. I would learn through this present journey as Peter learned with Jesus' response in Matthew 18:22, that there is no limit to forgiveness of someone who has wronged me or continually wrongs me. I am simply admonished as a Christian to forgive that person every time they offend me – no matter how many times that happens. Forgiveness has no limit with Christianity. However, I also learned that God doesn't desire for us to put ourselves in harm's way imprudently and He doesn't call us to be martyrs in a fruitless cause either, especially at the expense of fulfilling the mission He has for us in this life. So we are admonished to remove ourselves from unsafe environments and situations with His help and guidance.

As I prepared to take the girls to school and start my day, I stopped to do a "wellness check" and see how they were doing. I apologized profusely for what they had seen and heard, but they just looked at me with blank stares that troubled me. When I asked them what was wrong and what they were thinking, they simply responded that their dad belonged in prison. Completely stunned by their response at such young ages (10 and 7), I realized that I needed to probe a little deeper with them to make sure they weren't referring to more than what they had witnessed that day. I was completely floored with their indifference as they calmly asserted this explicit remark. So, I inquired if they had anything they wanted to share with me concerning their dad and they said no. However, I mentally registered that I would have to revisit this concern later after hearing their blatant response that morning because there was no time to delve into things sufficiently then. Later we would be able to talk unrushed and in a more comfortable and relaxed setting. However, for now, our concern was getting to school on time and talking to the administration and the girls' teachers about letting that day be their last day for school since the school year was almost at its end with only two weeks left. Their exams were already completed with the grades due the following week, so the school year was essentially over academically and at this point, they really wouldn't be missing anything. The last week would be for recreation as grades were finalized and any issues with the process resolved then. The request went well, and they were transitioned out of school that day without a problem. I was so thankful that this process was uneventful because I didn't want to deal with the possibility of their dad visiting the school and starting any commotion when he was released after being bailed out by his father who informed me of his plans when he learned of his son's situation. Concerns were also raised about the girls' peers and teachers inquiring about their family drama and putting them in an uncomfortable position where they may feel compelled to answer the inquiries. Therefore, ending their school year early gave them a much-needed break to begin to recover from the domestic trauma and its emotional sequela. It also relieved my uneasiness about all social interactions for the girls in their present vulnerable state. Thoughts of school options for the girls in the fall raced in my head as I figured that this family drama would not be short-lived, and the girls would be better off at another school until things were completely resolved. Their summer break was only a couple of months, and this certainly would not be sufficient time for them to mentally and emotionally recover and recuperate from everything. Nor would it be adequate time for the domestic dilemma to be fully straightened out. But that was a subject for another time. Right now, we had to focus on more immediate concerns which involved getting them through school that day. I also had to get to the office and see patients and perform a cesarean section that afternoon just before picking the girls up from school. With their father in jail after that morning's ordeal, all parental responsibilities fell on my shoulders and I was compelled to adjust my schedule to meet these additional duties now that I was suddenly and involuntarily thrown into single parenting. Thankfully, the girls successfully got through school that day without incident and I was equally fortunate in the office and hospital.

Chapter 2

~~

THE MINISTRY OF THE
WOUNDED HEALER

IT NEVER CEASES to amaze me how God answers prayers long before a request is ever uttered or the need for the request is even realized. The following testimony is a powerful example of this blessing and animates the Bible promise of Isaiah 65:24. Reflecting on this memorable moment arouses warm and tender emotions that still touch my heart as if the occurrence happened just yesterday. The story started with me dropping the girls off at school that day following that morning's fiasco. They were just 10 and 7 years of age at the time with fragile, unassuming, and innocent hearts and minds. So, our prayer that morning was for God to comfort them and to put a protective hedge around them as we separated temporarily for the day. Well, thank God for His omniscience and omnipresence. He knew exactly what was needed, who needed what, and how to deliver it. Kelly, my oldest daughter, had a different experience that morning than Haley, who was somewhat oblivious to what had happened and didn't witness the event visually – only audibly. Kelly lamentably witnessed both. She was actually in the same room when the life-threatening event occurred. Therefore, the mental and emotional anguish that Kelly suffered was unique when compared with that of Haley – not only because she was older and more mature, but also because she witnessed everything, which involuntarily involved her in this domestic incertitude. Consequently, Haley's initial response was less intense and less passionate than that of her sister's, and understandably so because she processed things differently being a couple of years younger and she didn't observe things directly that morning. However, Haley soon became my little bodyguard like her sister as she witnessed things moving forward. But on this particular morning, God chose to focus His attention on Kelly.

Digressing for just a moment, I saw how both girls became my official full-time bodyguards following the ordeal. I would jokingly refer to them as my two little "pit bulls" because from that moment forward, they were. They were aggressive and serious about protecting their mommy (me) and shielding me from all harm. And logically, this was my plan concerning them as well. I took advantage of this positive energy and assertiveness they exuded by mentally role-playing an emergency response for any similar threatening encounters they might witness in the future – whether with us or someone else. This emergency response plan involves one of them calling 911 to secure police backup while the other sister calls for help from someone nearby. Sounds like a CPR training course, right? Well, this drill can be lifesaving for someone in a toxic life threatening situation just like CPR is lifesaving for someone experiencing cardiopulmonary compromise or arrest.

In any event, now that I have digressed, I will redirect back to dropping the girls off at school that morning. This was very difficult for me to do as my maternal sentiments mentally fought against leaving the girls alone anywhere without my emotional support to buffer them especially on that particular day after all they endured that morning. But knowing all that I had to accomplish that day, I begrudgingly left them as I headed to my office with plans to expeditiously complete my tasks and pick them up promptly later. As I drove to my office, I was continually plagued with dreadful and anxious thoughts concerning the girls' emotional health at school that day as I recounted all that they had psychologically suffered just minutes ago. Refusing to be a worrywart, I chose to leave them in God's hands and trust Him to protect their emotional stability as we had prayed during our devotional time earlier. I knew that His watchcare trumped all others - including mine, so I resolved to be at peace.

Upon arrival at school that morning, the girls went to their respective classes as usual and started their day as if nothing happened. I had already reassured them that I would be withdrawing them from school at the end of the day and they wouldn't have to deal with the public after that day for a while. They were content and comforted with this plan and just concentrated on getting through the present day. Well, Kelly informed me later that day that she had an interesting encounter in the bathroom prior to starting class that day. When she went to the bathroom that morning, she was very emotional and attempted to get her emotions together before going to class so it wouldn't be evident what had transpired in her home that morning. However, she was unsuccessful and began crying. She was met by a close friend in the bathroom who saw her crying and inquired what was wrong. As Kelly divulged the profile of her morning events, her girlfriend shared a similar experience from her household that revealed some marital and domestic discord as well. The two began sharing freely about their concerns for their troubled families while they cried and comforted one another. This mini pow wow in its unusual setting proved to be a rather unique and impressive therapeutic session for the girls. It provided a sense of identity, belonging, security, support, and empowerment temporarily while they struggled with their hidden pain and shameful domestic secrets. Realizing they had limited time before the start of class, they committed to update each other often and be there for each other now and in the future as they prepared to go to class that morning. As they regrouped before entering class, they felt the strong urge to put their socially-acceptable masks back on for the day and pretend that everything was just fine to avoid drawing unnecessary attention to themselves that they believed could potentially make their domestic matters worse.

When Kelly relayed this experience to me later that evening at the end of the day, I was inundated with emotions as I recognized God's hand in orchestrating the entire encounter. I immediately began to praise and thank Him as my daughters looked puzzled by my response and behavior. I took time to explain to them that this occurrence was not by happenstance but was ordained by God to provide comfort and encouragement to them in their despair – an answer to my heart-felt prayer. Out of the myriad ways God chose to comfort Kelly that morning, He chose the relatable application of a personal peer to peer approach where two individuals on the same level could share and dia-logue about similar apprehensions. What a profound and impactful way to indelibly impress a young mind and heart. This technique is equally effective with individuals of any age and endorses the concept of support groups where individuals can find acceptance, encourage-ment, inspiration, and support. I am left speechless and amazed when I contemplate how God used the life-transforming tools of empathy and transparency with these two young girls who were clueless about its ability to uplift, motivate and comfort them. God knew that con-sidering the circumstances, professional counseling would have to be for a later time when things settled down, however, for now, He com-pensated perfectly. The more I contemplate on this scene, I can attest that God knows what's best for us. So, we make the best decision when we leave everything in His hands. This bond that was created that day, was just the beginning of future encounters where the girls and Kelly's friend would be there for each other in times of need. That therapeutic encounter Kelly experienced that day, impacted her powerfully and positively as no other incident has since then.

As time went by, our home became a haven for Kelly's friend to come and share her frustrations and concerns as we shared ours. It was a place where she could let her hair down, take the public mask off, and be transparent with the girls, and just bond together as they did the same. She felt comfortable sharing as she realized that this information would not traverse the walls of our home and there would be no criticism, censorship, or condemnation – it was strictly a "judgment-free zone". Therefore, an environment was provided for my daughters and her to feel safe, secure, and supported. The principle of bearing one another's burdens mentioned in Galatians 6:2 of the Bible was observed to be reciprocal and rewarding as the girls saw that as they supported their friend, they too felt supported. Their prayer life was strengthened as they came to know Jesus as their Confidant, Advocate, and Best Friend. I stressed that all the sharing, supporting, and bonding was futile if they weren't connected with the Life Source – Jesus. This connection I informed them was vital because He is the reason we "live and move and have our being" (Acts 17:28 ESV). When they felt deserted by family and friends, they saw how His promise to never leave or forsake them was proven to be true through their own experience. He was always there - just a prayer away (Hebrews 13:5-7). Although they were familiar with these Bible verses, these promises came to life through the trials they endured. I can attest that my spiritual life soared to new levels when I witnessed the promises of God firsthand in my life. They suddenly became real and my spiritual eyesight sharpened, along with my spiritual perception. I no longer had to resort to living vicariously through the lives of the prophets and disciples in the Bible to see the hand of God. I had my own stories to tell of His majesty and power through this journey that lasted several years and is still ongoing in its final stages. I found Him to be Jehovah Jireh, Jehovah Nissi, Jehovah Shalom, and Jehovah Rapha - all these roles intertwined into one in my life. And I was glad to see the girls make this discovery as well. As time went on, we had some "girl nights" where Kelly's friend came with her mother and younger siblings and we shared and emoted through the night. These occasions were treasurable during this unfavorable time in our lives.

Throughout our journey, I found it interesting that God seemed to frequently position us where we could empathize with someone else going through a similar experience and support them. I recall several women of various ages at my church who approached me at different times in this trial to inquire about my situation. Each time, I thought it was to help the girls and me in our current predicament. On the contrary, it turned out to be an opportunity for me to share my testimony with them about what God had done and was doing for the girls and me despite our existing plight, and to be a source of empowerment for them and others in similar crises, or to just encourage those suffering a low time in their lives to hang on in there while they awaited their change. I assured them that they too could be delivered mentally, emotionally, spiritually, and physically like me because God is no Respecter of persons and His love, comfort, joy, and presence are available to all. Praise God that His love is inclusive and not exclusive. Because of these divinely ordained opportunities, my outlook brightened, and my perspective on the situation changed allowing me to do a 180-degree turnaround regarding my current adversity. I began to see how God was using me in this current ongoing trial to minister along the way and to prepare me for the ultimate ministry He was designing for me when the trial was over.

The title of this chapter conveys a weighty message that speaks of the potential that one possesses to motivate and empower another life going through similar hardships and trials. This is not a new concept by any means, and we've all heard this message communicated in various ways. Motivational speaking and testimonies are some familiar methods employed. During the aftermath of this initial storm that destroyed my household and marriage, I also concluded that professionals are in a crisis when it comes to having resources and support groups to connect with when they find themselves in day-to-day "real life" situations that are destructive to their families, homes, and overall self-worth. Who can they turn to in their time of need? Where is their support in a crisis? They are so focused on the patient or client (or student), that they often overlook their own problems and needs. I can recall reaching out to the various medical organizations in 2012 in my crisis and I was disappointed that there were no feasible organizations or support groups specifically for professionals to aid me with my current dilemma. Although professionals pride themselves on wholeheartedly tending to the needs and issues of their patients and clients, a disservice is done to the patients and clients when the professional has no avenue to recharge, refuel, and exhale. Without this reprieve, the overall health of the professional is suboptimal which compromises their competency in dealing with the needs of the patient/client (or student). Hence, they are operating on "empty" and have nothing to give or contribute to the physical, emotional, and spiritual well-being of their patients (students). This then becomes a tragedy to the healthcare system and professional world on a large scale. For this particular problem that I viewed to be inconspicuously prevalent, I saw the vision God gave me to be a resource of hope in meeting the needs of this social dilemma as well as other social concerns and crises. In this vision, I would spearhead professional support groups and would become a motivational speaker, along with other professionals unafraid of being transparent concerning their vissicitudes in this life and how to navigate successfully in spite of them. Through this transparency manifested, other colleagues will have the opportunity to be empowered and inspired. This arrangement would also provide a safe atmosphere for professionals to exhale confidentially. In essence, this ministry would not only serve as an advocate for resolving the social needs of clients, but those of professionals as well - anyone in need - as lives are transformed.

As I recollect on other experiences revealing the positive impact of camaraderie, I think of the time when I went to get my TPO (Temporary Protective Order). The concept revealed in the title of this chapter was strongly conveyed in the scenario surrounding this event. Little did I know that pursuing this restraining order would be more than a notion. I was not prepared for the loopholes I would have to jump through to obtain this very important temporary court order that would serve to protect the girls and me. The antagonism faced during this pursuit was mind-blowing and served to give me more understanding as a provider when making referrals for patients to seek these much-needed social services. The light shed during this entire process served to ignite a spark inside of me to be an advocate for victims in these settings and somehow find ways to make a difference. I also felt the concomitant burden to advocate for assistance programs to help the predator as well because without dealing with the root cause of this domestic turmoil experienced in today's society, the problem would remain prevalent and essentially go on unchanged. It's synonymous with treating the symptoms instead of the disease in medicine, which only serves to mask the disease in the long run and not eradicate it, which can be deadly. For example, if a patient comes in complaining of nausea and abdominal pain and I (the healthcare provider) choose to forgo ordering laboratory tests and imaging studies in my evaluation, but just treat the nausea and abdominal pain instead with antiemetics and analgesics, I could have a real medical catastrophe on my hands that could possibly be life-threatening because I don't have a diagnosis. Therefore, the symptoms will continue to be a problem because I haven't identified the source to stop them. Bypassing the imaging and laboratory evaluation ignores the methods used to detect the disease and to treat it so the symptoms can abate and the disease can be eradicated. When only the symptoms are treated (e.g. nausea and abdominal pain), they will be recurrent and possibly fatal because their root cause (the disease) is still not treated but left to fester. Some of these life-threatening possibilities could be acute appendicitis, acute cholecystitis, bowel obstruction, ectopic pregnancy, and the list could go on and on. Pardon me, I was having a google and medical moment. Nevertheless, you get the point. Any one of these medical emergencies ignored or overlooked can end up in death.

Similarly, ignoring the perpetrator who is considered to be the disease in this analogy, and solely focusing on the victim represented as the symptoms, can lead to death which usually involves the victim, and seldomly the perpetrator in cases of self-defense. Well, now that I've digressed to my medical world briefly to explain my rationale in being equally intentional and passionate about treating both parties - the perpetrator and the victim, I'll drift back and continue with expounding on the powerful message in the title of this chapter. The courthouse setting, where sisterhood was illustrated at its best, depicts this message beautifully. It was definitely a memorable and life-transforming occurrence that ignited a flame in my spirit concerning the ministry God was preparing for me. It also served as an eye-opener to me as a primary care provider for women as I mentioned earlier.

Recalling this experience, I remember awakening early this weekday morning and planning to get an early start in applying for a temporary protective order. It was a month or so after the incident and although emotions had settled some, we still traveled everywhere together – the girls and me. We were inseparable unless I had to go to work, and then my mom would keep them. And at this time, we had relocated from our apartment and didn't have a permanent residence yet, but were transitioning. I was thankful that my mom – affectionately known as "Nema" to all her grandchildren - came from out of town to help me when all the chaos commenced. I didn't have any biological family locally, so we welcomed my mom with open arms as she came to support us. With the summer break being in effect and school officially out, all four of us made the trip down to the courthouse that day. Unbeknownst to us, the application process was done in a designated room of the courthouse where children were not allowed. The only individuals allowed in the room were the caseworkers and other staff from the Department of Family and Children Services, along with the applicants. Thankfully, mom was there to watch the girls during this long, laborious, and frustrating process. We were not prepared for this lengthiness, and all I could think about was this overwhelming inconvenience for the young ladies who lacked family support or who were financially challenged in this current crisis. With my newly adopted "VA" ("Victim's Advocate") mindset, I could sympathize with the ladies who were unable to afford childcare services so that they could apply for this desperately needed temporary protective order. Those who could afford the services through Medicaid or other government assistance programs were still put in a bind during this application process because the time required exceeded the coverage for childcare in most cases. So, these specific young ladies just had to take the risk of investing all this time and possibly having it wasted if they had to leave in time to get their children before the completion of the process. If this wasn't frustrating enough, they would have to start all over the following day or whenever they returned. The women who were too financially challenged to take advantage of any childcare services available and couldn't qualify for the government-assisted programs that provided free or discounted childcare, were really in a bind. They fell into this quandary because their household income disqualified them for government assistance even though it proved to be insufficient for their day-to-day needs. Other challenges involved being able to adequately articulate one's dilemma or traumatic experience and then express it in writing. In addition to these hurdles, one also had to sound and appear credible to a "no-nonsense" and "zero tolerant" judge later in the process that manifested an unfriendly and harsh demeanor. So, I found these discoveries to be very disturbing and unsettling as I witnessed these loopholes in the system that prohibited some victims in dire need from getting the help and protection that their cases demanded.

I also found it equally troubling that the spirit of nonchalance permeated the atmosphere as the staff appeared to be "doing business as usual" and to be outwardly numb to the pain that I thought I only felt as I sympathized with my fellow suffering sisters who were left hopeless and disappointed as they were devoid of options that day. This apathetic attitude disturbed me terribly because it manifested an insensitivity that was hurtful to these broken, mistreated and despondent females who needed just a little glimmer of hope manifested by a compassionate, caring, and understanding staff. A smile, an encouraging word, a warm greeting, an attentive listening ear, or an encouraging hug were gestures I envisioned seeing in such a setting to inspire, motivate, empower and heal these distraught ladies. Unfortunately, I didn't witness any of these signs of compassion and sympathy that day. Instead, I just sensed a cold and callous milieu that felt so inhumane. I later realized that the caseworkers and administrative help were most likely emotionally inundated and burnt out with the multitude of cases witnessed daily and not insensitive at all, but equally frustrated with the limited help. As I stood there as a victim myself, I was empathetic with the despair and anguish felt by my sister victims that day who found themselves in a conundrum because of the lack of support exuded by the system in securing the critical help and aid needed. Consequently, I committed to learning more about the resources available for females in these situations so that I could help bridge the gaps in the system that dealt with life and death issues. I felt this was paramount in providing real help and saving lives. I also came to grips with the realization that I couldn't be in the soup kitchen distributing soup when I was in the soup line myself. In other words, I felt that I couldn't be of any help to my sister victims when I myself was a victim seeking help just like them and was in no position to be of assistance to them in my current situation. Now, usually, this thought process would be logical, but God revealed to me that day a different way of thinking. He was showing me a new thing. Hallelujah!! After all, He says that His thoughts and ways are different from our thoughts and ways (Isaiah 55:8,9). He would reveal this new thing to me through this experience that I would treasure and remember forever.

Earlier I mentioned that the TPO (Temporary Protective Order) application process took place in a large room in the courthouse and children weren't allowed. So those devoid of childcare were not allowed to apply until these arrangements could be made. As I entered the room, I was immediately intimidated by the large size of the room and all the tables where applicants were engaged with the various caseworkers. Some were standing along the walls or seated by themselves indicating that they had already completed the process. After walking in the door, I was met by a woman at a desk with a blank expression who addressed me with a harsh and loud question asking why I was there. I expressed that I was seeking to obtain a TPO and she asked loudly in an unprofessional and nonconfidential manner why I was applying for it. Embarrassed by her lack of discretion and courtesy, I stated that my husband tried to kill me. Because I was compelled to speak up, my response was heard by others in the room and I instantly became the center of attention by default for the moment. Shamefully, I followed the instructions and began the process to expedite getting my TPO and then, hopefully, to mentally erase this nightmare. As I digested what had just taken place then and earlier with the childcare issues, I became perturbed and bothered by the overall insouciance observed thus far when initiating this process. I grieved as I personally felt the paucity of solicitude for individuals like myself that day in grave predicaments necessitating an immediate solution. This was a very uncomfortable and heartbreaking scene for me to engage in, but God sustained me (2 Corinthians 12:9). As I was led to a table to sit and express what happened in writing, I heard someone mention my professional name – not Lilith Whyte, but Dr. Whyte. My first thought tempted me to cringe due to the awkwardness and disgrace I felt that someone now knew of my deplorable domestic situation as a professional after witnessing everything in this embarrassing moment. But because transparency is usually my middle name, I quickly recalibrated and turned around to respond. When I tried to find the person who said my name, I was unsuccessful. Apparently, someone recognized me but stayed incognito when I attempted to discover who they were. So, I concluded that I didn't know them and they didn't know me. They only knew "of me". With the community outreach I participated in on occasion and as a healthcare professional in the commuity, this person could have been anybody. Nevertheless, I didn't waste time trying to figure this mystery out because I purposed to get things done quickly and relieve my mother and the girls from their long wait. It was just so odd and uncomfortable for me as a professional as I thought about the possibility of a patient recognizing me in this setting and deducing from this mishap that I was no longer capable of fulfilling my role as a healthcare provider. Unfortunately, this fear is real in our society today where we professionals are falsely viewed as demigods and not the humans that we actually are. This is where the ministry I envisioned would also be helpful to professionals because it would provide them with a safe place to download freely with their peers and colleagues and find support. So the large umbrella of this ministry would deal overall with the reconciliation of impaired relationships ("The Ministry of Reconciliation") while encompassing several ministries below this umbrella that would also serve to repair broken relationships and broken lives. Whether the problem was parenting or marital issues; social issues; bullying issues; substance abuse issues; domestic violence issues; grief issues, or financial issues, the ministry would offer support through resources and counseling. The ministry for the professionals would be under this umbrella also, but be physically separate to alleviate the negative impact that these issues could potentially have on their careers and reputations in the professional world. Hence, the threat of losing clients, patients, or students while suffering a life challenging event exposing their humanness as professionals, would not be a problem. For example, with teachers suffering misfortune, they wouldn't have to lose the respect of faculty and students just because they were facing a common vicissitude of life that is oftentimes inevitable.

In any event, I began writing the details of my incident as instructed in the application process to get things started for this TPO application to be completed. During this time, it registered to me that this was not a simple task for everyone. I loved writing, so I was not disturbed by this requirement in the application process for a TPO. I just had to organize my thoughts and give the pertinent details.

However, I realized that some people felt more comfortable articulating their experience rather than writing about it, which I noticed that day among some of the ladies. Consequently, this request served as an impediment to them as they tried to optimally convey their experience. But the desperation to be safe by procuring a TPO, compelled these ladies to complete the process as best they could. After completing the essay that described the event in detail, the caseworker reviewed it and then had to rewrite it in her own words to include what she considered to be significant which created a painful process of pure redundancy. This took some time, and before I knew it, two hours had passed by during this lengthy and burdensome process. After the caseworker completed her rewritten version of what she extrapolated from my essay, I was asked to wait along the side of the room for the court hearing that afternoon where the other ladies that had already completed the application process were also waiting. There was only one TPO court hearing that day and it was at 4:00 p.m. and would normally take about two hours which I discovered later was typical in these instances. The two hour process was explained by the fact that this court hearing was usually the only one for the day and it had to serve all the applicants for that day. This was another reason why this entire process was difficult for those with childcare coverage that typically ended at 6:00 p.m. Regardless of how early I arrived that day, the final decision would only be made after the court hearing that afternoon, which was at 4:00 p.m and would routinely take two hours. At that time, the judge would determine which case warranted a TPO. The judge would do this by reviewing the caseworker's revisions, scrutinizing the clients' responses to the inquiries made in the hearing, and then make her decision. Now that I completed this process, I just had to mentally prepare myself for this long wait before the court hearing which initially seemed like forever. Because it was only about 1:00 p.m. at the time, I was compelled to find something to occupy my time until 4:00 p.m. This wasn't easy because there were no televisions. We just had our cell phones and the batteries were almost dead. Furthermore, we were only allowed to leave the room to go to the bathroom or to briefly communicate with family or friends outside the room who had accompanied us. Many resorted to using their cell phones to isolate themselves in their private shells as they attempted to speedily pass the time away. Some ladies got into small groups and talked, while others fell asleep seated at the tables used earlier. As everyone seemed to settle down and prepare to wait patiently for the afternoon session, the caseworkers finished their last case and left us in the room with an attendant who would supervise things from that point on until the hearing. The attendant was a young lady who appeared somewhat friendlier than the staff earlier. She informed us that if we had anyone waiting outside the room they could come in and wait with us now that the interviewing process was over and confidentiality was no longer an issue. She made this allowance because she was trying to accommodate us since we were instructed to wait inside the room. So those outside came in and found their friends or family members who they would accompany in the long wait. I went to check on the girls, and the girls decided to stay outside in the hall with their electronics. I had been outside a little while talking to the girls to assure their safety and contentment before going back in. When I returned to the room, I glanced over and saw a large group of the women talking and emoting together. As I was approaching the group to see what was going on, I was stopped by two young ladies who asked me why I was there and I shared my story and they shared theirs and we consoled one another as we emoted together. We then decided to join the larger group and found them to be sharing their stories. I chimed in and shared my story as I gave praise and thanks to the Most High Who had seen my babies and me through our life-threatening tragedy and was currently sustaining us. Little did I know that there were many more hurdles of dismal circumstances to overcome that He would see us through along this seemingly endless journey. As I looked around and saw all the tearful and distraught faces looking hopeless and desperate, my heart was broken. My "provider mentality" as a healthcare provider for women was stimulated by this scene, and I sought to resolve this dilemma in some miraculous way, but only became more frustrated as I recognized that I too was a victim needing help and assistance in the same circumstance. That's when God showed me once again the ministry of the wounded healer where I actually could make a positive difference in someone's life. As I shared my testimony about His miraculous deliverance and expressed my gratitude to still be alive, all eyes were focused on me as they listened attentively to the miracle God wrought in my life. Those listening agreed that God had sustained us all through the difficult times we had faced thus far and we were grateful despite our current circumstances. We all witnessed a shifting in the atmosphere in that moment as Jason Nelson sings about in his song, "Shifting the Atmosphere" as we expressed our thankfulness to God. This was one of the songs that carried the girls and me through our journey. This shifting involved the Holy Spirit permeating the atmosphere with His presence creating a serenity that was almost surreal. As the sharing continued and others told their stories, emotional wounds surfaced and healing began right there in this "upper room" experience similar to what occurred on the day of Pentecost spoken of in the book of Acts in the Bible. Through all of the tears, embracing, consoling, and empowering, the Holy Spirit was transforming lives in this window of time. Troubled faces were instantly changed into countenances of peace and contentment. If someone was passing by and didn't know any better, they would think we were in a church service. Love, peace, and empathy permeated the atmosphere as everyone experienced a little taste of heaven on earth during these precious moments. These were precious and treasurable moments that were very inspiring, empowering, and life-transforming. Chains were definitely broken that day as individuals were emancipated from their hopelessness, discouragement, and dejection. It was a beautiful scene as the room was suffused with a nurturing and liberating spirit. All we needed that day was a pastor to make the altar call because the Spirit (the Holy Spirit, i.e.) was moving in a mighty way. Lives were being transformed and burdens were being lifted as prayers went up. It was so surreal that I felt like pinching myself to confirm that I wasn't dreaming. Remembering the pervasive attitude of nonchalance experienced earlier made this new shift in the atmosphere unexpected. But it was a welcome and refreshing occasion that had the potential to forever change the lives of all those involved.

As time elapsed and we got closer to the time of the hearing, we decided to band together and support each other through the remaining process. We did this by having everybody recite their stories in preparation for the court hearing, which was minutes away at the time, and then we helped each other make the necessary changes to strengthen our cases. We felt confident that each of our cases would unquestionably mandate a TPO, so we waited expectantly for what we believed would be a sure victory. We realized the challenge would be moving forward after procuring the TPO and not allowing ourselves to fall back into the same precarious situations. When the attendant in the room finally informed us that it was time to go to the courtroom, we lined up nervously and anxiously feeling that the time had finally arrived when we would be heard and our cases vindicated. Oddly, however, there seemed to be a spirit of ambivalence circulating that was unexpected. I soon came to realize that mixed emotions were developing because we knew that we would soon be going our separate ways after the hearing, and things would be back to the way they were. For some, this was depressing while others found this thought frightful (i.e. returning to their current environments). This dreadful and gloomy feeling was perceived by some as devastating because of their lack of support from family and friends in their toxic households and situations coupled with the thought of having to go back to these miserable and portentous surroundings with the risk involved. So, this moment became a bittersweet time in our lives because, although we were excited about the hope of finally obtaining a TPO, we were sad when we thought about departing from each other and going our separate ways with slim chances of ever reconnecting. For this small moment in time, we actually felt like a family. We all had similar experiences and could relate to each other's feelings and current situation which made a world of difference.

Remembering this moment brings back fond memories. It was truly a photo-op moment and video opportunity as well as we lined up and prepared to go to the courtroom - the long awaited anticipation. The courtroom was on the other side of the courthouse, so we had to walk across the lobby on the main level to get to the other side of the building. We locked arms and walked in groups supporting and empowering each other as we walked through the lobby and halls. I remember the looks from bystanders in the lobby and courthouse that day. I know that they had to think we were part of some women's empowerment movement the way things appeared. This camaraderie was viewed to be a strong representation of sisterhood among all races. This recollection will always evoke strong and warm emotions from me because I am reminded of how God transcended all cultural barriers that day as He moved miraculously by empowering, inspiring, and transforming the lives of these broken ladies all through the power of transparency. Or shall I say, through the ministry of the wounded healer as this chapter is entitled. God gave me a ministry through my current painful experience to help heal someone wounded like myself. Consequently, this became an epic moment for me where I was shown God's plan for my life through an epiphany surrounding these precious moments. I would not only be a victim's advocate in domestic crises but a perpetrator's advocate also because both need healing to resolve this prevalent problem in our society. God was also anointing me with the task and vision of focusing on the big picture with a broader scope dealing with impaired and severed relationships (parental, familial, marital, social, spiritual, and romantic). The vision He gave to me that day at that moment encompassed the "ministry of reconciliation" overall as described earlier and not just the issue with intimate partner violence that I experienced that morning when things changed.

As we entered the courtroom that day, we sighed with relief as thoughts of being moments away from our deliverance filled our minds with hope. The judge, who was a middle-aged Caucasian woman, appeared very compassionate and understanding as we watched her observe us seating ourselves before the process began. When the session was called to order, it was explained to us that this hearing was to determine if our case warranted a TPO. We were also given other details centered around this order. The first petitioner took a stand and explained her case to the judge, but to her dismay, she wasn't granted a TPO. The next lady expressed her situation and her argument was disturbingly dismissed also. This went on and on until I could barely stomach watching the hearings because the judge that initially looked sympathetic, turned into an apathetic and insensitive bully. I observed her interrogate each petitioner to the point of intimidation and then deem their situation as meritless and without credibility. She also insinuated to some degree that the petitioner was responsible for the current situation they were in and needed to walk away and stay away if they wanted a safer environment and a changed lifestyle. I thought to myself, "Gee, thanks Einstein for telling us something we didn't already know". Really?!!!! All I could repeatedly say was, "Really?!!!!" "That is a "no brainer" dear! What the heavens (smile) do you think we are doing here in the midst of this adversarial climate of embarrassment, insensitivity, shame, and disrespect we've encountered from the onset of this application process from those we hoped would be our advocates? Not to mention the danger we were risking hoping our perpetrators didn't discover our agenda that day and cause us more heartache! We are TRYING to walk away to a "safer environment and changed lifestyle", which is why we're here pursuing a TPO to help us do just that. Hello!!!! We need YOUR help! Can't you see our plight is HOPELESS without this? Can't you see that we NEED just a LITTLE love and compassion in our vulnerable and dejected conditions?" Well, thank God that He reminded me that He was in control, and not this emotionally detached judge. This reminder couldn't have been more timely when I was listening to the present petitioner conveying her story. It was a heart-wrenching story that brought tears to the eyes of everyone in the courtroom - except the judge. Her story dealt with repeated episodes of physical abuse that cost her many hospital bills as she was brutally beaten to the point of death. During our moment of sharing earlier in the room while waiting, this petitioner showed us her cellphone pictures revealing the bruises and injuries she suffered under the hand of her significant other. She would press charges, but they would always be dropped because his parents would repeatedly bail him out and financially clean up his mess. They were extremely wealthy and abused their monetary power and financial status. There were some pictures where her face was unrecognizable because he had used his pistol to administer his merciless blows to her face. This still surprisingly didn't elicit the slightest sentiment from the judge. It was amazing how heartless and indifferent she proved to be during this hearing as she maintained a poker face throughout the entire process. So, unfortunately, to this petitioner's chagrin, she was refused a TPO and asked not to come back unless she left the predator. But what the judge failed to understand was that she needed the TPO to do this and until then, she would be enslaved because she was devoid of family support and friends. Then again, maybe the judge was not ignorant of this fact but just didn't care. In any event, this was one of the most deplorable stories with the most hopeless and disappointing outcomes. There were a few other cases after this one that weren't even close to the severity of abuse suffered by this young lady in the previous case, but the judge threw the court a curveball that afternoon and awarded TPO's in these cases. I later learned that the judge was frustrated with the "frequent fliers" and this was evident by the cold-hearted behavior she had with them. Learning this information, however, did not move me to give this judge a pass card for her harsh actions and dealings with these individuals because they were in desperate need of help, not censure. For many, if not all, this was a life or death situation, which the system failed to acknowledge. Hence, these ladies weren't provided with the resources and support needed to be able to leave their predators. In essence, their desperate pleas were ignored and consequently, essential lifelines were not offered that day. The low self-worth that plagued their psyche stripped them of the confidence to leave and contributed all the more to their hopeless situation. As I daydreamed about this conundrum, I heard my name called as the next petitioner to be heard. I immediately mustered up the fortitude to even present my case and be motivated after all the confusion, frustration, and disappointment I had just witnessed. After all, I was not a longstanding victim of physical abuse. I only suffered a one-time incident that seemed so insignificant and trivial in comparison with the stories just heard. So, with the few TPO's granted that afternoon, I was not eager to hear how the ruling on my case would work out as I thought of the possibility of the judge underestimating the seriousness of my ordeal since I wasn't hurt and there were no obvious physical signs of harm associated with my one-time incident. This reasoning tempted me to seek a plan B option because I didn't want to waste her time with what I thought she would consider foolishness. Nevertheless, as I thought about everything I went through that day to get where I was currently, I chose to give this pursuit a chance as I perceived it to be my only option. So, I was sworn in and then questioned. I noticed while I was reciting my story, the expression of the judge looked disinterested and rote. This was very discouraging, but I continued anyway and tried to think optimistically. Then it happened. The appearance of this "no-tolerance" judge abruptly changed and looked frightfully disturbed in the middle of my story. Pain was written all over her face as she interrupted me mid-sentence to get clarity on something I said. Assuming she wanted me to analyze the details of the domestic incident between my husband and me, I began to repeat the chronology of the occurrence. As I recounted the incident, she abruptly interrupted me and asked for clarity on something I had just said. She wanted to know if she had heard me correctly. Surprisingly, her interest was centered on the mistreatment of my dog - not me. I had shared an incident that occurred in the past with the dog that caught her attention and apparently struck a nerve because she immediately stamped a document and the next thing I knew I was being congratulated by the staff as being one of the few that evening awarded a TPO. Now, one would think that I was thrilled and overjoyed with this long-awaited news, but I just stood there dumbfounded until I was beckoned to follow someone to obtain my copy of the documents for my TPO. I was momentarily stunned like a deer in the headlights. It was puzzling as I pondered what part of my explanation triggered a soft spot in the judge's heart and compelled her to grant me the TPO. Surely it must have been the part of my story where my life was almost taken. I felt confident of that. However, I was flabbergasted when I discovered differently. After getting clarification, I learned that the incident with my dog elicited those strong emotions observed by the judge that day and not the life threatening event that I experienced. Digesting that the behavior towards the dog – not the treatment I received – was the actual trigger that stimulated the decision for justice in my case, was hard to process. For a brief moment, I felt insignificant, worthless, and empty. I felt slighted that a dog's life was valued greater than mine. This was a moment for a blog entitled "human lives matter". In any event, I realized that however I obtained my TPO that day, I should be grateful for how God showed favor in my case and just praise Him. Well, that's just what I decided to do. I also mentally went to John 3:16 and came to grips with the fact that no human being will ever determine the value of my life - calvary does that. Christ felt that we were all worthy enough and valuable enough to die for even while we were still sinners. This is a "hallelujah" moment! So, from that day forward, praise was on my lips every time I told the story of how God moved that entire day with the ladies earlier in the room with a cathartic moment while we awaited our court hearing, and then with the judge later that day. It was truly an amazing day and many lives were forever changed that day. I was confident that seeds were miraculously planted that day that would bear fruit from these precious and treasurable moments in their designated time because lives were remarkably impacted.

Nevertheless, I found it difficult to forget my revelation that day in court that was disturbing to the uttermost. I grieved bitterly as I thought of all the ladies that were refused a TPO who lived in dreadful and precarious environments and who cringed at the thought of returning to these deplorable conditions. I even felt guilty of having my TPO when I knew of others worse off than myself and devoid of the resources needed to survive. They trusted that the judicial system would be of some help and assistance, but they were sadly mistaken. It appeared that no one even cared, and the charities and ministries in place were either already full to capacity with scarce resources, or apathetically "doing business as usual" with no real thought or concern about the urgency at hand. Support was lacking in this area of the judicial system, and I was determined to fix the loopholes when I found myself in better conditions. Thus, the vision I had stayed on my heart and mind by the constant unspeakable circumstances I observed. I was determined to do something about this when my situation would allow. For right now, I prayed for my sisters that God would put a protective hedge about them as we went our separate ways not knowing when or if we'd ever cross paths again. I had to realize that everybody has a different mission in life and a different cross to bear. However, with Jesus, we can all have a common endpoint - eternal life. This world and the problems it affords are only temporary.

When I reached the office where I received an official copy of my TPO, I experienced a sense of relief and accomplishment now after this long arduous process to secure this piece of paper. This feeling of victory, however, was short lived when I learned later on that this temporary order would expire in 30 days and a longer order could only be secured by going to court and filing for another one. This second TPO would usually expire in twelve months. The hearing for this longer TPO would be much different than the hearing for the first TPO which was temporary because the alleged abuser would have to be present in the court hearing this time. So, my husband would have to be subpoenaed. Now things would really get interesting.

Chapter 3

MY TPO EXPERIENCE

WHILE MY INITIAL TPO was obtained with blood, sweat, and tears, I was totally clueless about the challenge I would encounter when obtaining the second one that had a one-year expiration date. This was an interesting and extremely revealing walk that only Jesus saw me successfully through. It all started after I was awarded the 30-day TPO. Initially, I was so glad to have a TPO that I became complacent with the accomplishment of this 30-day order and almost lost the opportunity to obtain the one with the 12-month extension. You see, I wasn't aware that the current TPO would expire in 30 days and that the one year TPO would require another application process. However, I was made aware by my lawyer who informed me that after thirty days I would be back to square one if I didn't solidify a 12-month TPO before this expiration date which was the standard protocol. So, I realized this 30-day TPO was only put in place to allow time for a court hearing to see if the TPO was warranted and needed extension, or if it wasn't justifiable and needed to be nullified. I also was informed that the 12-month TPO could only be obtained with the presence of the perpetrator in court. Well, this is where things got real interesting because I didn't anticipate any difficulty in following these procedures to obtain the extended order, but I encountered some unexpected opposition and resistance along the way that made things more challenging and dramatic.

When I attempted to serve my husband so that he would attend this court hearing for the one-year TPO, I was repeatedly unsuccessful. Frustrated and exhausted with my efforts, I sought to make sure that the information I had documented for him was correct. After researching things, I confirmed that the information I gave to the court system pertaining to his address, phone number and vehicle were all correct and hadn't changed. Bewildered and clueless concerning the difficulty serving him, I decided to visit the courthouse and see what was going on because it had been almost two weeks of unsuccess and I was running out of time. With the clock ticking and my TPO's remaining days on countdown before the 30-day expiration, I had to think and move fast. I only had a few days remaining, and I dreaded the thought of having to repeat the entire process that got me where I was currently. It was my worst nightmare at the time. Upon reaching the courthouse, I explained the concerns and problems I was having with serving my husband, and consequently, was directed to the sheriff's office. I was unsure of the reasoning behind this directive, but soon I saw how it resolved the enigma related to the difficulty of serving my husband. I was able to view the records that documented the numerous attempts to serve him and how he appeared to be successfully blocking these attempts. I also saw that the attempts were made at different times of the day to serve him, accounting for all possible work-related shifts he could have had. So, the only explanation for this impediment with serving him was his avoidance of being served. Surprisingly and disturbingly, they had tried to serve him over twenty times.

With this new knowledge, I realized that I needed a plan B to obtain this extended TPO. So, I began praying and inquiring about what my next move should be. During this time, I remember talking to my close childhood friend who happened to be a psychologist. From the very beginning of this crisis, she recommended that I get a divorce, but just the word "divorce" pierced my heart and elicited strong emotions. I understood then what counselors meant when they said that a divorce is analogous to death because it is a loss. I first heard this perspective while participating in a seminar on grief where I presented a session on pregnancy loss and grief while other sessions focused on the grief experienced with the loss of a significant other through a breakup, divorce, or death. A psychologist discussed divorce during this seminar, and this is when I first heard this concept of divorce being considered synonymous with that of death because of the loss involved – the loss of a partner and a relationship. Nevertheless, as I mentioned earlier, I hadn't come to this point of finality with the relationship. Even with the domestic hiccup that occurred, I planned to separate indefinitely while my husband entered rehab for his substance issues which I believed to be the trigger for the mishap, but I planned for this to be a temporary solution until things improved - not something permanent. During this process, I planned to be supportive of him from afar to assure his success with the different programs and to expedite his treatment. I initially assumed this would take a couple of years or more and I planned to remain separate until then. In any event, because of my religious beliefs from my Adventist upbringing, I knew that divorce was not a favorable option. Because of this mindset, getting a divorce was not first on my list. I would try to make things work and pray for God's guidance as I separated while waiting from afar for safety's sake. After all, my pastor and church were strongly against any thoughts of divorce, but then again, they didn't have to live with him, I did. So I prayed to make the best decision for me through God's leading.

As time elapsed and things became more intense with the hearing approaching, I saw how uncooperative my husband was and noted his insensitivity overall with the issue at hand. I wasn't aware that someone could avoid being served by refusing to answer the door, and that the authorities weren't allowed to force entry. Therefore, I filed for divorce as recommended by legal advice (and my childhood friend) to get the ball rolling and "knock out two birds with one stone" when I saw how this was really my best option now for more than one reason. I was advised that if the divorce went uncontested after 30 days, it would be done in the state where I resided at the time, so I knew this would incite a response from him. In addition to this, I also hired a certified process server to expedite the process with serving my husband since he was intentionally avoiding being served. These individuals appear like regular civilians and are usually successful in serving individuals who strategically try to avoid any one in authority to delay this process or cancel it altogether. Therefore, this plan would take my husband off his guard and accomplish things inconspicuously. Instead of him seeing a sheriff at his door or an officer in a uniform in his neighborhood, he would see a man dressed as a civilian that would engage him in conversation and before he would know what was happening, the order would be served. And this is exactly what happened. The process server informed me that it was not difficult at all serving him for the TPO. He also shared with me that when he told him about the divorce as well, he became very vehement about contesting things, so I was sure to meet him in court, which was required to secure my TPO. Thankfully, this plan's outcome was successful and I considered it to be a major checkmate. The court-mandated order stated that the petitioner, as well as the respondent, had to both be present in the court hearing to extend the TPO and my mission was now accomplished. Now that I was free of the burden of serving my husband, I could begin preparing for the hearing.

In preparation for my court hearing, my female attorney admonished me to be focused, calm, and professional at all times. She warned me to eschew altercations with my husband and ignore any potential false accusations and allegations hurled at me during the hearing. She stressed that I should resist any attempts to be deflected from achieving my goal of obtaining an extension of my TPO. She explained that if this endeavor turned out to be ineffectual, there may not be another opportunity to secure an extension of my 30-day (soon to expire) TPO, and the girls and my safety would be in jeopardy. This resonated deeply with me because I already felt somewhat isolated knowing that I had no family locally. It was just the girls and me. We had some friends and church members who were local, but they were limited with what they could do. The TPO would provide legal protection from harm and endangerment which we were desperately in need of in our current situation. So, I took this preparation seriously and made sure that I cooperated with my attorney to accomplish this goal. I also felt the need to have my staff present in court to testify that my husband was a threat to my safety and to advocate on my behalf for an extension of my current TPO. Because they were in the office the day he manifested red flags concerning his mental and emotional health, it was only logical to have them as witnesses in court to validate my concerns for the welfare of the girls and me in the situation at hand. They saw his apathetic attitude when I instructed him to go to the ER (Emergency Room) without delay for evaluation and treatment when his blood pressure was noted to be out of control in the office one day. It was his habit to have his blood pressure monitored occasionally in the office, and on this particular afternoon, it was extremely high. Seeing his reluctance to go to the ER, I alternatively suggested that I would call in something temporarily while he scheduled an appointment with his healthcare provider. His nonchalant and cynical response as he turned a deaf ear to me with both propositions offered, led me to be blatantly candid in my response to him as I emphasized the gravity of his present physical condition. I remember jokingly stating that the girls would be devoid of a father if he didn't take this situation seriously, and he clearly and unambiguously articulated that they wouldn't have a mother either because he would take me with him since we loved each other. Unfortunately, I was so focused on the physical problem at hand that I failed to immediately see the mental and emotional crisis staring me right in the face. This statement was a definite red flag. When pondering this statement a few days later, I was troubled concerning the potential reference to a homicide-suicide act. And, a couple of months later when the life-threatening incident occurred, I reflected again on these words. Oddly, I misinterpreted this absurd statement at the time and felt that it was just an example of his cynical and twisted sense of humor and inappropriate conduct at times. I didn't realize that this may have been a cry for help on a much deeper level and I missed the opportunity to throw him a lifeline for which I am eternally sorry.

Although the deficit in his physical health was apparent, what was not as obvious was his impaired emotional and spiritual health as well. As a healthcare provider who believes in a holistic approach when considering one's "total" health, I understand that being healthy encompasses more than just physical health. One's mental, emotional, and spiritual health are all equally important. So, if there is a deficiency in any one of these areas, one's overall health is impaired. That afternoon the deficiencies in these other areas of health outside of his physical profile were revealed. This became more obvious one to two months later when the choking event occurred and I nearly lost my life. I only realized then how intervention on some level that day in the office could have possibly prevented what happened some months later.

On the court date, I brought the girls along because we were inseparable if I wasn't at work. From the day our lives were disrupted and family bonds were broken, we were glued to each other by the hips unless I was at the job. And they accompanied me there too at times. With the school year ended, this was permissible because the girls were on their summer break and summer school was not an option due to the current circumstances. So, that morning, they accompanied me to court as well. They were not allowed in the courtroom when the trial began, but they were allowed to sit outside in the waiting area with the other petitioners and respondents who were accompanied by family or friends while awaiting their court hearing also. My mother, who flew in from out of town to help me during this difficult time, was there to watch the girls during my court hearing. Because the girls came to court with me that day, they were able to see their dad and greet him although they were not allowed to interact with him by themselves during this time because of the TPO currently in place. And though this seemed cruel, it was prudent because the emotional state of their father was labile during that time and safety was a strong concern after all that had transpired. Nevertheless, they did have the privilege of interacting briefly, and it was uneventful. Now, the drama began when he and I saw each other in the lobby while awaiting the hearing. His entire countenance changed from that of a flat disposition to a sorrowful disposition right before my eyes, and the next thing I remember hearing was his whining in pathetic tones saying that he didn't understand why things couldn't just go back to how they used to be. He even downplayed the domestic incident and implied that I overreacted when he was just trying to calm me down. He accused me of being hysterical about some hypothetical altercation we supposedly had that morning which embarrassingly exposed my infidelity in the relationship and explained why he put his hands on my shoulders to calm me down. Now, he relayed this fabricated story right there in front of my attorney, his attorney, my mother, and the girls as if to cunningly persuade them to believe this lie. At this point, it registered to me that he was attempting to finagle this case in his favor with a weak and flawed alibi and persuade my lawyer, his lawyer, my mother, and the girls to believe him. Therefore, I abruptly stopped him by simply correcting his verbiage which suggested that we were just arguing when I was being choked instead, which made it difficult for me to argue, let alone to even breathe. So arguing didn't even factor into this equation. There was no dialogue when this incident occurred; instead, I was blindsided by this act of aggression and almost killed. Consequently, I chose not to engage with him any further prior to the hearing to prevent things from escalating. And I didn't even entertain the accusations of infidelity because he and I both knew this was absurd. I simply ignored him from that point onward as I recognized his attempts to provoke me to be angry and hysterical right before the hearing began in efforts to weaken my argument. I also saw this as an attempt on his part to deflect from the real issue at hand.

Nonetheless, I realized that day in court that he had set the stage from day one for deception when he was arrested and mumbled something under his breath to me while being apprehended. I later discovered the content of his mumbling to be a ridiculously fudged insinuation stating that I was cheating in our marriage, which he wanted the officer to hear as he strategically sought some substance to use for the police report that could explain the altercation that morning. Of course my husband knew that I had not committed adultery, but what better way to deflect everything from the real issue at hand - his drinking and anger management issues, which were the real factors responsible for his minacious behavior witnessed that morning. He also claimed and documented in the report that the girls did not witness the incident, which was not correct either. Kelly directly witnessed it and Haley indirectly witnessed it. Kelly was a direct witness being in the room during the occurrence and Haley was an indirect witness being in the next room hearing everything and being adversely impacted. Furthermore, to my chagrin, the offense was only categorized as a misdemeanor when my life was almost taken, which was ridiculously absurd. More light will be shed later in this narrative concerning that issue. But that morning as I awaited my hearing, I refused to enter into any altercation or controversy with my husband or entertain any of his strategies to dissuade me from my purpose that day. Being familiar with his tactics and cunning ways, I knew that he intended to nullify my testimony about him being a threat to the girls' and my safety by just making me appear cantankerous and difficult to get along with as a spouse. So, I greeted him briefly and then chose to respond with silence to all other inquiries or comments from him before the start of the case. In essence, I was intentional to ignore his wheedling and cajoling that morning as he strategized to invalidate my argument.

I hated for the girls to be caught up in the domestic circus witnessed at court that morning, but thank God it was short-lived and civil because I refused to engage in any way that could have potentially escalated things. Looking back on this day, I see the wisdom in the proverbs stating that a "soft answer turneth away wrath" (Proverbs 15:1) and that discretion will preserve and keep us (Proverbs 2:11). Also, from Proverbs 26:4-5, I learned that there is a time to answer someone speaking foolishly to alleviate any room for arrogance or pride that could potentially distort one's perception of his idiotic ranting being mistakenly viewed as intelligent. And then there is a time to keep silent when someone talks foolishly so you don't stoop to their level of imprudence. I was experiencing the latter on this occasion.

When our court hearing began, I testified about everything that had happened and arranged for a staff member to serve as a witness to validate my testimony. She confirmed my statements and to my amazement, my husband did not refute anything. This was puzzling after recalling his conduct and accusations just prior to the hearing in the waiting area. For a moment I thought that maybe he was convicted about his wrong and experiencing feelings of remorse. Contrary to this thought process, my husband had something else up his sleeve that I soon discovered. The shenanigan he pulled that day in court was a direct attack on my reputation and career. He attempted to make me responsible for his violent behavior that morning when he choked me. He blamed his actions on the side effects of a medication that I prescribed him per his request. This was another trick he pulled out of his hat that day. First, the infidelity and now this. The falsifications, lies and deception just never stopped. At any rate, as he witnessed his brother's success with this medication, he felt compelled to try it. Now, while he was attributing his harsh and life-threatening behavior to this medication, and then strategizing to put my license along with my medical career at risk, I simply confirmed that I had prescribed the medication fully aware of the potential side effects that were possible without any denial or rebuttal. I also elaborated that most – if not all - prescription medications have some adverse side effects that have the potential to occur so this was not a revelation. I also mentioned that he knew that drinking alcohol was contraindicated and dangerous to one's health while taking medication of any kind, which he was guilty of while taking this specific medication that day. This combination most likely served as a contributor to the bizarre and violent behavior witnessed that morning. I'm just thankful that things didn't get worse because the potential for worse to occur with this cocktail was definitely possible. This is what he failed to tell the judge that day, as well as the plans we discussed for his doctor to manage this medication. Of course, he was noncompliant with the safe usage of this drug and his nonconformity contributed to what was witnessed that day. I gently reminded him of this while on the stand, along with the fact that he had manifested belligerent behavior in the past on more than one occasion where this medication wasn't involved, but only his alcohol usage in these cases. However, I had never been the recipient of his aggression until that morning which I attributed to his behavior worsening over time with the habits he employed. I stated that drinking is dangerous while on prescription meds because it can adversely affect one's health and behavior and this wasn't something new for him. I reiterated to him the well-known facts of alcohol abuse and its potential to cause aggressive and harmful behavior, which is only exacerbated when feelings of anger, irritation, or annoyance coexist with the usage of this substance. These were well-known facts that were not foreign to him, so, after highlighting these pertinent points, his argument was curtailed. The judge quickly moved on to other topics, which addressed my husband's firearms. At the time, my husband owned numerous firearms and notably had them in his possession all this time since the incident, which was over a month ago. Sounds insane, I know, but it just validates God's omnipotence and protection with situations that are out of our control. We were surrounded by His protective hedge and no demon in hell could touch us. With my husband in his deranged state after the repercussions of this incident, he was in no condition to possess these firearms all this time until now, yet they were disappointingly never confiscated. I was disappointed that I had to bring this oversight to the judge's attention instead of my lawyer doing so while I was on the stand in order for it to be addressed in the hearing. Surprisingly, there was no effort made to secure his firearms when he was released from jail on probation although he was established to be a threat to the safety of the girls and me, which is why we were awarded a TPO. So, the logic here will forever escape me as the laxity of the legal system was exposed in court that day. The court proceedings got even more strange and bizarre when his attorney convinced the judge to allow my husband to take his multiple firearms unchaperoned out of town to his father's house over the holiday weekend that was soon approaching as if they could trust him in his angered and troubled state. To my astonishment and outrage, I could barely mask my reaction as I heard this preposterous court order proposed by his attorney approved that day. Everything I had researched about an individual under a TPO or convicted of a misdemeanor in a domestic violence setting, stated that the court was to assume possession of their firearms immediately, which is a no brainer. No research was even required to conclude what is simply common sense in this critical situation. So, once again, I was baffled with the reasoning wielded here where a TPO was granted to us because the judge agreed that my husband was a threat to the girls and me, yet my husband was permitted to transport his guns out of town to his father's house unsupervised over the holiday weekend that was approaching with no legal concerns of danger or risk. I can vividly remember this moment. It was extremely disheartening, but, on a more positive note, we did succeed in getting our 12- month TPO despite this major legal screw-up that we suffered during this hearing.

Digressing for a moment, I recall another memory involving his guns that took place when I had to go back to the apartment Saturday morning – two days after the incident when he was arrested. I had left my business check book and made plans to get it. Exercising caution, I went to the county website to see if my husband was still incarcerated, and thankfully, it showed him to still be confined. I remembered his father's plans to bail him out and wanted to see if he had already done this. Feeling safe that he was still incarcerated, I decided to venture back to my apartment briefly to recover my checkbook this one time. On the way there, I recalled that the policeman informed me that if I needed to go back to the apartment for anything, that I should stop at the entry gate and be escorted in the gate by them, but not to go through the gate alone because, at that point, I would be on my own. It was tempting not to be inconvenienced by this extra step since my husband was still confined as I confirmed via the county jail's website, but I decided to be compliant regardless. With that being said, I called the police just before arriving at the apartment and waited at the gate until their arrival. A police officer greeted me not too long afterward and I told him the reason for my return to the apartment after I briefed him on my current situation. Because everything had just happened two days ago, I hadn't obtained a TPO yet. He said that he would accompany me through the gate and then further to the apartment to assure my safety. When we were just about to do this, I glanced in the rearview mirror by habit and you would have thought that I saw a ghost. Observing my astonishment, the police officer asked me what was wrong as I looked horror-struck with what I saw and gasped in disbelief. Right before my eyes, I saw my husband looking well-groomed and casually dressed in his Ford heavy-duty truck. Not at all like the website picture I had just pulled up on the internet supposedly confirming him to still be in jail. It was so eerie because all I could re-member was the Fulton county jail website showing his mugshot and confirming him to still be locked up and now I was seeing him right before my eyes as I realized that the website was not in real-time and obviously slow to be updated. Nevertheless, I came to grips with the fact that he was released from jail and apparently had been out for a while because I noticed that he had a haircut, was clean-shaven, had his truck, and was dressed in a different outfit from what he had on the day of his arrest. It was the most uncanny feeling as I sat there in a daze - paralyzed from the shock of everything. Somehow, however, I was able to mentally regroup and process everything that had just occurred before answering the police officer who was puzzled by my reaction and behavior. I told him that my husband, who I assumed was still incarcerated, was right behind us in his truck. I thought to myself, how coincidental that I would run into him now. I realized later that he had been using the mobile phone tracking feature that we shared on our cell phone account as a family and his presence wasn't coincidental at all. Although it was just two days since the incident, I was very cautious and intentional about amending all of our joint accounts, but had not gotten to the cell phone account yet. Knowing that my plans were to separate and start anew, I had every intention to amend our joint accounts immediately when I had a break in my schedule as a physician, entrepreneur, and, now, a single mom - all thrust on me suddenly after the domestic upset while I was trying to figure everything out. I just prioritized other accounts dealing with our finances on that Friday - the day after the incident. These other accounts involved our auto, health, life, and disability insurances, along with my will - among other things. Thank God we didn't have any joint bank accounts, which I'll talk about later. So, that Friday I was flooded with things to do, which not only included amending those joint accounts just mentioned, but also relocating the girls, Ruby (our dog) and me with the stuff we chose to take to our new safe space until we found a new home. This was no easy venture because of the emergent nature of things, which didn't allow me time to recruit help, or to even think about where we would go. I was left to secure a UHaul at the eleventh hour and pack up everything that the girls and I wanted to take with us as we embarked on our new journey. We later got help with unloading our UHaul at a safe storage place over the weekend while still looking to solidify a safe residence. I also failed to mention that amending those accounts mentioned earlier required a person to person encounter because handling things over the phone was not an option for the sake of authenticity. But once I shared my story, the different offices worked with me to set up an impromptu appointment quickly that got me seen on that day. However, this still took a great deal of time considering everything else that needed to be done that day. Needless to say, we couldn't get everything done that Friday following the incident, but we sure tried. So, the next day, which happened to be this Saturday when I had to return to the apartment to get my business checkbook mistakenly left behind, he was still able to manipulate our family cell phone account that I had not cancelled yet. It was this account that had the mobile tracking device feature and gave my husband access to my whereabouts that morning. The discovery later on in our journey of his usage of this mobile tracking feature, however, led me to secure a new cell phone account and even purchase a new cell phone altogether, which minimized our drama with him significantly for the time being. Thankfully, our bank accounts were separate from the day we married and remained that way as aforementioned. This was decided from the onset of our relationship because he was divorced and I didn't want to get entangled - personally or financially - in any baggage from his previous marriage.

Redirecting back to the scene with my husband standing behind me at the gate of the apartment complex with his truck, I had no clue that he was using this mobile tracking feature but sensed something was fishy. A quick phone consultation with a friend's lawyer the night of my husband's arrest raised my suspicions of a tracking device on my car because this attorney mentioned the use of various devices and gadgets that are habitually used by perpetrators to maintain control of their significant others. The cell phone just didn't come up in that conversation. So, being cautious, I decided to trade in my vehicle as you'll see in detail in a later chapter to remove the possibility of a tracking device on my SUV. At any rate, I warned the police officer that there was some hanky panky going on with his presence at the gate that morning and I didn't think this was by coincidence. Hence the trade-in of my vehicle not too long after this incident, which followed the discontinuation of the joint cell phone account and purchase of a new phone altogether. We were starting anew and breaking any remaining ties with him completely for the time being while safety was an issue. For a moment I wondered how he was even allowed to come back to the apartment complex - let alone our apartment - where the girls and I were supposed to be still residing when he was considered a threat to our safety after the incident. I realized that he had been bailed out just recently by his father and later learned that he was on a six to twelve-month probation contingent on his compliance with his anger management program. There were other details, but since the communication was prohibited between the two of us - and understandably so - I wasn't aware of all of his restrictions during his probation and whether they were monitoring him for any substances (e.g. alcohol). Reflecting on all of the significant oversights experienced with the legal system in this case (e.g. failure to confiscate his firearms; failure to restrict his return to the apartment; and failure to give me my TPO when he was bailed out; among other things), I realized that these crucial oversights could have cost the girls and me our lives. Nevertheless, I had to quickly remind myself Who was actually in control (God) while I claimed Isaiah 26:3 daily in order to maintain my sanity in this obviously insane ordeal. Because the present hideout for the girls and me wasn't made public yet to the authorities, they had no clue that the girls and I had relocated. So, their lackadaisical approach concerning our safety could have been devastating when they allowed my husband to return to the apartment where he left us and where we were still presumed to be. His return could have been toxic and life-threatening for us if we were still there. Thank God for His providence and wisdom in leading us elsewhere to avoid this certain endangerment. He should have been banned from returning to the apartment. If he needed to get his things, he should have been escorted or accompanied by a police officer. This was a huge legal screw-up again that could have cost us our lives before our uphill journey even started had we still been residing there in the apartment.

In any event, he was now behind me and the officer told me that he would see what he was up to. I warned him that my husband was very intelligent and had the potential to be very manipulative. I also stressed that this situation could get risky because he possessed firearms and was currently angry because I had him arrested and didn't follow through with his plan. This incident occurred prior to the court hearing where his firearms were arranged to be removed from his residence. At any rate, my husband's plan was for me to bail him out and act as though nothing happened which was insulting and disturbing at the same time. He reasoned that since it was his first offense in our relationship and he had never put his hands on me in a harmful manner prior to this episode, I should just forgive him and forget everything else. But one time was too much. His father sought to persuade me to do the same as he excused his son's violent behavior with the passcard that he was stressed. Insulted by this insensitivity he manifested concerning our well being (the girls and me, i.e.), I told him that he was preaching to the choir in terms of stress and informed him that I would not be complying with my husband's plan. I didn't need his next episode of stress to finish what he started and to be choked to the point of suffocation this time. Within those last two years, my job had become very stressful as I juggled between the increased business at the practice and family time. So, I wasn't hearing stress as an excuse for anything. Thankfully, God revealed his strategy to me and opened my eyes. I saw how if I had picked him up from jail and bailed him out, this would have nullified my argument that he was a threat to the girls and me, which would have caused the authorities to drop all charges. But I refused and he was bailed out by his father who I notified the day I had him apprehended. Nevertheless, the officer found my warning concerning my husband to be amusing and just chuckled on his way to see what was going on with him. While he was there, I immediately called for police backup feeling nervous about the whole encounter. My youngest sister, who was visiting from out of town, was in the car with me at the time and she looked nervous too. She had asked to accompany me during this attempt to get my checkbook that I left at the apartment. The girls and Ruby (our dog) stayed at the apartment of a friend of ours while I made this trip. Meanwhile, the police officer appeared to be detained for a while with my husband, and I decided to call my close childhood friend who was a psychologist to get some insight. As a side note, she and I had many conversations throughout this journey and oftentimes, she was left speechless with some of my intriguing, inspiring, and mind blowing anecdotes. She anticipated our talks because she acknowledged that as a mental health professional, she wasn't aware of these loopholes in the system that were expressed earlier. Now she could appreciate the stories her clients shared with her about their experiences with the legal system while trying to get help with their pernicious circumstances because my experience validated their stories. So, we gleaned from this symbiotic relationship and kept the lines of communication open. Nevertheless, I will redirect back to our scene with the police officer going to see what was going on with my husband. Suddenly, I saw the officer at my window in a frenzy as he frantically tried to get my attention after returning from talking with my husband. He abruptly interrupted the conversation I was having with my girlfriend in a perturbed manner asking who had called for police backup. I told him that I did, and that's when he began telling me about his skills to comfort me, but I remember referring to him as "Rambo" jokingly and telling him that he needed to exercise caution in this venture with my husband because he didn't know who he was dealing with but I did. I told him that we would need another officer now that my husband showed up on the scene and was angry although he masked this emotion and appeared sorrowful for the sake of the police. One officer would escort me to the apartment to secure my checkbook, while the other officer would watch my husband until I finished everything. The officer agreed and it was only a matter of minutes before the second officer showed up on the scene. However, he canceled the backup request I made earlier in hysterics, and for a moment, I forgot that my friend was still on the call until I heard this roar of laughter. I quickly remembered then that she was still on the line and was laughing after hearing me tell the cop that this was no time to play Rambo. We were dealing with a very angry and emotionally unstable husband and father that felt desperately hopeless about losing his family and was prepared to take his family back by force especially when learning of our unannounced relocation. His discovery was most likely made when he returned to the apartment after his release and found us, along with our most vital things, gone. I was sure he returned there because his keys to the truck that he was currently driving and his change of clothes he had on were all there. There was no time for frivolity that I sensed from this police officer as he used this tactic in an attempt to calm the situation down. We were in a very virulent setting although my husband did everything to conceal his true intent and appear remorseful, sorrowful, and reconcilable. He even became dramatic as he whined and wailed saying repeatedly that he was sorry and I should be forgiving and take him back. The police officer and my sister wondered why I appeared so insensitive and apathetic, but I would catch his furious glare at me when they weren't looking and when he thought I wasn't looking as well. So, I recognized his strategy for what it was – an insincere and conniving act to manipulate me to fall for his pretentious grief about what he had done. He showed no sincere regret for his violent actions a couple of days ago. And reconciling things to the point of placing the girls and myself back in that baneful environment was the furthest thing from my mind that day. Things were far from safe and stable in that environment, therefore, I continued to ignore his futile attempts to cause me to feel otherwise. When he finally realized that he was just wasting his time, he became more enraged as his fury intensified. I was determined to wait for him to seek counseling, anger management, and rehab before entertaining anything amicable between the two of us for the sake of the girls, as well as myself.

However, getting back to the scene, when the second officer arrived, she was very brutal and abrasive with me as she instructed me to get out of the car while she checked me for any weapons. She addressed me roughly and dealt with me as if I was the criminal or the assailant in this offense on record. I was sadly disenchanted as I expected to be shown some empathy or sympathy from this African American female cop, but I was terribly mistaken. I felt more sympathy and compassion from the first officer that came – a caucasian male. Anyhow, after being ordered harshly and insensitively to get back in my car, she proceeded to escort me to the apartment to get the checkbook while the other officer stayed at the front gate with my husband. There was no time for me to throw myself a pity party in my despair and sulk in response to her crude and callous behavior towards me as if I was to blame for everything. Instead, I quickly got my checkbook and headed back to the front gate to leave. But right before I left, I informed the male officer that my husband's firearms were inside the apartment and how I would feel much safer if he would confiscate them. The female officer that escorted me to the apartment ignored this same request I made with her while I was at the apartment getting my checkbook, so I was determined to bring it to the attention of the first officer who I believed would honor my request because he actually cared. He told me to wait at the gate while he went to the apartment. When he returned, he informed me that he couldn't take the firearms without an order, but he dismantled them and left them in the apartment on my husband's bed. I didn't know how to respond to that news, because, essentially, what he did was pointless as the guns were still left in my husband's possession and all my husband had to do now was reassemble them. Being beyond frustration at this point, I desperately yearned for someone to truly understand my dangerous dilemma and offer me some real help.

From that moment on, I concluded that the legal system would not be our fail-safe. Since the time of the incident, I was not impressed to solely rely on the legal system because there were too many inadequacies - specifically in safety measures. I was also convinced that the system was inundated with these domestic cases which explained the numbness in their response. Because of the overall pervasiveness of this issue in society, manpower and resources are lacking. Here again was another defining moment for me as I saw the hand of God allowing this challenging time in my life to occur so that I could be aware of Who really was in in control, as well as to see the overwhelming need for the ministry Christ was inspiring me to launch at His appointed time. When the arm of flesh failed me (the social and legal system at the time), His omnipotent arm carried me all the way. Despite the limited help from the legal authorities, I recognized again Whose hedge of protection encircled me 24 hours a day and 365 days of the year.

This awareness gave me great peace of mind as I recognized that I was safe under His wings as Psalms 91:1-4 puts it. And through this experience, this is exactly what God was showing me. If everything had been perfect and accommodating for the girls and me, we would have felt no need to call on God for help. We would have missed the opportunity to see Him work His wonders and miracles on our behalf. With everything appearing stable, I would not have appreciated Acts 17:28 (KJV). Consequently, we would have wrongfully attributed our favorable circumstances to man discrediting God's intervention when He (God) is the sole authentic Source of every good thing. Therefore, I praise God for all of the hurdles and hiccups along our journey that served to remind us Who was in charge without any ambiguity, because despite the mishaps encountered with the legal and social systems, we were safe in His arms.

Regardless of my disillusionment with the legal authorities that day, progress was still made to secure a 12-month TPO as I stated earlier, which was my main concern that day in court. My attorney was also able to arrange for supervised visitation which I initiated realizing that this would be healing for both the girls and their dad. I had no vindictive intentions or vengeful emotions that day, or throughout this journey. I only wanted to move forward with the girls in a safe environment as we accepted our family's new norm in our current predicament. Thankfully, I had a girlfriend residing in D.C. who was (and still is) an esteemed attorney who gave me good legal advice and was extremely supportive. She informed me about a local supervised visitation and exchange program with robust surveillance and was instrumental in getting us enrolled in this program. This program was such a blessing to us as we were able to "kill two birds with one stone" – allow the girls to interact with their dad and to do it safely with the

TPO in place. This program was well structured and wisely devised for the safety of victims and their children interacting with their abusive partners. It provided video surveillance during the visit and an officer on duty who would hold the abuser after visitation until the victim and children were gone long enough to prevent stalking and discovery of their whereabouts. The atmosphere was very homey and welcoming with couches and a television, along with toys, movies, and whatever was age-appropriate for one's family. Because appointments were mandatory and interviewing of the family was done before participation in the program, most of the visits were personalized for one's family dynamics and structure. This was a pleasant change from the standard visitation sites that were known to be lifeless and sterile and located in obvious legal facilities that I was familiar with as a clinician. At this facility, the visit for the children and the abusive parent took place in a house that was devised as a low-key supervised visitation site and appeared like a family residence. The girls loved it and looked forward to the visits. The policies and procedures of the program instructed the present legal guardian and the children to meet with the attendant 30 minutes before the arrival of the abusive partner in a building adjacent to the visitation site. The children would then be escorted to the visitation site next door while the victim would remain in the locked and secured building adjacent to the visitation site until the one hour visitation was over and the children were escorted back. The visitation site was a 3-story house that had surveillance cameras throughout the house on all levels and officers present to escort and supervise the abusive parent to the level where the visit was to be held and then to the car when the session was complete. The 3-story feature of this house used for visitation allowed three families to be utilizing the facility at the same time because they were on different levels. The attendant who escorted the children would prime them about what questions they should avoid answering and what to say and what not to say. The abusive spouse was also warned against using prying questions with the children in an inappropriate fashion in efforts to discover their residence, their daily routine, or their schedule of activities during this visitation. He was also informed that the visit was being videotaped, as well as audiotaped. I felt that he never should have ventured down this deceptive path when I was the one who suggested this arrangement in the first place in efforts to provide a way for him to safely communicate with the girls despite his TPO prohibiting this privilege for the lifetime of the order, which was one year. I realized that he and the girls both would benefit from this gesture as long as he cooperated with the rules of the facility and program to keep everything secure. Unfortunately, this supervised visitation did not last the life of the TPO because I had to stop it after the girls told me of numerous attempts he made to find our location and to find out other vital information despite the warnings to discontinue his probing. Well, as the idiom says, "all good things must come to an end" and they did. But at least they were able to have several visits before everything culminated and this proved sufficient for the time.

Overall, my TPO experience was enlightening and I learned that these TPO's can be very challenging to obtain - especially when the offender is required to be in court for the victim to receive it. This requires the defendant being served to appear in court to address the allegations of the plaintiff and this is where things become difficult because the offender often resists this process. The resistance from the offender lies in the fact that he is not enthusiastic about helping his victim get a restraining order (a TPO – Temporary Protective Order) to protect herself from him. So, he avoids the court hearing where his presence and the petitioner's presence are required to obtain the one-year TPO. These defects in the system, along with others discussed earlier, prove to be impediments for the victim to be liberated from a life-threatening situation at times. Why the victim's safety is contingent on the predator's cooperation in this legal aspect is puzzling and dangerous at the same time. Therefore, many individuals feel hopeless and forever trapped because the judicial system has not filled or fixed these loopholes.

I'll never forget what a police officer said to me when I was seeking help and guidance from the authorities concerning my husband's noncompliance with the TPO. He turned to me and pitifully uttered that just in case I wasn't aware of how the system works, he wanted to inform me that there are many loopholes in the system when dealing with domestic and intimate partner violence. And, these loopholes can impede victims from getting the help they need. What a terrible reality to deal with in my situation. I was tempted to feel that all hope was gone, but then I looked up and remembered Who my Advocate extraordinaire was and is - my omnipotent God. I knew then as I know now where my help comes from - my Jehovah Nissi as Psalm 121 reminded me at that time. My help comes from the Lord Who created all things, owns all things, and controls all things, and therefore, I would look to Him - the true Source of my help. Although the law didn't seem to be working for me, I knew that if I put my trust in God, all things would work out for my good in the end (Romans 8:28).

As I looked at the restrictions in a standard TPO and viewed the many ways my husband was in noncompliance right from the very beginning, I was amazed. According to the restraining order, the no-contact order prohibited him from contacting me at work, school, or home personally or via phone. So, as the order mandated, all communication was prohibited and was to cease between us when this order was enacted. I informed my church of the circumstances and they asked me if I wanted them to forbid him from coming to the church while the TPO was in effect or, in other words, if I wanted them to temporarily disfellowship him for the duration of the TPO order. I immediately declined that option as I believed that he needed the church now more than ever. As I mentioned earlier, I wasn't interested in being acrimonious or vindictive; I only desired to be safe. So, I just told them to execute my TPO, which stated that he was not to come within 500 feet of me. As far as communication went, he was not to call the girls or me while his TPO was active for the 12 months and not to contact my office staff either. He was also prohibited from involving himself in any of my personal or business matters during the life of this restraining order. Strangely enough, however, he was contacting me from the day of his arrest. That morning after his arrest he was contacting the office from a payphone in jail where he called the staff collect asking them to accept his call and to allow him to speak to a member of the staff and then to me eventually when I became aware. I was not privy to the conversation he had with the staff member, but I had already given the staff permission to accept the call when they were puzzled about what to do. After accepting the call, he apparently asked to speak to this staff member while I was seeing a patient and unaware of what was happening. I later learned that he and this staff member talked for a while during the time I was seeing patients before he and I did. So, from day one, he violated the order with no fear of retribution. Ironically, he was committing the violation from the sources we relied on for our protection and support - the jail (i.e. the legal system). However, interested to see what he was up to, I talked with him and he pleaded with me to forgive him and forget everything that had happened. He also asked if I would come get him out of jail and give him another chance. I told him that I couldn't do that and questioned him on how he was allowed to call me right after he was apprehended for violently offending me. He said that there was a payphone in the hall that anyone could use, so that's what he was on at the time unsupervised. I was still in a state of shock with this occurrence but finished the conversation with him anyway, which I ended shortly thereafter and mentioned that I would be praying for him. After hanging up, I quickly informed the staff of that morning's details concerning the domestic incident and how my life was almost taken. I also told them that I had him arrested, which was why he was calling the office collect from the county jail that morning. His father shared with me his plans to bail him out after I informed him of the situation.

I then quickly snapped back to my reality, which involved caring for my full load of patients on the schedule that day and then promptly getting to the hospital for my scheduled surgery that afternoon. I had a full day ahead of me and no time to waste as I was already somewhat delayed because of that morning's incident and as I stated before, I was thrust into single parenting all of a sudden with this fiasco so I had to pick the girls up after work too. So you can see that my plate was full!

But, as you can see, from day one, he was aggressively contacting me against police orders shortly after he was arrested. Not only did he call me at work, but later that night at home as well. I was bombarded and harassed by numerous collect calls from him all night as the girls and I were packing in efforts to relocate from the apartment in the morning assuming that he would be getting out the next day or so when his father bailed him out. My youngest sister who was visiting me that weekend from out of town and who witnessed the incident, was there helping us with plans to leave the next day. She was equally amazed by the many phone calls I received from him that night, which was the same day of his arrest. All of his calls were attempts to persuade me to come to pick him up in the morning and reconcile the relationship as though nothing happened with no plans for intervention of any kind. This suggestion was outlandish as our family was in desperate need of counseling among other things. Nevertheless, I kept focused and packed up everything I thought we could fit in a U-Haul that I planned to get in the morning and then retired for the night. However, throughout the night, I continued to get calls from him that I felt compelled to answer because I felt worried about him in jail. Although I agreed with his arrest that day, I still felt awful about the details and outcome of the day because I still loved him and cared about his well being as his wife.

Nonetheless, it was clear how he violated the order from the onset of this drama on more than one occasion. These occasions involved the numerous phone calls made against police orders, his coming to the parking lot of my job and calling the office on more than one occasion, and his efforts to communicate with us at church and then follow us home. I also never knew the content of the conversation he had that day with the staff member when he called the office collect from the payphone in jail. So, fast-forwarding things a bit from all of these examples where he was seen to be in violation of the order from the beginning, I was encouraged when I obtained the 12-month TPO later on because now I would be able to enforce the previously ignored orders moving forward, so I thought. This is when major disappointment set in because, unfortunately, I still experienced his noncompliance from time to time with the court order. Hence, the statement made by the police officer that day became clear to me and still resonates with me today.

Looking into my face pitifully as I returned to press charges again for another one of my husband's violations of the TPO, the officer addressed me politely and gently while informing me that the legal loopholes that currently existed surrounding this issue of domestic violence would serve to make it difficult to get the optimal help needed in my dilemma. When he glanced at my records and saw the multiple attempts I made to this police station to get help in my situation, he felt compelled to enlighten me of how the system works. His blunt statement was difficult to process at the time and I wrestled with feelings of hopelessness, defeat, and bitter disappointment. However, my experiences with seeking assistance, resources, and overall help in the area of domestic violence (or intimate partner violence) proved his words to be true that day.

Later while reflecting on the police officer's words, I saw this to be a defining moment for me where I concluded that I would have to advocate for myself and the girls because of this deficiency in the system where women, children, and minorities are devalued, and thus, considered unimportant. Unfortunately, as victims of the system, I realized we can be viewed as insignificant; therefore, equity of treatment is just a dream instead of a reality in these situations because victims are considered to be underdogs and thus discardable. Regrettably, I came to the realization that the girls and I fell into this category. Hence, the justice system would not be our friend nor our advocate along this journey. Sadly, this mindset subconsciously exists in some churches where females have no voice when suffering in a toxic marriage for example. I will expound more on this in later chapters. In any event, I saw the seed being sown for "*Three Women and A Vision*" to be born at God's appointed time. The three women represent my daughters and me and the vision is the insight that God gave me in our storm. This vision would help to provide hope for all of those who are hopeless and broken from impaired relationships, addictions, unemployment, poverty, and low self-worth. After witnessing utter disappointment and hopelessness during my courthouse experience with my sister survivors of intimate partner violence in chapter two, I realized that God was prepping and fertilizing the soil for the seed of ministry He was giving me through this walk of life. This ministry entails ministering and advocating for the social needs of others. In other words, I would be a social service advocate and assist individuals in getting the help and support that they need in various situations. After experiencing the unnecesssary struggle and fight to secure my extended TPO for the girls' and my protection, which I considered senseless, I knew that advocacy in these areas of justice was warranted. These experiences, along with others in this journey, aroused an unquenchable passion inside of me to make a difference in these areas of injustice in society. Thankfully, the seed was sown during these trying times and now, I would have to wait on God for the rain with its ultimate harvest and reaping.

Chapter 4

OUR CHALLENGING SHIFT

NOW THAT WE had our one-year TPO, we sought the next step to solidify a residence. After staying with a friend over the weekend when we left our home, we opted to stay in hotels until a permanent place was found to alleviate jeopardizing anyone else's safety. The challenge was finding a place with high surveillance and security due to our present dilemma, along with procuring a dog-friendly environment for the breed and size of our dog. It wasn't even an option to leave Ruby in that toxic environment while we were transitioning. She was family and her well being was just as important as ours. The challenge was just to find a place for us all in a timely fashion. Ruby was an American Bulldog who weighed 118 lbs at the time - mostly solid muscle - and she could be quite intimidating by appearance alone. Her demeanor and behavior could be even more menacing if she sensed by any means that we were in harm's way. She was often mistaken to be a pitbull. So, we realized that solidifying a place would take some time and thought and wouldn't be a quick fix venture because of her size and breed. Because renting was our best option in the essence of time, we moved forward with this option realizing the challenges we were up against. Finding a permanent residence was out of the question in the urgency of our situation. We didn't want to make a quick decision about anything permanent for fear of having regrets, and our situation called for a quick move. Also, rental properties were preferable in our immediate and precarious situation because as we saw on the day of my incident, the close knit community added safety in comparison to single family homes. If you recall, the neighbors of my apartment complex called security for me because they heard everything that morning. I, on the other hand, called the police, but security was able to respond faster because they were on duty there at the complex. The policeman responded not too long afterwards, but the security response from the apartment complex was more immediate. So, rental properties were definitely in our best interest at the time. However, most rental properties prohibited aggressive and intimidating breeds like Ruby and had size restrictions that excluded dogs over 60-80 pounds. We would just have to keep looking for those few properties that did take dogs like Ruby.

While looking for the right place for our new home, we enjoyed our hotel excursions which the girls found to be intriguing and exhilarating as we enjoyed the amenities and ambiance that afforded us the much-needed vacation in all of this chaos. The pool became the favorite amenity for the girls where they spent most of their time relaxing from all of the stress and anxiety precipitated by the horrific incident. However, at the tender ages of 10 and 7, the girls were totally oblivious to the seriousness of the issue at hand for the most part and I was happy to experience the truth in the old adage that says "ignorance is bliss". Fortunately, they didn't fully understand the stalking concerns and the potential violence that could flare up at any time if unexpectedly confronted by him even though we were currently separated from him and no longer in that toxic environment. Because of my awareness of the potential danger involved, I hired a private investigator temporarily until I felt things were more stable. I was prompted to do this after an experience we had one evening when returning to our hotel room. The concierge seemed to be less friendly this evening and asked me several questions. When I asked why I was being questioned all of a sudden after being there several days with no problem, he informed me that he was confronted by a man alleging that his wife had abducted his daughters and he needed the hotel to help him find the girls. Of course, the pictures of the girls that my husband presented to the hotel staff alarmed them and prompted them to initiate an investigation. I immediately showed the management office my TPO and they xeroxed it and kept it for documentation. They were very apologetic for the unnecessary and inappropriate inquiries and overall inconvenience. I also provided them with my husband's mugshot with the misdemeanor charge and they dropped their internal investigation. Thank God by the time we were in this hotel we had already secured the short term TPO that helped to shed light on this shady situation because, at the beginning of our hotel hopping, we hadn't obtained a TPO yet. We were hotel hopping because staying in these standard hotels longer than a couple of weeks was uncommon and we didn't want to draw unwanted attention to ourselves. Because we were locals, we were also extra cautious not to be seen by anyone we knew so that our secret place wouldn't be made common knowledge and compromise our safety. So we avoided long stays in one place and therefore didn't use extended stay hotels at the beginning of this journey. With extended stay hotels, one-month stays or longer were common because these hotels were set up just like apartments or efficiencies for situations requiring longer stays. However, during this phase of our journey, lengthy stays were not in our best interests for the reasons cited above. Be that as it may, I was relieved that the hotel had discovered that my husband's accusations were false. We were still aware, however, that we would have to transition to another hotel since my husband knew we were there and we didn't want to meet up with him by surprise. Knowing that he was irate with the sequence of events – the arrest, our relocation, the TPO, and his public exposure – I was unsure of what he would attempt to do. I didn't want to be put in a precarious situation like that morning when the choking incident occurred. So, I prayed and then felt led by God to move without hesitation - immediately. Now, I want to pause just a moment to address the importance of his "public exposure" that I just mentioned. Besides the picture on the fulton county jail website that is posted to the public that we have nothing to do with, we also realized the need to inform our circle of friends and family of the incident for safety reasons. But just in case there are any questions about this, I want to explain the rationale. If someone's life is threatened by a significant other, it logically and prudently behooves that person to alert family, friends, and coworkers for safety reasons moving forward.

This is extremely crucial because without one's social circle of family and friends knowing that the relationship has changed and is now dangerous, they may give vital information to the significant other (e.g. your whereabouts currently, your revised schedule for safety reasons, etc.) not knowing that this information could cause danger and cost a life. The news has shown numerous accounts of homicides at the workplace or hideout of the victim because the assailant discovered their new work schedule or their place of refuge by a friend, coworker, or family member who didn't know the relationship had turned toxic and was now dangerous. I recall a patient of mine in Atlanta that was killed this way. With her first pregnancy, her significant other accompanied her on almost every prenatal care visit, but when she started prenatal care with her second pregnancy, she mentioned that this baby had a different father. Unfortunately, she did not inform her family, friends, nor me (her provider) that the father of the first baby was furious and hostile with her about this current pregnancy because it wasn't his. She had a new significant other and the old boyfriend was so angry that he threatened to kill her. This was vital information that she should have relayed to her village and me. Had we known, we could have directed her to social services to secure a safety plan that could have saved her life and the unborn child. Because everyone was unaware, no one knew that she needed help. In any event, this angry father called my office one day to see when this patient's next appointment was and my staff told him that he was not privy to this information because of HIPAA (Health Insurance Portability and Accountability Act) rules and regulations. Although he wasn't successful in obtaining any information concerning this patient from my office, the staff and I later discovered that he found the patient's sister to be very resourceful. Uninformed of the current perilous situation that her sister was in, she divulged her sister's new residence to this aggrieved father not knowing that her sister (the patient) was currently estranged from him for safety reasons. Our office received a call two days later from a person wailing uncontrollably on the phone. It was a family member notifying us that our patient had been killed by this enraged father. Later that day, we saw that this story made the news and revealed that this father came to the patient's new residence, forced entry, and shot her in the stomach and the chest killing her and her unborn child right before the eyes of their two-year-old son. When the ambulance arrived, they found the patient lying dead on the ground in a pool of blood with the two-year-old crying and asking his mommy to wake up. His father not only mentally and emotionally traumatized his son by performing this atrocity in his presence at such a young age, but then abandoned him in this devastating moment leaving him terror-stricken, fatherless, and motherless all at once. This was the assailant's son from the patient's first pregnancy. What a tragedy and heart-wrenching scene that possibly could have been avoided if danger were communicated and the ex-boyfriend - the predator - exposed.

Redirecting back to our hotel scene where my husband had visited and falsified the girls' abduction, we checked out quickly and went to another hotel across town in a busy locale where we would have lots of traffic and make sure we weren't isolated considering our circumstances. The girls were so tickled as if they equated this move with the game "Hide and Seek". They enjoyed these hotel excursions during their summer break where we happily took advantage of all the amenities and found lots of family bonding and quality time in these close-knit settings. These were some memorable times that we treasured.

Although the girls were out of school for the summer, I had to get up and go to work from the hotel while my mom, who came from out of town to help me, would watch them. Usually the girls only got to see her maybe two to three times a year because I was the black sheep of the family who left my birthplace in Chicago, Illinois, and moved down south after undergraduate and graduate school. My three siblings and my mother, on the other hand, still lived in Chicago (my father was deceased) and they had no intention of leaving anytime soon. So, the girls took advantage of this bonus time to make treasurable memories with their Nema as my mother was affectionately called by all of her grandchildren. My mother enjoyed this bonus time with her only two granddaughters as well. They indulged in all kinds of scrumptious baked treats and namkeen that summer as they relished every moment with their one and only chef extraordinaire. They were in their own little unique heaven on earth and for this, they were appreciative. In addition to the delicious meals and finest desserts, they learned quickly that Nema was the Uno queen and they were deeply amused that she won most of the matches effortlessly despite their finessing, manipulating, and even cheating. Well, it was all in good fun anyway.

These hotel experiences weren't exclusive to just the girls, Nema, and myself either. When my nephews and sister-in-law came down to visit during these hotel excursions earlier on in our journey, we pow wowed together and had a good time. The close confinement of the hotel afforded an intimacy that allowed us to have some real relaxing, releasing, and exhaling moments. One particular time I fondly recall is when my nephews and I had some quality bonding time while my mom and sister-in-law went running some errands for me so that I could rest. We all gathered in one room (my room) and I decided to play some meditative gospel - particularly of the praise and worship genre. It was Friday late afternoon in the summertime and we had a couple of hours before sunset, but I wanted to usher in the Sabbath early as we took time to reflect on God's goodness. So, as the inspiring and thought-provoking music set the ambiance, the Holy Spirit sweetened the atmosphere with His presence. I was overwhelmed and ecstatic to have this time with my nephews all to myself during these precious moments where I talked with them and got to know them on a deeper level. Because I was their "out-of-town" auntie, our time together was limited and scarce, which saddened me as I reflected on how much I was missing while they were growing up. I wanted to be there for every milestone in their lives and share in their joys and sorrows, but this obviously wasn't God's plan for me as my residence was not a hop, skip and jump away. And God made it clear that He wanted to uproot me from my childhood environment by relocating me down south where He obviously had a work for me to do. By God's grace, I blossomed in my new locale and established a flourishing practice that became my ministry as well. As a gynecologist, it was of paramount importance to me to establish a practice where I could provide a holistic approach. This would allow me to minister to the social, emotional, and spiritual needs of females in addition to their physical needs, which I considered to be essential for one's total health. Therefore, my role would include that of a life coach for my patients as well as their healthcare provider.

At any rate, as I accepted the fact that I was the "away auntie", I still remember praying for God to allow me the opportunity to create a strong bond with my nephews and to make many memories to cherish with them. Although my other nephews were not able to come down during this time, I had some fun and memorable times with them as well when visiting Chicago on occasion - especially during this particular chapter in my life. God opened doors for my relationship to grow with all of my nephews and especially during this time in my life in the midst of the crisis we were undergoing. Right in the middle of the confusion, He (God) blessed us with some tender and comforting moments. His way is always the perfect and best way if we just wait on Him and exercise a little patience. If I had the privilege to see the future, I wouldn't have it any other way. Just a reminder of Isaiah 55:8,9.

As the Sabbath drew near, there was a shift in the atmosphere and ironically, we were playing this powerful song by Jason Nelson. This shift created a comfortable, judgment-free zone that stimulated a time of exhalation. Everyone seemed to be encouraged to let their walls down and open up about concerns that were troubling them. And as all of us shared different trials plaguing us at the time, we comforted and encouraged one another. This was motivated and encouraged by me sharing some of our story (the girls and my story) with them to answer any questions they may have been hesitant to ask. Realizing transparency begets transparency, I didn't hesitate to lead out with my testimony for starters. Without getting into a very detailed account of our current storm, I conveyed a synopsis and kept it simple. I didn't want to inundate them, but I knew that clarifying misinformation would be helpful and give them the correct perspective on things. The age range I was dealing with spanned from about six to eighteen years of age, so I had to take this into consideration when explaining things. I simply told them how the devil had wreaked havoc in our home and severed family bonds compelling us to relocate for the moment. They quietly listened and as I realized that I had their undivided attention, I took this opportunity to reveal how God was so good to us despite our present circumstances and how He delivered us that morning. At this point, they all started opening up and sharing some of their concerns as we prayed and comforted each other in this very emotional and nurturing setting. I just praised God for answering this particular prayer about my relationship with my nephews as I mentioned earlier. I also realized that had it not been for our current crisis, I would have never had the opportunity to talk with them on a deeper, more spiritual level because most conversations with family members who get together are surface. We all wear our masks and hide our pain well in these large family get-togethers and usually don't experience the freedom from constraint to just be open and honest about current situations that may warrant prayer and support. It's unfortunate that sometimes one may not be able to trust some family members, which blocks transparency.

Also, in these settings with family - whether immediate or extended - children and adults separate as their interests differ, which

doesn't offer enough mingling to bridge the gap between the generations and allow the youth to glean from the wisdom of the matriarchs
and patriarchs of the family. This is a huge misfortune that is especially
prevalent in today's society where the youth feel such autonomy and
independence in facing life's challenges because of their knowledgeable
and resourceful friend Mr. Google. Now, I'm not discouraging Google
by any means. I use it quite frequently and consider it to be one of
the most intelligent, convenient, and useful innovations in the world
today. There isn't an excuse for anyone to be devoid of knowledge with
this powerful resource tool available. However, knowledge is nothing
without wisdom because wisdom teaches one how to use knowledge,
and the youth of today can learn so much from the wisdom and experience of their elders. So, this time with the nephews that Friday
provided was a unique setting where the gap was bridged and there
was intermingling freely and openly. Looking back on this memory,
I thought of it jokingly like a "Cancun moment", where one would
say "what goes on in Cancun, stays in Cancun" because we trusted the
information shared would remain confidential and not transcend those
hotel walls. This was one of the special moments that I count dear during my journey that I will treasure.

Nonetheless, I will focus now on the urgency to restructure the
practice after the incident and the need to redistribute the work my
husband used to do in the office to someone else. I had to replace my
husband's information as my contact person for the practice temporarily with mine instead while we were in search of a permanent re-
placement. The hospitals, insurance companies, vendors, and various
medical offices were immediately notified of the change. All this was
done within the next one to two days after the incident. What I didn't
anticipate was moving my office space to a new location. With my
husband's unpredictable and unrestricted visits to the building, phone
calls, and other suspicious activity, I was compelled to relocate my
practice to assure a safe environment for my office staff and patients.
I chose a professional building further down the street and began the

move quickly while I notified all of the entities mentioned above of the change of address at the same time. This all occurred within the first couple of weeks from the time of the major incident.

After this task was complete, I resumed looking for a residence which I knew would not be an easy endeavor as I explained earlier because of the various rental property restrictions for my dog's breed and size and the overall safety concerns for all of us. So this would take a little more time, research, and lots of effort which meant that our residential situation would be left in transition for now. In the meantime, I sensed that the girls needed a break from all of this fast pace transitioning so I planned a trip to my hometown Chicago. The girls and I were in desperate need of a vacation and this would be somewhat of a vacation for them as they would be able to bond with family and friends. With the completion of one assignment, we could pause to breathe and let our hair down for a much needed reprieve. This assignment dealt with the office move, which was the most urgent at the time. So, we headed to Chicago with the plan to free our minds from the aftermath of this recent domestic upheaval.

Although it was early in this journey, it seemed like forever because of all the transitioning that had to be done right away, and yet, I was still working full time. So there were a lot of long night hours for me as I essentially had to restructure my personal and business life suddenly due to the urgency of the situation as I became a single parent entrepreneur who was an obstetrician/gynecologist. How I found time for the kids and myself is only explained by God's miraculous intervention through it all. Therefore, I welcomed the option of this temporary stress-free atmosphere away from all of the present turmoil where I could comfortably vegetate for just a moment as I collected my thoughts and sought God's guidance without worrying about the girls. They would be among family, so they would be safe.

This time away proved to be perfect for me also to unwind and prepare for the court date coming up in a week with my husband concerning the misdemeanor as it was sadly categorized. My lawyer and

I had made some preparations before the trip and we would be in contact while I was away. She and I were confident that things would rule in my favor at this upcoming court date with the violent ordeal I suffered. I had hoped to have my sister serve as a witness to strengthen my testimony as she was present in the apartment when the incident occurred, but she was not comfortable doing this. Nonetheless, the lawyer and I felt that my testimony alone, along with his arrest on the scene that day, would suffice. Unfortunately, I learned later that this held no weight when my mother and I returned for this court date a week or so after relaxing in Chicago. We were shocked to learn when we arrived at the courthouse that morning that the trial was cancelled without our knowledge. My lawyer and I were extremely disturbed because neither one of us was notified and I felt like I had been bamboozled. My mother and I drove back to Atlanta together leaving the girls in Chicago for a week or so to be present for this court hearing and then to solidify a residence before bringing the girls back, which they didn't object to and which, surprisingly, didn't take long to do either. My Ruby (my dog) was in the kennel, and my aim was to get her out and reunite as soon as we could. However, when faced with the news concerning the cancellation of this court date, we were taken aback in perplexity. Needless to say, I was beyond being disappointed as indignation surfaced while I fought to maintain my composure. It was then when I spotted a friend of the family who I remembered was a social worker. She was my babysitter on a few occasions and we both sang in the praise team together at church. I wondered what she was doing there as I saw her walking down the hall between the courtrooms as she was approaching where I was. Strangely, she didn't appear surprised to see me there and looked as if she was coming to tell me something. I didn't wait for her to reach me, but met her midway and began to ask if she knew what was going on. I don't know why I thought she would know, but I got a sixth sense at that instance that she did. Before I could ask the question, she just calmly stated that he wouldn't be there because he was categorized as a ward of the state in this case and the court hearing was cancelled. I thought to myself, "What does that mean, and what about the safety of the girls and me?" She just continued shaking her head as if she was in total disagreement with this action, but then I wondered how she even got involved with our file and had this knowledge. When I asked her how she knew all of this, she informed me that she knew about our case from its onset because the file had come across her desk when the incident occurred. That's when I became upset with her and questioned why she behaved as if she didn't know what was going on when she saw us at church. She responded that she wanted to avoid breaching confidentiality and professionalism in our case. Because this sounded reasonable, I accepted her response and was receptive to her advice to attend this courtroom hearing that was about to start where I could initiate the process of getting my 12-month TPO. An appointment was not required and this would make my courthouse visit that day worth the trip after my disappointment with the cancelled court session. She appeared to be in the hot seat in retrospect and I was tempted to believe that she only used this gesture to distract me from asking her any further questions about things. This deflection was not suspect initially, so I consented with her suggestion and this is how and where the laborious process mentioned earlier with obtaining my extended TPO started. My attorney who was with me during this encounter later disclosed some concerns about what had transpired and recommended that I be cautious when dealing with mutual friends of mine and my ex-husband's. She felt strongly suspicious about things at this point and wanted to forewarn me. From that day forward, I was circumspect when dealing with mutual friends. This situation, however, proved to be another example of how God can turn a negative situation into a positive one because, despite the foul play with the initial hearing, I was still able to initiate the process to obtain my extended TPO before the temporary one expired not initially knowing that this was required. The first example of God turning a negative situation into a positive one was illustrated when I saw how God used our misfortune to allow some treasurable bonding time with my nephews as we made precious memories amid this mess.

And now this disappointment with the court cancellation that turned into an opportunity to get the 12-month TPO process started. By trusting God through it all, I saw Him work over and over in our favor. Another interesting discovery during this process involved the rationale for the misdemeanor charge which didn't match the offense. Because this behavior was considered a first offense and there was no presumed history in the system, this charge was given. However, later when applying for my temporary TPO, I was questioned about my stepsons because the caseworkers recognized my husband's name. There was some history in the social system after all, but it mysteriously was unavailable at the onset of this case.

When I met these two handsome and brilliant little clones of their dad and mom, it was truly love at first sight. They were just five and two years of age then and I considered them to be my two precious gifts that God gave me when I married their dad. It was truly a love thang as BeBe Winan's song says. Shortly after I married, my husband and I had two daughters to add to our clan creating our very own Brady Bunch scenario. The Brady Bunch was one of my favorite TV shows when I was growing up and I felt that this popular TV show's blended family reminded me of our blended family at the time. However, by the time of this incident, the boys, who were now in high school, had decided to live with their other (biological) mom, so they were not present that morning when my life-threatening event occurred because they were living with her at the time. Nevertheless, when my husband's name appeared in the system that day, I tried to investigate things, but to no avail. All of the attempts by my lawyer and me to address this finding were blocked by one thing or another, which made matters worse and caused our situation to appear hopeless …. but God! (my mantra always).

Well, despite the monkey wrench thrown into our plans with the court case being cancelled, my mother and I began our apartment and condo search as planned now that we were back in Georgia. We started where we left off before taking our Chicago vacation and hoped to find something in a week so we could bring the girls back soon. Unbeknownst to us, we had other interesting encounters awaiting us. One specific encounter of note was my recollection of a package my husband and I received from Ford prior to this unhappy shebang. I never knew what it was, but it was for my car with instructions. I wasn't the least bit disturbed at the time because I figured my husband had just ordered another gadget for my car. Of course, with the current status of our relationship, this initial nonchalance concerning this device transitioned into an uneasiness that prompted an investigation. I decided to call Ford and inquire, but it was to no avail because they weren't able to give me any helpful or additional information other than it was sent from his brother who was an employee of Ford at the time. My husband's father, who was retired during this time, was also once a Ford employee, however, my husband was self-employed. Refusing to ignore the apprehension that was in my spirit, I decided to be more proactive and go to a local Ford dealership for answers, and once again, they discounted any concerns of mine in regards to this device as if I should not have been concerned. So, just when I was tempted to let it go assuming that I was reading too much into everything, a family member pointed me to someone she knew who owned a Ford dealership in Georgia where we were residing and he just happened to be someone that my husband and I had recently met at a wedding and my husband had become good friends with him. I called him and he asked me to fax the papers that came in the packet with the device, which included a picture of the device and installation instructions. Hours went by and there was no response from him. Additionally, my attempts to reach him were unsuccessful. Meanwhile, I recalled that I had faxed the paperwork at 8:00 a.m. and it was now 4:30 p.m. and still no response. At this point, we perceived this option was disappointingly nonviable as well and just concentrated on completing other tasks before sunset after wasting much precious time that Friday afternoon. Arriving back at the hotel that summer evening, we noticed that the latch on the door was broken and immediately notified the front desk. A hotel attendant was sent up at once to fix the problem and we retired for the night. Falling asleep, however, was difficult because my spirit was disturbingly troubled. Thoughts were racing through my mind as I wondered if the door latch was a warning sign. My mind quickly went back to the day we checked in two days ago. This door latch was perfectly fine then and for the two days of our stay until later this evening upon our return to the hotel. Since our short stay thus far, there had been no problems. Was it just coincidental that the door latch broke this evening? And, if so, how did this happen and who broke it? Or was this a sign to evaluate things further? I chose the latter and reviewed the day's activities closely looking for any obvious red flags that would validate my concerns. The most apparent one was the lack of follow up with the local dealership owner who happened to be a friend of my husband's but made it clear that he wanted to be helpful in any way he possibly could considering the circumstances. The other red flag was the door latch being broken only after my contact with this friend of my husband's who I sent a fax to revealing our hotel location. The possibility was real enough for me that he could have informed my husband about my inquiries concerning this device and my location. Not wasting another second, I called downstairs to the front desk and asked them if anyone had checked in to the adjoining room to ours. Upon my check-in, I requested a single room without an adjoining room because of safety concerns, but the single rooms were all taken and I was regrettably left with this single room that had an adjoining room. Sensing my frustration and concern after learning of my situation, the hotel staff assured me that they would not check anyone into that room during my short stay there. However, to my astonishment that night, I learned that a single man had checked into this room that afternoon with plans to leave first thing early in the morning. The safety concerns obviously were not passed to the night shift staff who checked this gentleman into my adjoining room, and at this point, I wasn't going to sit around and second guess things. I immediately made arrangements to check out without delay.

Because I consulted God on everything through prayer, I was familiar with the voice in my conscious spelling trouble, so I adhered to the warning, not a second too late. I told my mom, and she and I were packed and ready to go in less than fifteen minutes. Fortunately, we hadn't unpacked everything just yet as we planned to stay for one week and we had only been there a couple of days. Nevertheless, confirmation of my decision was validated further when I had a clash with the bellhop who began questioning why I was leaving at that time in the morning (close to 12:00 a.m.) and tried to discourage my decision. According to him, all the surrounding hotels were full to the limit and I wouldn't have anywhere else to go. Although this could have been the case, I didn't recall asking him for any advice or input on anything and wondered why he assumed I was going to another hotel. For all he knew, I could have been going to a friend's house or traveling out of town after checking out. I was also curious why he was so overly concerned with my desire to leave. But by this time, things had escalated as one would expect with the unwelcomed concern and interrogation I suffered from him. Therefore, I was no longer asking politely, but now in an urgent manner and demanding an immediate response. For anyone who knows me, it is a well-known fact that when I am determined to do something and it's God-endorsed, no demon in hell can stop me. God sees to that. So, I reminded this gentleman in a cordial fashion of his duty as a bellhop - to attend to the needs of his guests. I also offered to call someone in administration if he needed assistance in doing his job. This gesture nipped the present foolishness in the bud and he quickly took our luggage to the car and our stay there was history. This hiccup with the bellhop as aforementioned just validated my feelings that something had gone awry that night and I wasn't gonna stay there and try to figure it out either. His overly concerned interest in our plans was extremely troubling to me, along with his aggressive gestures to dissuade and deter me from leaving at that moment. But it was this questionable and bizarre behavior that sealed the deal and prompted me to check out with a sense of urgency. My conversation with our dealership friend was history as well as we never heard back from him again, which additionally substantiated the actions taken above. Not only did he fail to call me back, but he avoided my follow up calls and never returned a call at all - not even to this day and my number hasn't changed. Nonetheless, I remember this early morning of wandering around Atlanta trying to find a safe place to go after leaving that hotel after midnight. It was frustrating and unnerving trying to free myself in this quandary. After reaching out to the police officer assigned as my advocate (my victim's advocate) for the first time in this case, I discovered that he was unavailable because he was with his son for visitation that weekend and wasn't available until Monday after the weekend despite my current emergency. It was early Saturday morning at this time and to wait over 24 hours or more for a solution in our emergency was senseless. Ironically, as I mentioned, this was the only time I had ever solicited his help since the incident, which was a couple of months ago, and disappointingly, he was not available and unconcerned. My pastor informed me when I contacted him that he was at the airport and about to board the plane soon which made his availability nil as well. It hurt that he didn't even bother to offer up a quick prayer for me right there on the phone to calm my fears, but I figured that he had a lot on his plate while preparing to board the plane and then to solidify his plans upon arrival, so I gave him a passcard. I only wish that he had an elder or deacon (someone!) that he could have referred me to as my situation was urgent. I only thought to call him because he asked me to keep in touch with him and update him on occasion after learning of my domestic mishap. While taking a deep breath during this desperate moment, the idea to go to the hospital and sleep in the call room came to my mind. Because it was the weekend, the call rooms for obstetricians like myself were more likely to be unoccupied, so I headed there and prayed all the while that this plan wouldn't jinx the present quietude of my obstetrics and gynecology practice. I needed a break and didn't want to have to deal with any medical emergencies at this particular time. Nevertheless, I felt so grateful to have an "ever-present help in trouble" (Psalm 46:1) and took the time to praise Him all the way to the hospital for reminding me of this option. Our God is awesome! My mother and I had a restful sleep knowing that we were in secure surroundings and attended church later that morning where we lifted up a heartfelt praise thanking God for all of the victories of that week and then resumed our apartment hunting the next day.

Sunday was a new day and after my devotion that morning, I felt confident that we would find our new residence that day, and that's just what happened. The place God led us to that morning was safe and dog friendly just as we desired and we made arrangements to move in within the next couple of days, which was perfect. Prior to moving in, I decided to trade in my SUV for another one since my concerns about the device on my car were never resolved, along with other concerns mentioned earlier on. After our successful and uneventful move in, we made plans to get the girls who were currently in Chicago and bring them back to Atlanta, and then ultimately bring our Ruby Duby (our dog) home from the kennel too. Ruby was in a local kennel for an indefinite period until we were able to find a new home. Words wouldn't begin to do justice in describing this reunion. It brings tears to my eyes just thinking about it - my very own love story with a canine. It broke our hearts when we were compelled to make temporary arrangements for Ruby to go to the kennel indefinitely when we began our apartment hunting following the domestic incident. Knowing that Ruby was clueless with everything going on and that she probably thought we were leaving her there for good, was also very difficult for us. Oh how we wished for a way to communicate to her that we loved her, that we weren't mad or tired of her, and that this would only be temporary. In any event, we mustered up the strength, courage and tough love to place her where we knew she would be safe from any harm and we had no regrets.

Even though it was never my intention to get a dog, I simply fell in love with her from day one when my husband brought her home as a puppy and she sat at my feet. Then it happened right before my very eyes. In just a short while, she quadrupled her size and grew into the big fierce dog that my friends and neighbors saw her as until they got to know her. She was really a tender and gentle sweetheart - our very own teddy bear as long as you weren't considered a threat to the family. In this case, she would render you the business as expected as our guard dog. Her new intimidating and robust appearance that transpired rapidly from just a tiny adorable puppy, put the fear in everyone - including me. I'll never forget when I came home for lunch one day and she barked at me so viciously that I mentally succumbed to being eaten alive. When I suddenly stopped in my tracks and she saw that I was paralyzed from being frightened, she surprisingly stopped barking and looked at me intently while leaning or tilting her head from one side to the other as if she was confused with my timid behavior. She was only trying to communicate that she was hungry too and didn't want to be forgotten as I learned later on. God forbid if I got my lunch that day and forgot to feed her the tasty meals I always made for her. In retrospect, I believe this was my saving grace that day and what kept me from being eaten alive. Ruby dared not bite or harm the hand that fed her.

In any event, I still wasn't comfortable with this new ferocious bark yet, so it continually petrified me, along with many others. Nonetheless, as time went on, she interpreted that I didn't like her terrifying bark and substituted it with a more gentle bark when communicating with me. Consequently, she and I became emotionally in sync from that day onward. When she died in her old age, she was sorely missed and I often recall fond and dear memories of her that I'll eternally cherish. I'll take time to digress for a brief moment as I share some precious and comical memories below of our Ruby.

The first memory I can recall is when I was returning from a trip and I was anxious to see her. I remember coming in the back door and being met by her aggressive barking. Startled, I attempted to calm her down by gently and fondly saying her name as I talked to her and tried to hug her, but this only resulted in the barking progressing to growling as if I were a stranger. Of course I was hurt beyond words and somewhat traumatized as I entertained the ridiculous thought that maybe she had forgotten me while I was away. However, after a few more unsuccessful attempts, my husband and his father who were lying there unbothered on the couch watching television, turned to me and calmly instructed me to put my luggage down. I was trying to greet and hug her with luggage in my hands which frightened her because she was unfamiliar with it. As soon as I complied, Ruby attacked me with love. The luggage was clearly intimidating her and making her feel uncomfortable, which undoubtedly put her on defense. Because I didn't have a dog growing up, I had no clue what was going on, but I must say that I was glad to be in company with the dog whisperers that day.

Another memorable event was when I was walking Ruby in the neighborhood one day. Now, I lived in a wooded neighborhood at that time surrounded by forested areas with some sections devoid of sidewalks along some of the streets as well. This particular morning, Ruby and I were out on one of our usual strolls when a car appeared out of nowhere going a little faster than usual in a residential area. Because of the quietness of this area with low to no traffic at this time in the morning, I allowed Ruby to walk without a leash, which she did on occasion with no problem. This was a street that somewhat resembled a trail and I could see if anyone was coming long before they reached us and apply the leash if necessary. We had Ruby well trained and when her name was called, she responded promptly without hesitation and was overall very obedient. When I saw this car coming from a distance behind us at this time in the morning and going unusually fast, I immediately called for Ruby by reflex in an emergency just trying to see where she was. Ruby was across the street from me at the time in one of the forested areas and hearing her name she immediately responded by starting to come towards me as she located me across the street from her. However, this was not what I wanted at this instant because the car was coming and would hit her if she crossed the street at that time. I was merely trying to locate her by calling her, forgetting that she was trained to come when called. Well, in a matter of seconds I quickly shouted for her to stop - hoping that it wouldn't be too late because I knew she was prompted to come to me when called right away. As I shouted I saw that she was in motion to run already. It was at this moment that I confirmed my Ruby was special and that my God is good. What she did next will testify. In this desperate moment, I whispered up an inward cry to God for help and just as Ruby started running, I shouted for her to stop by yelling "no" and then "stop" at the top of my lungs, and thank God she responded. Just as this car passed by, Ruby fell back. This driver was obviously oblivious to what was going on and didn't stop even once to see what had just happened despite all of my hysterical shouting as if someone were dying. I was so sure that the driver heard all of this commotion, but apparently not. In any event, what happened next was amazing - essentially a miracle. While in full motion to run to meet me, my warning shout registered to Ruby and she saw the car just in time. Discerning the danger involved, in the middle of her lunge or mid run she pulled her torso up and back to prevent landing on her front legs which would have placed her in the street where she would have been hit by the car just at that moment. Instead, she fell backwards and avoided being hit by this car. Yes, my Ruby executed the "Matrix" move (borrowed from the movie) as she dodged being hit by this car. At this moment I began thanking and praising God profusely for sending an angel to save Ruby that day. Ruby and her "Matrix" move were the topic of every conversation for a good while. Then there was the time that we had family and friends over in the summer and my young cousins were running around excitedly. One of my younger cousins noticed something on Ruby that caught his attention. He had to be about four years of age or a little more at the time and surprisingly unintimidated by Ruby although Ruby was more than two to three times his size. Equally surprising was the fact that he didn't really know Ruby because he lived out of town, yet he didn't appear fearful of her menacing and robust stature at all. So, with a childlike boldness that still remains inexplicable, he walked right up to Ruby and got directly in her face almost rubbing noses and put his finger close to her inner eye showing us where there was something in her eye. His act was so quick and unpredictable that we didn't have time to stop him, or grab him for that matter in efforts to prevent him from being presumably bitten. We all sighed deeply with indescribable relief and amazement at Ruby's response, which was a calm and loving demeanor through it all. Not once did she appear agitated or angry, but just sat there unperturbed as she tolerated this cute, young, intrepid preschooler who was unaware of the potential endangerment involved with what he had just done. These anecdotes of Ruby serve to attest to the gentle and compassionate spirit she possessed which was consistent with our research prior to getting a dog. My husband and I did our homework and discovered that her breed was very affable with children. So Ruby was a precious dog and anyone visiting our home saw the royal treatment we donned on her in the way her water bowl had ice (especially in the summer) and how she ate warm and tender tasty meals from time to time to break the monotony of her usual dry, hard, and boring dog food that was room temperature. I made sure of this and defended my indulgence by reasoning that because I wasn't sure of a dog heaven, so to speak, Ruby was definitely going to get all the heaven I could possibly give her down here.

Well, after things calmed down a bit, my mom and I went back to Chicago and got the girls and brought them back. When I brought them to our new found home, they were ecstatic and speechless. Seeing Ruby just added to the excitement. We were all elated as we looked forward to settling down and relaxing. We were all back together again. It had been a whirlwind and now it was time to take a moment to breathe, unwind, and catch up with our circle of love - the ferocious four as I affectionately saw us as during that time (the girls, Ruby, and me).

Chapter 5

———— ❧ ————

THE SECRET PLACE OF
THE MOST HIGH

AFTER SEVERAL WEEKS of ongoing planning, investigating, transitioning, and restructuring, I finally took a moment to breathe and exhale. From the day of the incident to the present time, I had been nonstop in a survival-mode mindset as I mentally repeated the old adage that "only the strong survive". Things were in a state of overall chaos and confusion, yet I struggled to make sense of things with all of the unaddressed concerns and unanswered questions. New discoveries, quandaries, and problems were constantly being hurled at me and I was doing my best to maintain my sanity and peace of mind. Interestingly, however, I had an inexplicable peace that came over my spirit from the time I relocated and moved on with my life. From a spiritual standpoint, I attributed this unanticipated serenity to be from my liberation from an unequally yoked relationship, and consequently, an environment devoid of peace. Contrary to what was expected after a tragic separation, I actually felt relieved as if I had a huge weight lifted off my chest. It was ironic but refreshing. This experience revealed my true emotional status which was an eye opener for me. Overall, I thought that I was happy for the most part, but apparently not. My family life was more stressful than I realized because Jesus was missing in our relationship as a couple. I made efforts to maintain my personal connection with God daily, but my efforts to do so as a couple were often rejected and dismissed leaving the marriage's spiritual fuel tank on empty. Of course, there were times when my husband and I didn't see eye to eye on things and this was frustrating and discouraging at times. But then, there were good times where we shared lots of laughter and good ole fun. But with Jesus missing in this equation, over time we experienced marital estrangement that served to considerably distance us and substantially weaken the relationship. Apathy set in and all of our interactions from that point on were met with indifference. We were like two ships passing in the night in desperate need of counseling. We were in a woebegone state that needed spiritual intervention before it was too late.

Unfortunately, we didn't get the counseling we needed and the spiritual decline observed in our marriage was left unchecked and consequently reached its nadir. Hence, on the morning of the incident the curtain was lifted and our marital defects were glaringly exposed as we allowed the enemy (Satan) to wreak havoc in our home. His (the enemy's) true intentions were unquestionable that day as the Bible verse came to mind in John 10:10 disclosing that he only comes to "steal, kill, and destroy". But although the enemy was hell-bent on destroying our family bond, which he succeeded in doing that day, he was not allowed to destroy us. On the contrary, God was there to pick up all the broken pieces and give the girls and me a reason to start all over again. We were thankful for His protective watch care and ever abiding presence that showed up in our defense and blocked the enemy's diabolical purpose of taking my life that day. It was a close call, but with God all things are possible (Matthew 19:26).

As I reflected on everything that happened over the last month or two, I knew I needed to just stop and process everything that had occurred thus far. It was mind boggling and hurtful, which made it difficult to digest, but I knew it was necessary for my healing. So I allotted this time for the girls and me to begin our mental, spiritual, and physical recuperation, as we allowed God to shower us with His tender loving care and speak to us words of hope, comfort, life, and healing. We recognized that we also needed this quiet time to listen to His voice for direction in this domestic mayhem. It was in these quiet moments that I felt an irrepressible sense of gratitude as I thought about all that God had brought the girls and me through in spite of our current state. The fact that we were in our right mind and still standing after being hit by what felt like a whirlwind, was a definite testimony of God's goodness to us. It was clear to us that we were still standing only because God was holding us up through it all. His intervention was evident in how He reversed the evil that Satan meant for us along this journey and turned it around for our good instead. God was constantly working positively through our misfortunes. Amidst all the confusion that bombarded our lives from the onset of this domestic catastrophe, God graced us with an unbelievable serenity in our storm that allowed us to navigate along this journey prudently and optimistically. The inconsistencies and loopholes we encountered in the legal and social systems, along with the foul play we discovered left us no other recourse but to rely totally on God. And this is the best decision anyone could ever make because no one can love and care for us like Him and He is in control of everything. We didn't know how to make sense of anything that had recently transpired, but knowing God was in control comforted us. This knowledge was sufficient for us to press onward with the fortitude essential to see brighter days with God as our omnipotent Leader.

Thankfully, we took this time to reflect, unwind, exhale, and worship after settling down in our new place. It was time to get in our Secret Place as I would mention to the kids on occasion. They were familiar with this reference and appreciated the time spent in meditation, prayer, song, and reading God's Word. This precious time with God refueled, refreshed and fortified us on a daily basis to face the anticipated and unanticipated agenda of each new day. One of our favorite books of the Bible was Psalms. I love and appreciate King David's (the author's) transparency and humility as he shares the vicissitudes of his daily life with us through his praises, supplications, prayers, and reliance on God's promises.

Because I could empathize with his psalms in various areas of my life, I found them very helpful when we were confronted with this tragedy. We learned like David in Psalms 23 that God is all we need and want - the only One we can trust. During our reflections, we were grateful for His guidance as our Shepherd in our troubled state with its uncertainties. We trusted Him to guide us safely through this current adversity and to re-establish us on our new path. After all of the domestic turmoil recently witnessed, along with the abrupt transition from what we called home, we welcomed this respite in the "green pastures and beside the still waters" (Psalms 23:2) where we could let our hair down, kick back, and exhale. We longed for peace and tranquility now that we were safe and sound in our new home. Having somewhere to call home was meaningful also as we were establishing our new norm. So I took a vacation for a couple of weeks from work to stay home and connect with the girls and spend some quality time - after all, it was their summer break. We enjoyed playing games, watching movies, and doing activities together outside and inside the home. We also enjoyed our devotion time. This was special because I was able to share with them how God was blessing us in spite of how things looked at times. I also stressed the importance of their personal relationship with Him aside from mine and warned them that they could not get to heaven by riding on my coattails, so they would have to get to know Jesus for themselves. During these devotional times, I encouraged them to express their feelings about everything including the situation with their father. They were allowed to be honest and open about their feelings and I did my best to address all of their concerns. Unceasing prayer, forgiveness, and unconditional love were highlighted as powerful tools every christian should possess. One's mental, emotional, physical, and spiritual health depend on these character traits. Journaling became one of our favorite pastimes and we were often entertained and inspired when sharing some of the contents of our journals with each other. We expressed our concerns and needs, as we offered our praise through this powerful communication tool we used to talk to God. Cooking some of our favorite meals and leisurely enjoying each day with no agenda was wonderful. We relished this time together just the three of us. My mom had gone home to Chicago temporarily to take care of some business, so it was just the three of us during this quiet time and we made precious memories.

Our new found place that God blessed us with set the ambiance for our little heaven on earth as it beautifully exposed the magnificent celestial sphere on a daily basis. Residing near the top of this high-rise building that possessed over forty floors, our condo was situated as such where we were afforded a breathtaking view that set the tone for our worship every morning as we witnessed the sunrise up close and personal being almost completely surrounded by windows. The aesthetic and stunning view of the sunset was also appreciated daily, which motivated us to stop if just for a minute and meditate on God's awesomeness and goodness to us at the end of each day. God's favor on us during this time was evident by our occupancy of one of the few units that had both views - the sunrise and sunset. He knew we needed this therapeutic, peaceful, and awe-inspiring atmosphere to begin and end each day as we looked to Him as our Jehovah Rapha (Healer). And what better way but through reflection on His creation that testified of His omnipotence and love. We were thankful for His favor and ever abiding presence along our journey (Hebrews 13:5,6).

My older cousin who was like a big sister when we were growing up, came down and spent a few days with us during this vacation time I set aside. We had a lot of catching up to do and had a good time doing it. While updating her with our current situation and then reminiscing about our past, we shared some laughs and tears along with some testimonies on how God had seen us through from childhood to adulthood. Once again, God was giving us sunshine in our storm by letting us have some precious and endearing memories with special people in our lives. She came to be a source of help for the girls and me while my mom was still in Chicago. So the girls were able to develop their own bond with her while I was at work and to make memories of their own.

Well, the two weeks went by quickly and my mom was on her way back. I said my goodbyes to my cousin and thanked her for coming. We promised to keep in touch and I promised to update her with our situation. As far as work was concerned, I was inclined to extend my vacation from the office another week to visit some places and take care of some unfinished personal and practice-related business. While restructuring the staff and administrative duties in the office, I discovered some concerns that I needed to address. My plan was to visit the various entities and offices during this additional week in efforts to appropriately resolve these matters. My mother came back the next morning and we updated each other and I shared my plans with her for the following day.

Chapter 6

———— ∿ ————

FLABBERGASTING MOMENTS

THE NEXT DAY I decided to make a visit to the IRS Center downtown to answer some questions I had about my taxes because my husband, who usually took care of this, was no longer available given the current situation. As the practice manager, he met quarterly with the accountant to do taxes and to take care of all the other accounting matters of the business until the day of the incident when he no longer served in this capacity. However, prior to the incident, I remember inquiring why my taxes weren't done for the last couple of years only to discover that it was longer. He was evasive with his response and informed me that he was transitioning away from the accounting firm that we had been using from the start of the business, yet I was never made aware of this plan until this conversation and this information left me feeling totally out of the loop of things. I not only felt disturbed, but perplexed also and, consequently, sought to get to the bottom of things. This new accounting firm he was transitioning to just happened to be the one he used for his own business. So, I assumed that because he was pleased with their services, he wanted to switch my business to this firm as well. Anyhow, I never was displeased with the accountant I had from the start of my business, so I was slightly confused with the decision to switch and this didn't explain the lapse in filing my taxes over the years noted. My husband was a commercial and residential inspector, as well as the practice manager for my medical practice. However, when things slowed down with real estate, he spent more time managing the business and financial affairs of my medical practice and less time with his business of commercial and residential inspections. For some reason or another during this time, the negligence with the practice's tax filing occurred and he seemed to be at a loss for words when I inquired about how this happened.

Seeing that I was perturbed with this unexplainable delinquency, he suggested using another accountant that could handle this matter promptly and rectify the situation before switching to the new firm. He rationalized this plan because the new firm didn't have an appointment for the next three months and this particular accountant had one in the next couple of days. Because he ascertained my urgency to get things done as soon as possible, he went with his current plan of using this accountant just this one time. Unfortunately, things didn't materialize with this plan because this accountant's estimation of the taxes owed was astronomical and incongruent with what my knowledge of the company's revenue, along with my income was over that period of time. So, logically I wanted some questions answered before paying anything. My husband, at this point, became very aloof in his dealings with this tax dilemma and distanced himself from it completely as he avoided any further conversation concerning it. His behavior became strangely awkward when I made attempts to follow up as I assumed he was resolving the issue. Sadly and surprisingly, after our domestic incident, I discovered that he never did resolve things, so I was left to reconcile things on my own with very limited information considering the circumstances and no accountant who had a clue of what was going on. Everything I could recall surrounding this accounting dilemma prior to the domestic incident was vague leaving me destitute of any possible logical solutions.

So my visit that day to the IRS center was to get clarification on my taxes owed, among other things. When it was my turn, my mother and I went to the cubicle and I inquired about my business and personal taxes over the last couple of years or so after recently discovering my husband's inexcusable delinquency with tax filing during that time. The IRS attendant confirmed this lapse in tax filing and attempted to hide the concern and confusion that was written all over her face as she appeared to be browsing through my IRS electronic file for the business and for my personal taxes trying to make sense of things. During this time in the interview there was a brief, but uncomfortable silence that was finally broken when she made eye contact with me and politely suggested that I take steps to rectify this dereliction of duty with my taxes as soon as possible. Upon leaving the IRS center that day, I looked at my mother in amazement at what we had just learned and witnessed. She too had an astonished look on her face as we walked to the car in silence. When we got in the car, she told me that she wasn't sure if I should have made this inquiry with the IRS. She felt that I was opening a can of worms that would possibly lead to tax violations with potential auditing and serious fines. I informed her that the steps I took that day were taken after much prayer and forethought and I was confident that I was doing the right thing because I was being led by the Holy Spirit. Furthermore, I explained that it was only prudent and imperative for me to be assertive in getting clarity with my tax filing status and taxes owed so that I could resolve any issues if necessary. As I retired that night, I realized that I had some additional questions I needed to ask and that I should have obtained some documentation of everything discussed with the IRS attendant that day as well. This thought process led me to make plans to revisit the center first thing in the morning. This time, however, I would not torture my mom or the kids with this redundant and time consuming task. Instead, I would let them stay home in bed and sleep because my plans were to leave before the crack of dawn and aim to be the first one in the line in order to expedite my visit. Well, I made it there early, but I was third in the line which I found equally satisfying. Either way, I accomplished my goal to be in and out in no time since I was there before the office opened and at the front of the line. When the doors opened, things went rapidly and it was my turn to be helped before I knew it. I recited the same spiel from the day before and anticipated things going quickly. I just had a few additional questions from yesterday that I forgot to ask. As the IRS attendant was authenticating me prior to assisting me with my inquiries, he looked disturbed as he viewed the monitor displaying my profile. Strangely enough, he informed me that he couldn't discuss my IRS file with me and just continued staring at the screen with a very concerned countenance. I immediately assumed that he opened the wrong file by mistake and insisted that he re-enter the information I gave him. The IRS attendant that helped me the day before had no problem reviewing my file with this same information, so I suggested that he try again presuming that a mistake was made. My persistence only served to unsettle his demeanor even more as I noticed that his face turned beet red by now. At this point, he could no longer hold his composure as he appeared to be getting extremely uncomfortable. All of a sudden he abruptly blurted out that he could not discuss "my" business account with me because the representative noted on file for the account was the sole contact to discuss all business matters with, so this would prevent him from assisting me with the questions I had concerning the account. Bizarre as it may seem, I was restricted from my own IRS business account because of a representative placed on the account serving as the sole contact for my business who I didn't even know. Even more strange, was how this apparent amendment to my account occurred literally overnight without me having any knowledge of it prior to this visit. I found it hard to believe that this insane gesture excluding me from accessing my own account was now actually being implemented and supported by the IRS that morning. This change on my account precisely occurred within less than 24 hours - from the time I left the center in the late afternoon the day before to early this next morning. Well, of course, this situation left me flummoxed and speechless for a second because of these puzzling facts that I was struggling to mentally understand and process. Thoughts of my interview the day before kept racing through my mind. There was no difficulty inquiring about my account during that first IRS visit using this same sensitive information. However, this information was now counterproductive on this second visit because it now blocked my access to the account which was extremely frustrating and bewildering. How things took a one hundred and eighty degree turnaround this particular morning left me baffled. Suddenly, I began directing inquiry after inquiry toward him because of the perplexing situation at hand until he turned beet-red from his frustration and all of the confusion. He immediately began writing on a piece of paper and then handed it to me. The paper essentially said that our interview was being audiotaped, but not videotaped, hence his written message to me. The message instructed me to go to the Secretary of State's office, which happened to be right across the street. and check my business profile. He also handed me a small pamphlet with IRS phone numbers for business solutions and I deduced that the interview was over since there was nothing else either one of us could do at this point. I also learned later that the card I showed this IRS attendant with the new accountant my husband had planned to use, was the name on my file representing the sole contact for my IRS account, yet I didn't even know him. Furthermore, I didn't recall following through with the switch to this accounting firm from the one I was already using. Things were really left up in the air when my husband became evasive after the tax hiccup mentioned earlier with my business and personal taxes creating this dilemma, which was why I visited the IRS center in the first place.

Stunned at what had just happened, I mentally and emotionally regrouped before starting my next undertaking which was to go to the Secretary of State's office across the street. What had just occurred was difficult to mentally process and I was tempted to pinch myself because this scenario was just that unreal and mind blowing. Fortunately, this shellshock was short-lived and I was able to follow the advice and visit the Secretary of State's office right after this nonproductive interview that same morning. At the Secretary of State's office, I discovered that my husband's name was placed for every position on the board of officers for my business. During the restructuring of the office, my husband was removed from all affiliation with the practice, which included removing him as an officer from my business profile on the Secretary of State website. He served as CFO until the incident and then I replaced his name with mine on the website temporarily until this position was filled. Therefore, that morning when I witnessed his name back on my Secretary of State business profile as the CFO when I had intentionally removed his name after the incident, I was flabbergasted, to say the least. Not only had his name been replaced, but now it was placed for all of the positions of my business excluding my name altogether. It was at this very moment that it dawned on me that I had not changed the username and password for this account since the incident, so this became a priority. After spending the time needed to correct my account and set up new authentication codes, along with checking on other business affiliated matters, I was exhausted - mentally and physically - and chose to call it quits for the day and go home. I felt an eerie feeling on the drive home as I pondered the IRS and Secretary of State findings. This enigma certainly provided food for thought to be addressed moving forward as it appeared that someone was trying to block my access to my business information to hide some corruption. My lawyer documented the information learned at the first IRS visit, along with the second visit's discoveries, and assured me that we would address these concerns in court. Disappointingly, these concerns were eventually overlooked and forgotten after a while because of weightier matters that developed over time. Nonetheless, I decided that afternoon on the drive home to make yet another visit to the IRS the following day, which would be a third visit. I would see if my IRS profile was rectified and reattempt to get my questions concerning the account answered and to obtain the transcripts that I presumed I needed now that I rectified things at the Secretary of State's office.

The next morning I took the girls and my mom with me and we went to a different IRS center which was outside of the major city this time. We arrived there an hour or so before noon and noticed right away that this center had much less traffic than the one downtown. Thus, the atmosphere was less hurried and less stressful, which was a welcomed change. As I awaited my turn, I noticed one of the IRS assistants who looked as if he really didn't want to be there and was just aimlessly passing the time away. He stood out from all of the rest of the staff with this nonchalant attitude and I remember hoping that I would not be the lucky one to receive his assistance. Unfortunately, I hit the jackpot and before I knew what was going on, he was calling for the next person in line which happened to be me. I reluctantly approached his work station and he asked how he could help me. I told him and then gave him my information which is when things got really interesting. All of a sudden his face looked horror-stricken as if he was seeing a death threat on his computer screen when he was accessing my account information on his monitor. While he was glued to the monitor, he was rapidly typing and I waited to see what his response would be. I couldn't help but think, "here we go again" with another flabbergasting moment after considering yesterday's discoveries. We were on a roll now with discombobulating news, so I waited with bated breath to see what mystifying information I would learn today. The gentleman continued typing swiftly and then slowed down and turned to me smiling as his countenance took a one hundred and eighty degree turnaround from his horror-stricken appearance just seconds ago. He then excused himself briefly to go to the printer and retrieve my transcripts. He stated that he didn't see any reason for the trouble I had the previous day with obtaining them and put them in an envelope as he handed them to me. Instantaneously, I released a sigh of relief as I felt I was finally getting somewhere after forty eight hours of frustration and disappointment with trying to solve this enigma with my taxes. I took the envelope and thanked the assistant who now exuded a very convivial demeanor in lieu of the indifferent one evinced earlier. It was a refreshing change. Excited with my victory at last, I completely forgot to address some other concerns and questions I had, which was one of the primary purposes for my return visit. As I began to walk out, the assistant bade me farewell and made a comment that took this visit to another level. He told me to take it easy and be safe as he saw that I was in my South Carolina office yesterday. I smiled before I realized what he said and nodded my head. Then, I did a double take after acknowledging what he had just said and exclaimed, "what?!". By this time, he was helping someone else and I chose to just forget about it at that moment instead of having to wait in the line all over again. Well, now I was back to square one with trying to figure everything out in this state of mere confusion! What was going on?! Surely, something was not right and I wasn't sure if my account was merged with someone else's account or had just been corrupted. Whatever the situation was, I knew that further investigation was warranted.

Well, enough of that flabbergasting moment and moving on to another one that is of equal interest and befuddlement. This one involved my business banking relationship that suddenly became estranged after my domestic mishap. I began to feel alienated from my business banking partners after relaying my domestic misfortune to them, and this feeling became pervasive throughout my entire banking experience because my relationship with my local banking branch was not welcoming and genial anymore either. The managers I was once jovial with suddenly became evasive and too busy to engage in conversation. In fact, one manager relocated from Georgia to the west coast all of a sudden and I considered this to be a huge move. Other eye openers besides my recent awkwardness experienced with my bank's local branch, involved my rapport with my online banking manager, which changed abruptly also. Inquiries that I made about my business line of credit were blocked and unfamiliar changes were made without my authorization while my business online banking account manager remained totally unavailable during this exasperating quandary. In fact, I was informed that my line of credit was no longer available because of the unfavorable change of my recent credit score. This was unusual because until that day, I had never had credit score issues before. Therefore, I found this information to be quite disturbing and puzzling as well. More troubling, was the fact that this explanation took weeks to obtain as I unsuccessfully kept attempting and reattempting to procure money from my business line of credit, but to no avail. Needless to say, with this new credit concern, the Equifax Center downtown was next on my agenda. I would aim to obtain my business and personal credit scores and reports - among other things - and see what was really going on.

My visit to the Equifax Center was uneventful in comparison to my previous experiences with the other entities mentioned above. However, it still had its share of surprises. Upon my arrival at the center, I learned that the area for credit inquiries from the public was in a small section of the building. The lobby was fairly small as well and consequently, didn't offer much privacy when dealing with personal questions or concerns at the window. Fortunately, there was only one person ahead of me in this closely confined space and his visit was ending as I walked in the lobby to await assistance. During subsequent visits, I learned that the low traffic was the usual and the wait was never extremely long. At this first visit, however, I requested personal and business profiles, but was informed that the center only provided personal credit scores and reports. Business credit reports and scores were obtained by calling a phone number to request the information and then following the required steps to obtain it. So, after securing my personal information, which took only a few minutes, I decided to go home and review my credit report in detail. I viewed my credit score immediately, however, and saw that it was good and shouldn't have been an impediment to me when requesting money from my business line of credit. Nonetheless, I planned to view my credit report that afternoon after running a few errands and then I would call and request my business credit profile afterwards. Later that afternoon when

I had settled down, I began reviewing my personal credit report. You probably guessed already that I was faced with more unsettling news. As I looked at the different aliases on the report that were used to represent me, I was speechless. Along with these unfamiliar aliases, I saw an address in my residential history that I didn't recognize at all. After taking a deep breath, I reviewed the report further and saw all of the fraudulent financial activity with revolving accounts in my transaction history that I knew nothing about as well. It was almost unbearable as I struggled to wrap my mind around all that I was learning from this report. In a state of frustration and aggravation, I called the number on this Equifax credit report and immediately reported identity theft. The representative explained that this would be documented on my account immediately and my account would be locked and monitored. I called the other two credit bureaus also - Experian and Transunion - and alerted them as well. Later along this journey, I reported this identity theft to the Federal Trade Commission too. I also filed a police report to my local police department and notified the IRS as well later on in the journey after failed efforts to resolve things. Consequently, the IRS issued a pin number for me when filing my taxes to authenticate me on their records as additional revelations continued to be forthcoming.

At this point, you would think nothing else could surprise or ruffle me. However, with the ongoing excitement from the new surprises and revelations, I couldn't help but be anxious to learn of the subsequent discoveries to follow. This next occurrence was on a level tantamount to the previous situations in its awkwardness and bewilderment. With all the excitement going on in the office, along with the current confusion and concern about the present discoveries made, I decided to get forensics involved. I got a referral to a computer forensic and data recovery expert and this is where I made my biggest investment. It was an extremely expensive route to take, but I felt the information obtained would be well worth the financial sacrifice. In my initial interview with the chief expert, I shared my story along with the red flags I had encountered. Key terms and key names of people were given as leads to help assist with securing the information needed to connect the dots and put the pieces of this mystifying puzzle together.

Because this forensic investigation was a significant financial sacrifice, I wanted to assure that this team of experts had all the information required to obtain the essential information I was seeking. The chief expert informed me that this would not be a small task because there was an overwhelming amount of data over the nine years of my practice's lifespan at that time. So, I patiently waited for them to complete the investigation and divulge their findings. A couple of times during the investigation I was asked to come and answer some questions to assist with their research. This was done to help them sift through and discard unrelated and unnecessary information in regards to the recent findings. Finally, I was called by their office to come and meet to discuss their findings. The appointment was set one week from the phone call and I anxiously awaited this day as I did a mental countdown. Thoughts ran through my mind as I could only imagine what these experts had uncovered and what my next steps would be. Disappointingly, my expectations were crushed when I received the call just a couple of days prior to my appointment informing me that this set time would have to be indefinitely cancelled due to a nearly fatal automobile accident suffered by the chief expert. I sent my condolences and decided to revisit things after a month or two. During this time, I asked the office if there was anyone else I could talk to concerning the findings of their report and I was told that there wasn't. After two months, I called to set up another appointment with the chief expert since I hadn't heard anything from his office yet, and I was told that due to the severity of the injuries, it would have to be another two months. The chief expert was on leave from the office for 16 weeks and was unavailable during this time while he was recuperating. I was beside myself with anguish as I was sitting there frustrated after being beset by yet another impediment in resolving this quandary. What could possibly happen next? Being devoid of options at this point, I patiently and anxiously waited while occupying my time wisely during this small break. Finally, I was called from the office to meet with the expert and I immediately got excited as I made preparations. However, my anticipatory excitement was brief in nature when I came to the realization that the meeting was not like I had expected. I was informed that after they browsed through the voluminous amount of data involved, they were unsuccessful with finding anything that raised a red flag. Of course this was another disappointing and frustrating moment for me that I had to mull over as I started to suspect some clandestine operations of some sort going on blocking all of my efforts to connect the dots with my recent discoveries. Nevertheless, I moved on and redirected my attention to other puzzling findings and events that didn't add up. These questionable concerns and incidents started to accumulate and I sought to find answers to unravel the present mystery of what was really going on.

While on the subject of computers, there was another incident that baffled me that I'll call attention to now that dealt with a letter I sent to an insurance company concerning some unresolved issues with my reimbursements. At that time, there were unpaid claims that were accumulating with no rhyme or reason for such a delinquency. Inquiries made with attempts to resolve things via correspondence were unsuccessful and I was frustrated with the lack of progress with this disturbing matter. Reviewing the responses and feedback sent by emails and letters, I concluded that the issue was with my practice profile at this insurance company. This became more apparent when my attempted calls to discuss the present problem were met with a roadblock. There was no difficulty authenticating myself over the phone with the sensitive information of the practice. However, there was much confusion when discussing unpaid claims over the phone because it appeared that my profile had different banking information. The roadblock was with my reimbursement information. Some of the claims yet to be reimbursed were documented by this insurance company as being paid which really threw a Monkey wrench in things. This eye-opener led me to do an internal investigation and audit that raised some questions in my mind warranting a conversation with this particular insurance company to rectify this troubling and serious dilemma. However, communication via the phone concerning reimbursements was always met with a roadblock as mentioned earlier because there was apparent conflicting reimbursement information documented on my practice profile with this insurance company that I was not aware of, which made it impossible for me to authenticate myself via this avenue. Because of this apparent discordance between my practice profile at the insurance company and my profile at the office, I decided to write to them and inquire about what information they had documented concerning my reimbursements. For example, I needed to know what banking information they had on file for starters. I wanted to get to the bottom of this and get my claims paid. With the noticeable inconsistencies that existed in my insurance profile at this company, it became a hopeless situation for me to try to verify myself over the phone in order to reconcile these outstanding claims. As previously stated, I needed to know what banking information was on file because any mix-up here could explain why I wasn't receiving the payments that this insurance company claimed they paid already. Therefore, I decided to write a letter to them requesting this information since phone calls were futile in this present pickle I found myself entangled in. And this is where something puzzling happened. One evening I decided to go back to the office and write a letter to this insurance company requesting the information on their profile for my medical practice. More specifically, I needed to know the bank information for my reimbursements. I communicated that the reimbursements that they documented as paid, were never deposited into the practice's bank account, and therefore, I needed to know the bank account that they had on file. I then went to the post office that had late hours so that I could mail this letter that evening after 6:00 p.m. The postal attendant informed me that the letter would most likely get there within three to four business days.

The next morning I went to the office just to do some administrative tasks although the office was closed temporarily for the next couple of days while this internal investigation was in sway. While I was there,

I received a phone call from a gentleman who identified himself as a representative of this insurance company. He informed me that he was ten to fifteen minutes away from my office and wanted to have a conversation about the letter I wrote last evening. For a moment I was speechless because it was only 9:00 a.m. that morning and this letter was written late in the evening the day before with a scheduled arrival at this insurance office three to four business days later - not the very next day first thing in the early morning. So, here was yet another question mark in my head about this strange occurrence. Things just didn't add up and now I was becoming more suspicious about foul play. At any rate, I told the gentleman that there was no need to come to my office because I hadn't scheduled an appointment with him and, at this point, I was feeling extremely uncomfortable about this entire ordeal and would prefer to schedule an appointment with him the next day at his downtown office instead. This would authenticate him for me and I would discuss the issues of concern at that time and at that location.

The next day I brought EOBs (Explanation of Benefits) and other paperwork from this insurance company to our scheduled meeting to resolve the mix-up that was interfering with reimbursements. The EOB is the insurance's summary of the service rendered by the health provider with the billed and paid amounts, along with the patient's financial responsibility if there is any. My goal was to show the insurance agent these denied EOBs confirming no payments were made to the practice when the insurance company somehow had documented payments for these same EOBs. The reasons cited on the EOB's for denial were because of "duplicate claim"; wrong date of service; wrong date of birth; or wrong social security number. After researching these reasons for denial, I saw that there were actually no errors on the claims, so I wondered if there was a glitch with the insurance company's system when processing these claims. In any event, there was a definite screw up that had to be fixed and it was paramount to see where these payments went because I had not received them.

When I entered the insurance building that morning, I received a thorough security check and then was escorted up to the agent's office after a call was made to verify the appointment. Upon meeting the gentleman, I initially felt comfortable and relaxed as we introduced ourselves. He then led me to a conference room where he asked me to wait as he went to get other coworkers for this meeting.

After a while, a small group of people came in with him and they asked how they could be of help. I began explaining things when all of a sudden this gentleman interrupted me and said he would summarize everything. His summary was very general and only addressed denials briefly that he informed the team he was going to work on with my office to resolve in a timely manner. He completely omitted the fact that I sought to see the reimbursement information on file for my practice as I discussed earlier with him because of the incongruencies cited revealing some serious concerns. It was as if he had something to hide from me and the billing team attending this meeting. He also abbreviated the meeting stating that my questions were something he could resolve later because they didn't require the assistance of the current team present at this meeting. He also told me that he would review the EOB's with me later at a scheduled time in my office, hence, there was no need to review them at that time. As he began ending the meeting with some more closing remarks, he assured the team that he would be in touch with my office manager who called him yesterday morning right before he decided to attempt to come to my office and discuss things. This is when a red flag went off in my head and I casually asked him to repeat what he said in an imperturbable manner to prevent alarming him about what he had just said. And this is when it happened. He repeated what he said, but with more details this time stating that he received a call from my practice manager. At the time, I didn't have a practice manager and was still looking for someone to fill this position, so of course this was an eye-opener and I realized that this gentleman was totally oblivious to the concerns involved. Therefore, I realized I would have to suspend this much-needed conversation for a later date with my attorney although my curiosity was immediately at its peak. Besides this discovery, I realized that there appeared to have been some unauthorized computer monitoring via spyware allowing illegal remote access to my computer activities. This speculation was derived from the fact that the letter I typed the night before hadn't even reached the insurance office, yet I was contacted by this agent referencing this letter and discussing some of its content the very next morning - literally less than 24 hours ago when the postal service predicted three to four "business' days before the letter would reach its destination. According to the insurance agent, he had received a phone call from "my practice manager" regarding the letter the following morning although it hadn't even reached its destination yet. So things were getting more interesting by the day and I continued to observe and make a mental note of everything. I also documented what I observed so that I could review things later on in efforts to understand this enigma. This would have been a perfect time to inquire with the forensic team we mentioned earlier, but after our prior experience with them, I realized that this wasn't a viable option. Also, the money expended to have them tell me essentially nothing was astronomical as they had to check the data on four computers, which proved to be costly. In addition to these expenses, there were attorney fees, personal investigator fees, and other substantial investments that were made to discover meaningful information obtained thus far, but more information was needed to completely resolve everything. So, it was prudent not to exhaust my finances any more than they had already been at this point because practice revenue was on a standstill with reimbursements presumably being redirected. Also, with all that had been spent for legal services, as well as the other services just mentioned, my expenditures were well beyond my anticipated budget - deep into the five figure range. So, I just took one day at a time and kept my eyes and ears open to any possible leads of what could possibly be going on with what appeared to be cyberespionage.

Another interesting occurrence involved my post office box around my office. I used this post office all the time and obtained the mail from my post office box myself almost daily as well. I did this myself because I didn't want to tempt anyone with the nonelectronic reimbursements (physical checks) that were mailed even though my instructions to the billing team from the beginning were to keep all reimbursements electronic. However, this instruction was not heeded and things became skewed and inconsistent concerning the billing of the practice. So here was a loophole for confusion and double-dealing to be looked into further. Being a child of a physician, I was familiar with some of the avenues that could lead to possible theft and fraudulence as I got a sneak peak of this from my dad's experiences. So anyway that I could be proactive in preventing this, I did just that in order to be prudent. Therefore, I was the only one who had a key to the post office box because I would be the sole receiver of this mail. Over time, I developed an amiable relationship with the post office staff where we all knew each other by name and one particular employee there became my patient. Of course our relationship grew and she looked out for me and often had my mail set aside waiting on me for my convenience. However, over time, checks that were mailed to this post office box were unaccounted for and everyone seemed to be totally clueless - including the post office staff. This discovery was made when the payments documented by the insurance company did not match the deposits in the bank account of my medical practice. This glaring incongruence not only raised a red flag but also prompted me to keep the activities of this post office high on my radar.

During this period of awkwardness and ambivalence with this post office, I decided to write a letter to the postal service expressing my concerns. Unfortunately, their response revealed that they didn't take my concerns seriously because they weren't considered to be significant. Therefore, like all of my other flabbergasting moments, I would have to wait on God because my attorney was unsuccessful in getting any leads or solid information to corroborate my thoughts.

I experienced another queer experience when I made efforts to find another biller after removing the previous staff when I noted a perpetual spirit of deception and dishonesty in the office. This was noted when I asked questions of the staff about certain billing red flags that I noted and the answers I received were incongruent with what I had found out. I later found that there were apparent integrity issues with some of the employees and business consultants because they never once brought the billing concerns and red flags to my attention that I discovered while investigating on my own for over a short period, and these were blatant errors and concerns that were obvious, yet ignored. This left the financial health of my practice in a pernicious state. So, my goal at this point was to move forward with total new staff - out with the old and in with the new. During this time, I began looking for a new biller from different employment-related search engines that helped me secure some potential candidates that I interviewed by telephone. This helped to narrow the list down significantly and I found a young lady that I was interested in for the billing position.

Now, this is where things got intriguing and suspicious. In other words, the consistency was maintained with jaw-dropping discoveries as seen earlier on. When I expressed my interest in her for the position, she was excited and I told her to call me at the office the next day where I'd be able to access my schedule and we would arrange for an interview in person. I shared my plans to have her start within one week and she was content with these plans. The next day she called the office and while we were discussing our availability for the interview, she informed me that my office manager had already reached out to her and discussed some of her expected duties. Flummoxed with this information, I questioned her about the phone call and that's when I learned that someone outside of our office had called her discussing the details of the job I was hiring her for and said they would be the point of contact. This information left me extremely frustrated because she was already speaking with the office manager - me! Currently I was the interim office manager until I could secure someone else for the position. After releasing the previous office staff from the office during the ongoing investigation - except for one person - I was compelled to wear many hats in the interim. So, at the time, this female employee remaining from the original staff and I were the only two working at the office. However, according to this potential candidate for the billing position, she had already spoken to someone who perpetrated to be our practice manager and had already interviewed her for the position on behalf of the practice. I took a deep breath and exhaled before responding to her and then informed her that the practice was experiencing episodes like this from previous disgruntled employees. Therefore, I warned her to block these calls and to let me know if she had any further issues. However, reflecting back on this incident, I realized that information seemed to be leaking from the office, so I finally just removed that last person who was part of the previous staff that I allowed to remain when I let everyone else go. This helped tremendously with maintaining some confidentiality, but because there were other avenues for leaks as explained earlier with the computers and phones, I still had to be cautious. And, unfortunately, this action of removing the final person connected with the previous office staff didn't occur until several months after the biller was hired, and there were all kinds of queer things occurring during these several months. I soon realized that this employee was probably being harassed and badgered by previous disgruntled employees who harbored bitter feelings against the practice and had ill intent. Hence, her removal from the practice was most likely liberating for her as she escaped from the stressful and toxic environment of harassment.

At any rate, I recall another questionable occurrence involving the new biller that was concerning and raised my suspicions that someone was communicating with her in a menacing manner. This interesting episode took place when she and I arranged to meet up one evening to exchange some office information at the new post office location which happened to be near her residence. By now, she had been working at the practice for a little over a month and things seemed to be going along smoothly although it was too early to make a complete and thorough evaluation of her billing skills. In any event, I had planned to check the mailbox that evening and mail something, so she planned to meet me there at the post office and give me some papers to look at for billing purposes since my new post office box was located near her residence. She had her own billing office in a designated office space connected to her house and did remote billing for my practice, as well as some other medical practices at her home office. When we met up in the parking lot that evening, the sun had already set and it was dark. I noticed when she got out of her car, she looked very serious and slightly timid. I wasn't sure what her body language was communicating, but it appeared to be conveying an apprehensive message that confused me as I watched her cautiously approach my car. As she got closer to my car, I rolled the window down in anticipation of the package dropoff we discussed earlier and this is where things got really interesting with this appointment. She anxiously and timidly stuck her head in the window suddenly and peered in the back as though she was looking for something or someone in particular. I asked her if she was alright and she acknowledged that she was, although she continued peering around the car - inside and out - as if spooked by something or someone. It was very strange but she seemed relieved when she saw my daughters in the back seat and realized that there was no one else in the car, or lingering around for that matter. Reflecting on things later that evening, I suspected that she was contacted and possibly threatened by someone trying to interfere with my billing because of the way she conducted herself when we met up, yet she denied these suspicions. However, her actions that evening made this suspicion very viable and I made a mental note to myself after this ordeal to be very observant of her medical billing practices with the office and her future behavior.

As the weeks and then months elapsed, we were successful in getting some claims paid, but I noted that the outstanding ones were denied for frivolous reasons. While performing my own random audit on a few claims, I discovered that some claims were denied because they had me documented erroneously as a mental health provider and then others had diagnosis codes that were changed from the correct codes to incorrect codes impeding reimbursement. When I reached out to the biller with these concerns, she stated that she was unfamiliar with what I described as happening with the claim denials, so we agreed to meet. Since she was off site but near my post office box, I suggested that I would swing by her place after going to my post office box the next day. The following day I was able to show her the concerns and she made the necessary corrections. She rectified my dual role with the credentialing departments of the insurance companies as a primary care provider and specialist in my field of obstetrics and gynecology and removed any erroneous information that documented me as a mental health provider, which was showing up occasionally on some claims at this time. I also asked her to clarify things with me before changing any diagnostic codes as my original diagnostic codes were verified to be correct and payable by the insurance companies for reimbursement. She was apologetic and everything went well for the next month in terms of billing with reimbursements. However, shortly after the first month from our meeting where corrections were made and billing strategies discussed, the same cycle seemed to repeat itself with a significant amount of denials observed for the very same reasons aforementioned. I figured that since we had just recently been down this road before with these particular denial reasons for the claims, a simple call alerting her of the situation would suffice for things to be immediately rectified. Unfortunately, this was not the case and this is where I had some eye opening experiences. As I continued to be vigilant about my billing, I noted that the same patterns continued to occur occasionally. I would have periods where reimbursements would soar, and then times where denials would be overwhelming for the previous reasons stated that should have been fixed permanently the first time they were discovered and corrected. These billing concerns were different from the prior ones seen before this biller started. The vacillating state of my billing history at that time led me to do some independent investigating as I sought for stability of the financial health of the practice. Upon completion of my preliminary evaluation, I noticed that there was one insurance company that stood out as having the majority of the denials. Researching things further, I also was able to conclude that this was the company that had the wrong credentialing profile for me. They had me as a mental health provider instead of a primary care provider and specialist. Sad to say, this error was still not corrected although it was identified and corrected several months before this new investigation even got started which raised a huge red flag. Consequently, this led to several meetings with the biller to resolve this problem and recoup reimbursements. Each time she expressed how sorry she was for the mix ups and promised to get these billing issues cleared up. Feeling confident that our meetings were goal-oriented and productive, I trusted that the biller would get things worked out and prevent these same recurring billing glitches from impeding the practice revenue. On the contrary, things got worse instead and the bottom line of the practice was adversely impacted. In other words, reimbursements almost froze completely with very little, if any, revenue appreciated during this time. As I recollect, I wasn't sure if the illegitimate credentialing profiles that I discovered earlier with the reimbursement issues were blocking my efforts to rectify the errors and inconsistencies now surfacing with this new biller. As you recall, these profiles that were set up by previous employees appeared to have fraudulent bank accounts set up under my practice's profile in addition to the bank account I originally set up with these insurance companies. This conclusion was made when the insurance companies had documented payments to my practice that I didn't find in the only bank account for my practice that I was aware of as discussed earlier on. In other words, unbeknownst to me, there were selected claims rerouted to these fraudulent accounts. Nevertheless, this was difficult to prove and correct because I didn't know the sensitive information used by these employees when they created these accounts. And without this information, my identity with my own practice could not be validated. Consequently, I was blocked when trying to secure the details of this account (e.g. banking information, contacts on the account, etc.) in order to see what was going on and correct it. As a result, the business reached a stalemate and I saw this as the hand of God divinely orchestrating a hiatus or timeout for me during this storm. He did this by letting the revenue stop altogether which compelled me to close the doors of the practice momentarily. All of my efforts to correct my insurance profile to resolve these reimbursement issues were futile because I didn't know the authentication codes for these fraudulent accounts set up by previous employees with ill intent. Therefore, I couldn't communicate with the insurance companies by phone, mail, email, or in person to resolve this serious issue because of my compromised insurance profile which blocked me from being verified. This was a true fiasco and God was giving me a rest from it all. With reimbursements at a stalemate during this time, practice revenue plummeted resulting in no working capital to cover practice operating expenses. Therefore, eviction - which consequently came about - was inevitable with no money to cover the current lease of our practice suite along with the other overhead expenses. Nevertheless, we saw God's hand in this situation as He orchestrated this eviction to be exactly one year from the domestic incident that occurred 4/26/2012. So, April 26, 2013, we closed the doors temporarily for a hiatus as I acknowledged God ordering my steps in this frustrating and grueling process. I arranged for a colleague to cover my practice during this hiatus that lasted a year or so. It was the best thing for the girls and me during our time of recuperation and healing from all that we had been through. Our battle scars were still healing and we had just started this arduous journey. Unbeknownst to us, it would be a long uphill battle and we had just got started. Nonetheless, we took the time to breathe, relax, exhale, and enjoy each other during this much needed break from my practice. Thankfully, God had already prepared me financially for this unforeseen time, and the girls and I were able to withdraw from the ongoing ruckus and to heal.

Another situation of interest in the office that occurred prior to this hiatus dealt with the office mail being received at the local address. This mail that was previously filtered by the office staff before

I ever saw it now fell on my desk as they were no longer there. Now, the exposure that came from the review of this mail was where the big bombshell took place. After removing the staff from the office and investigating things on my own, I started discovering mail from the office that I had never seen before possibly because it had been hidden from me in the past and discarded without me ever seeing it. Ironically, I found insurance checks addressed to the physical office instead of the post office box like the other insurance checks were, and then I found property secured in my name, which was the most outlandish finding. If you recall, I discovered this unfamiliar property affiliated with my personal identifiable information (PII) while reviewing my credit report during my Equifax experience. Interestingly, it was in Florida where I have never lived. In addition to these shockers, there was mail referring to durable medical equipment ordered for the girls and me associated with falsified diagnoses of back and knee injuries for us. This was absolutely mindblowing and inundating to say the least as I dealt with yet multiple other bewildering moments. But, despite the frustration, I considered this to be a reality check of my current situation and resolved to look into things on a much deeper level. Attempting to maintain a level head while trying to mentally process everything with these discoveries, I just took a deep breath at that moment and counted to ten. This was definitely a "Jesus dial-up" moment as I fought not to lose my mind and have an emotional breakdown with the weight of all this unwelcome and burdensome news. I realized that this was organized financial corruption on a high level involving many facets - so much more than I had ever envisioned. In that moment, I whispered up a prayer to God as I struggled to keep myself at peace through all of this confusion by reminding myself that God was ultimately in control of everything so I had no need to worry. One can only imagine what I was experiencing during this period of discoveries that took place over the several months following my domestic mishap that unleashed everything. These experiences were so surreal that I had to frequently remind myself that I wasn't dreaming or in a trance.

Other interesting happenings involved my occasional visits to the office in the evening well after office hours for one reason or another and finding the lights on in my office as if someone was in there working. Strangely enough, I would see the lights on in the parking lot while parking, but when I got up to the fourth floor where my office was, the lights would be off when I entered my office and of course there would be no one there. After this happened repeatedly on two other subsequent visits, I had my daughters and mother, who accompanied me on these occasions, stay in the lobby of this office building while I went up alone to see what was going on this particular time. What I learned this time was just as shocking as my previous eye-openers earlier on. The lights were off as before with no one found in my office, but this time when I returned from the fourth floor and met my daughters and mom in the building's lobby, they informed me of some enlightening news. First they made me aware that when I was going up the elevator this time, they observed that someone was coming down the elevator from the fourth floor at the same time so that we never crossed each other's paths or saw each other. However, because they didn't accompany me this time but stayed to wait for me in the lobby instead, they witnessed not one or two, but six people getting off the elevator. Ironically, all six of these individuals came from the fourth floor and were carrying briefcases, papers, folders and files coming out of my office (the only office on that floor) and appearing as if they were coming from work this late in the evening at 9:00 p.m. The fact that I knew they were coming from my office was very disturbing because I couldn't prove it and they were very deceptive with their actions as they apparently knew when I was entering the building and always left without me seeing them as if they had an informant. But they were exposed this time because they were unexpectedly surprised by my daughters and mother being in the lobby to see them leave with their evidence.

Then I realized that the security guard in the building at night was their informant, and the other times when the security guard wasn't there, I suspected someone from the gas station adjacent to the building was the informant because I would see individuals who looked suspcious.

In any event, when I received this troubling information that particular evening, I immediately called the police and filed a police report about the incident detailing what happened. The next day I noticed that management was installing an alarm system right down there in the lobby of the building and arranging for the lobby to be well lit at night. I assumed that the police department contacted management about this incident. About a week later, I decided to make another visit to see if the police report I filed was effective in putting the fear in these individuals to stop the nonsense, but I was terribly disappointed because this was not the case. As I witnessed before, I noted activity going on in my office from the parking lot and sought to get up there immediately and put an end to things that night. This time, however, the lights in the lobby were out, which I found strange after witnessing management take painstaking efforts to assure that the lobby was adequately lit in the evening by scheduling certain lights to turn on during the evening hours. Nevertheless, I resolved to enter the elevator and pretend to go up to the fourth floor to get to my office. This time my daughters and my mother were left in the car awaiting my return. Instead of going to my office, I paused for a moment when the doors closed and delayed selecting a floor allowing the elevator to remain on the first floor and for the doors to reopen without ever leaving the main floor. When I exited the elevator, the culprit had not come down the elevator from the fourth floor yet. So I decided to go to the car with my mom and daughters and wait to see who we'd see come off the elevator. I had baited them and wanted to see what fish I had caught in this sea of confusion, so we waited anxiously and then suddenly it happened. All of a sudden out of nowhere, a dark shadow-like form ran across the lobby and out of the door. At that moment, without giving it a second thought, I took off in my car following the person that I quickly saw was a young man running across the street into a residential community where I followed right behind him. During this interesting pursuit with the gentleman weaving himself in between and around houses making it difficult to keep up with him in my car, I never once thought what I had planned to do once I caught up with him. Well, that time came soon enough and I can tell you that it was a paralyzing moment for the both of us. We just stood there staring at each other for a good minute or two after undergoing an intense, high strung and fast pace chase. Prior to our little staring contest, I cornered him into a dead end street where my car was in front of him and a tall metal gate behind him. He was sandwiched in between the two and looking rather hopeless. Right before this apparent moment of inevitable defeat however, he turned around immediately and looked in the car and made eye contact with me as if he was looking for some specific cue to know his next move. For a moment, I believe he thought that I was his pickup since I didn't do anything once I cornered him. Believing this to be the case, he ran to the door and tried to open it briefly. However, when he viewed the startled and petrified faces of my daughters in the backseat of the car, he quickly aborted this plan realizing his mistake and instantly ran to the gate and climbed over it. At that point, I didn't try to stop him but decided to end my pursuit realizing it was futile without legal assistance to do anything other than what I had already done - identify him and validate the foul play in my office. Calling 911 now would not give sufficient time for the police to respond quickly enough because he would be long gone by the time they arrived. Therefore, I just went home feeling hopeless about this situation, but took time to thank God that my foolhardy response that night didn't get us killed. We were lucky that he didn't have a weapon and that he wasn't meeting up with anyone armed either during my impulsive exploit. So, as we retired that night, we just praised God for His protection and mercy and planned to file another police report at the office in the morning. As I slowly fell asleep that night, I came to the conclusion that this road of discoveries was intended to be an uphill journey, so I purposed in my heart to keep my eyes and ears open continually to see where God was leading and not to get discouraged (Psalm 119:105), because this was a situation only God could resolve.

There were other shocking and scandalous findings which revealed mail showing businesses affiliated with my name, social security number, or tax identification number (or all three) that I didn't even know about. Some of the mail showed my actual business name, while other mail showed alias business names closely associated with my business name. And then there was mail with my personal name used as a business entity. Also, there were EOB's showing two different payment methods for some of the insurance carriers when there should have only been one method and I later discovered this to be an avenue for the fraud. Simply put, reimbursements were made by direct deposit and paper checks sent by mail. These paper checks would either be mailed to the post office box or directly to the office. The mailed checks were often intercepted by staff as explained earlier. What a scandal! As stated before, I wasn't aware of these other payments paid by paper checks sent to the office until this time of discoveries. I just knew of the payments by check sent to my post office box. To add to the confusion, there were still yet other payments that were sent to the business entity using my personal name, which presumably had its own unknown bank account where its electronic payments were deposited. And all of this was discovered after the domestic mishap that opened Pandora's Box exposing all of this chicanery.

Chapter 7

WHERE DO WE GO FROM HERE?

WELL, ONCE I processed all these discoveries, which took some time to mentally and emotionally absorb, I looked into scheduling a self-care day where I would get a full body massage for an hour along with a pedicure and manicure in order to free my mind from all this nonsense. Contemplating this spa excursion alone gave me a sweet peace for the time being that was sufficient to eliminate all the ongoing ruckus in my life. I looked forward to checking out of my current state of commotion and being saturated instead with an ambiance of tranquility, relaxation, and lucidity. It had been a while now since I recalled a peaceful time in my life. After being hit by what felt like a whirlwind and a mental and emotional tsunami that morning of the domestic mishap, a serene and self-nurturing respite couldn't come soon enough. Yet I felt that God was leading me onward to connect the dots that I could with the new information now available. So, I began gathering and reviewing the information that I was able to obtain and answering questions concerning things that initially were an enigma. During this process, pellucidity ensued allowing me to understand things that seemed ridiculous and illogical before.

So what were some of the revelations that surfaced after connecting the dots? Well, starting with the IRS scandal, I came to realize that I was represented more than one way to the IRS which was startling all by itself. But, in addition to this, I learned that these different representations were either affiliated with my tax identification number or my social security number and I had no clue that these other entities outside of my business even existed. I discovered this when I requested information from my IRS profile. What was interesting during this period of inquiries, was the discovery of incongruent information I received in comparison to what this accountant received who was referred to me by a friend. This accountant received different details and data concerning my business when he requested information from the IRS concerning my profile. Interestingly, when I secured my business credit profile as instructed at the Equifax Center, I saw these counterfeit businesses under my business tax identification number also on that report. They were identical to what I saw on this paperwork from the IRS. The business credit report also exposed unfamiliar activities involving trade and other transactions that I wasn't familiar with, yet they were also associated with me. It was obvious that my BII (business identifiable information) and PII (personal identifiable information) were being illegally manipulated for ill gain. There was no question about it. So I was witnessing here firsthand the different ways I was represented to the IRS by my business tax identification number when there was only one authentic way I should have been represented using this number and that was solely with the business I incorporated under this number. All attempts and efforts to notify the IRS of this incongruence were to no avail. My tax identification number was being used illicitly, although its usage appeared to be legitimate because these alias businesses all connected to me. And, as frustrated as I was with this discovery, I was powerless to do anything legally about it at the time because information was insufficient to show my innocence with this fraudulence using my PII and BII. These businesses had names closely associated with my authentic business name and served as counterfeits. So, now I would have to gather some concrete evidence to expose this disinformation and sham because what I discovered and retained as documented evidence was exiguous to exonerate me from this huge mess. In addition to the lack of substantial evidence at the time to unveil this subterfuge, I also lacked the resources to obtain legal help. My finances were exhausted from all of the earlier legal and investigative costs involved when efforts were made to get to the bottom of these shenanigans that were unfolding.

Furthermore, I had to keep reminding myself that I would have to be prudent and wait for sufficient evidence to prove that I wasn't tied into this fraud before trying to pursue anything legally because my BII and PII were used in this scam which again traced everything back to me. So here I was literally trying to make sure that I was not blamed for the fraud that defrauded me. Therefore, in prudence, I decided to wait on God and let Him vindicate me from this debacle that could have left my career and reputation in shambles. In His timing, He would expose the serious shenanigans and treachery employed against me and exonerate me when He saw fit to do so. For now, however, I would have to let everything go and let God have His way despite how disturbing these discoveries were at the time. The felonious intent involved with the misuse and abuse of my sensitive personal and business information made this waiting process even more difficult and troubling, but I was left without any other options at the time as stated previously. Meanwhile, I was left dumbfounded with how all of this happened and how these things had been ongoing now for several years and yet I was clueless. During this period of underhandedness and double dealing, my business and financial history became tainted as my credit plummeted. It also became apparent that prior to opening my practice and having my BII misused, my PII was already being abused, misused, and tainted for several years prior to the establishment of my business. However, over time, I saw how God actually divinely orchestrated this legal standstill in mercy to allow the culprits to confess and acknowledge their wrong. Unfortunately, this has yet to occur - even to this day. Nevertheless, at that time in my life, I was content with the revelations that God had shown me and I sought only to follow His guidance on how to handle each new finding as I waited patiently on Him to end this fiasco and to recoup what was lost. This entire unscrupulous ordeal was a big pill to swallow and I realized that I just had to trust that God would resolve things in His time because we didn't know who we could trust.

As far as the change in my banking relationships was concerned, there was a definite new awkwardness observed locally within my bank shortly after my domestic incident that created tension. This uneasiness was enlightening, however, as it was eventually exposed for what it really was. Apparently some of the banking personnel had developed a very strong relationship with my husband and felt uncomfortable with the new status of our relationship. My husband and I both had our personal and business accounts with this bank, so things became a little complex as the bank tried to accommodate us both in our sensitive situation. Neither one of us had access to the other's accounts. We were the sole contacts on our own accounts with the bank and didn't have anything to do with each other's banking on a personal or business level. Things were structured this way from the very beginning of our marriage due to the fact that my husband was married before and had financial obligations from that relationship that we both agreed he would handle and would not involve me from a financial standpoint. However, shortly before the domestic incident, I allowed my husband to sign off on some things on my business account for the first time ever in order to decrease my work-load. This gesture was immediately reversed as I terminated this authorization on my business account without delay after the incident. With all of the new drama in my marital relationship at the time, the bank seemed to distance itself from me, which made my account less accessible. I found this observation to be strange and unsettling because my domestic issues should not have had anything to do with my banking affairs. Nevertheless, as mentioned earlier, I now faced challenges with securing working capital via business loans and lines of credit when this was never problematic before and my credit history (my authentic credit history - not the credit history connected with the fraud and marred by the perfidy) was never a problem either, which made this financial hiccup with the bank all the more peculiar. So, I became reasonably suspicious of these new financial impediments that I now faced as I questioned the credit profile that mysteriously made an abrupt plunge downward coincidentally after this domestic upheaval. This sudden change in my financial and credit profile with the bank became even more dubious when I recalled what I saw on my business credit report that revealed transactions and trading that I was totally unfamiliar with and that I had successfully disputed with Equifax at the time. Regrettably, however, I also recalled my disappointment with Equifax when my efforts to research the details surrounding these exposed transactions were blocked. Equifax said they could not delve into such details, but would remove them from my business history. Of course, this didn't allow me to get to the source of the fraudulence in efforts to end it, which was most upsetting and left me feeling temporarily defeated. In the meantime, things got murkier still when I stumbled upon a questionable occurrence. It all happened when I decided to extend one more effort to obtain funds through a line of credit with my bank after becoming inconveniently frustrated with the unsuccessful prior attempts. After reconciling the fraudulent accounts noted on my business credit profile that I was able to review, I thought my credit would surface somewhat from its deplorable drowning state. Unfortunately, this was not the case; instead, it ironically got worse which I discovered later had to do with my personal credit profile being perpetually tarnished. If you recall, I mentioned that my IRS profile had linked my personal and business information because it appeared that some of the ongoing fraudulence had business entities set up under my social security number, while other entities were solely incorporated under my tax identification number. So, this established link between my PII and BII created a relationship where one was affected by the other. Therefore, the efforts made earlier to clean up the business profile were futile because the personal profile that was connected to it was constantly being targeted with fraudulence keeping them both tainted. A case in point occurred this particular evening when I called the toll free business banking phone number to inquire if I was able to procure some working capital from a line of credit that was available prior to my domestic event. Unsurprisingly, I was met with the same familiar and discouraging message stating that my application was declined. However, this time my flawed credit profile was not the reason for my credit ineligibility according to the representative on the phone, and strangely, this time I wasn't told that the line of credit was no longer available either as I had been informed before when making this request. Instead, I was told that I could not secure two loans this close together. In other words, I had supposedly secured a loan already two days ago in the amount of $10,000 as I was so kindly reminded by the representative on the phone. At that moment, I did everything possible to hold back the gasp in my astonishment as I immediately realized this to be yet another case of identity fraud. Sitting there concomitantly speechless and aggrieved because I felt helpless with the muddle I was in, I remember being awakened out of my two to three minute paralyzing trance by the voice of the representative repeatedly calling my name over the phone. At that instant, I realized I had mentally checked out momentarily into some twilight zone with this alarming news. I quickly snapped out of my state of shock and asked the representative for some clarity as I asked her to repeat herself seeing that I was dumbfounded with what I believed I had just heard. Everything seemed so bizarre and unreal as I just sat there hoping someone would nudge me afterwhile and tell me to wake up. But of course this didn't happen because I was fully conscious and in my right mind as I heard this disturbing news. All I could think of was, "here we go again" and, "what next". As I regained my composure, I inquired about the details concerning this transaction and obtained information overtime that proved to be unverifiable. I already knew that the profile for the individual who received this loan would be bogus because the individual was perpetrating me and, therefore, the information would not be accurate. The frustration I experienced that day was inexplicable. And I found my efforts to inform the bank of this identity fraud to be equally frustrating. Without information and documentation to substantiate my argument of fraud, all efforts would be pointless, and at that time, I had no documentation to work with in proving my case. Besides, I was additionally challenged with vindicating my cause in this situation because I discerned that no entity wants to acknowledge that they've been defrauded or bamboozled when it comes to money, and proving this realization was the next obstacle to getting things elucidated. Also, it appeared that the perpetrator had an internal hookup and contact within the bank that was in cahoots with the chicanery involved because this person only approved the loan when the perpetrator applied and not when I applied - the "real" Lilith, which was inconceivable. Clearly, there was a fictitious profile strategically set up for me internally that had distorted and skewed my personal identifiable information (PII) with phony facts and had created a corrupt data bank for me, which served to block me from accessing my own account - the intention sought. However, it provided an avenue for the perpetrator to secure funds by using this fictitious information placed on this phony account or profile for me that only he or she knew. You see, because I didn't know this skewed information on this fraudulent account that supposedly represented me, I couldn't be authenticated to get information on this account or to do any transactions with this account. This left me totally helpless as I witnessed how my perverted bank and credit profile had become so misrepresented by the creation of this phony account that it was difficult for me to prove who I was - the authentic and DNA proven Lilith Whyte. My speculation attributed this forged account to be an avenue created and manipulated by the perpetrator's internal connection with a bank employee somehow who apparently facilitated this double dealing. They were in cahoots with this treachery witnessed and there was no other rational way to explain things at the time. So, for the time being, I could do nothing but wait for justice to take place because I believed it would. Two biblical texts that I stood on at the time and still stand on today, speak on exposure for "unconfessed" secret sins and deceit (Ecclesiastes 12:14), along with reaping what you sow (Galatians 6:7).

Nevertheless, I was at another roadblock and extremely frustrated this time with the news of this recent substantial loan granted to the perpetrator in my name. Things became more disturbing as I received a lot of hostility and suspicion from the representative on the phone that was assisting me at the time. The representative was annoyed with my continual inquiries because she wasn't aware of the fraudulence involved. This made things even more exasperating and bothersome, but I knew that I had to persevere and work through this in order to get to the bottom of things. I was determined to get answers about this pseudo account and to have this scandal unveiled. Even though I knew I would have to ultimately wait on God, I gathered what information I could to help unravel things later as I saw this situation as an opportunity orchestrated by God to do just that and nothing else for the time being. So I continued my questioning with the representative until I learned that there was an unverifiable phone number and other fabricated information dealing with the perpetrator's employment and address. I asked for a copy of this fabricated profile to be mailed to me and was only able to have this request granted when I gave some other information that apparently matched what they had on file, but was in fact, incorrect information concerning me. You see, at that moment, the Holy Spirit brought to my mind the falsified information I found on the internet immediately after the domestic incident earlier on that was affiliated with my name and I used it. Surprisingly, this information I found on the internet and gave to them was what they had documented on this fraudulent banking profile. So now I was allowed to inquire further and secure more particulars with this account using this falsified information. However, because of my unfamiliarity with all of the spurious details of this account, I was at an impasse with finding out who initiated this deceitful gesture and illegally procured the $10,000 loan in my name. Having knowledge of just some of the details and not all of them would not suffice for further investigation.

The representative was adamant about me knowing more specifics concerning the account before she would release any additional information. And what she agreed to send me concerning the account when I told her it was fraudulent, turned out to be just a fictitious address and business name in Baltimore, Maryland where I did my residency training. Although this information appeared to be of little worth because it was nothing but deceptive concoction, it did highlight a critical fact worth pondering. As I studied the fake facts, I noticed that the addresses were places I had once lived while in school and later in residency. So, strangely enough, this appeared to be someone very familiar with me and my history, which proved to be valuable information as the pieces of this mystifying puzzle were coming together. This seemingly no-win situation was now coming together - slowly, but surely.

Nevertheless, I still find it disappointing and frightfully disturbing that the bank had my correct social security number, but the wrong date of birth associated with it. The other erroneous demographic information was not as unsettling for me as this fake date of birth falsely associated with my social security number. Knowing that the databank for social security numbers is one of the most reliable and authentic tools for providing accurate information, I was not able to give the bank a pass card on this screwup. Being the prestigious and professional institution that this large worldwide bank is today and was then, I held this bank to be responsible for this screwup because, as a reputable institution, it should have been more scrutinizing with this bogus information used to create this phony account. If the proper vetting had been done, it would have exposed this account to be the scam that it was. In fact, if things had been audited and analyzed properly, the perpetrator's sham would have been blocked and this account would have been nonexistent. However, because of this bank's dereliction of duty, the identity fraud and theft were successful with this account. I also found it to be equally disturbing that there was an age gap of more than 20 years between my imposter and me. So, as God assisted me with connecting all the dots, I realized that the mail I had received in the past while at home from medical school during summer break or on vacation on more than one occasion was revealing. This mail would solicit my membership with AARP and Medicare prematurely which would perplex me at the time. However, with the hindsight gained I could clearly see how these puzzling moments all made sense as I learned that my imposter was more than 20 years my senior, and this all stemmed from this double-dealing. Interestingly at the time, no one else in the house (my parents or siblings) seemed to be alarmed by it, so I discounted it as a simple mixup by the sender and didn't linger on it. Hence, this chicanery was going on long before I married and had a family. It was going on while I was in medical school, and I had no clue.

Nonetheless, with this new information, I was momentarily at a legal standstill once again, until I could gather more facts and resources to identify this imposter. So I placed everything on hold temporarily with this aha moment and made plans to revisit this situation at a later date. Unfortunately, I would still remain monetarily paralyzed in terms of securing business loans or lines of credit until resolution of this pecuniary impropriety. I would also be financially paralyzed salary-wise as well because of the rerouting of my insurance payments (reimbursements) to these fraudulent bank accounts instead of my business bank account leaving me financially drained. Without money, seeking legal help would be momentarily impeded and I would be at a standstill with resolving things.

My focus now goes back to the other IRS shocker in 2012 that occurred with all of the other flabbergasting moments I experienced that involved identity theft and fraud with my sensitive personal information. I realized that my PII (personal identifiable information) was not the only data misused and manipulated for corrupt purposes at the time, but my confidential business information was tainted also. We talked about this IRS shocker not too long ago and saw how all of my efforts to unravel this financial muddle were futile and appeared to be blocked. However, this particular IRS shocker that I chose to investigate at the time dealt with a mysterious South Carolina office referenced by the IRS representative as he farewelled me while leaving the center that day as you recall in one of the earlier chapters. My sole office was in Georgia and I knew nothing about a South Carolina office, so this revelation left me understandably befuddled. Of course, I wondered what was going on and if my profile was mistakenly merged with someone else's profile. After researching and investigating some things on my own, I discovered a post office box in South Carolina that was associated with some of my business and personal information. Of course I found this interesting, but disturbing as well. This led me to conclude that the office in South Carolina referenced by the IRS representative at the center that day was not a physical location, but rather a post office box only, which raised red flags. According to this representative, he was able to see that I had visited this office the day before, which was puzzling to me because I didn't know anything about a South Carolina office. To digress momentarily, I believe this is why a physical address is required when incorporating a business in lieu of a post office box solely to prevent corrupt practices like what I was experiencing. This will prevent the scams involved with fake businesses. Unfortunately during this time, office addresses with only a post office box were allowed, which supported many business scams around this time. However, since the COVID 19 (Coronavirus disease 2019) pandemic, post office boxes for business addresses may be acceptable again because of the home jobs created now. Nonetheless, as I reflect back on this post office box address that I discovered during that time, I was initially clueless with connecting the dots that would explain its involvement. Its purpose still remained an enigma to me at the time. After some thought and consideration while navigating through the mare's nest that I was caught up in, I had some suspicions about insurance reimbursements probably being rerouted illegally to this post office box, but I couldn't substantiate these thoughts initially. I wanted to collect more substantial evidence to corroborate this conclusion even though this would be the only logical explanation for its surreptitious existence. However, at the time I didn't have sufficient information to make the essential connections.

As far as my Equifax visits were concerned, I notified the entities (Equifax, Transunion, and Experian) as soon as I saw the aliases, unknown addresses, and fraudulent transactions made on my profile without my knowledge. I alerted them that I was a victim of identity theft and they proceeded to lock my profile to prevent illegal manipulaiton of my sensitive personal information. The business credit profile was handled differently and had different contact information as I stated in a previous chapter. They allowed me to dispute the bogus and corrupt information on the account while they assured me that nothing else needed to be done at that time. I eventually closed the practice, which made further steps in that direction pointless. Therefore, I chose to trust God moving forward knowing that He would take care of everything according to His timing. Besides, the inquiries I made when disputing fraudulent transactions on my business credit profile were denied and I was told that this fraudulent activity would be removed only, but could not be investigated. So, I was blocked from getting any additional information concerning this dishonest and counterfeit activity on my business profile. This is where legal support would have been able to pursue things further to get to the root of all of this fraud, but I would have to await God's timing. However the credit bureau handling my personal credit history immediately locked my account and issued me a pin number to unlock it as I saw necessary. This step was required to end the fraudulence with my credit profile because whoever was falsely manipulating my profile with pseudo facts, obviously already had my sensitive information that allowed them to modify my credit profile as needed to falsify information as they had already done. So the pin number would impede them from continuing this unscrupulous duplicity because they would not know it and therefore, would not have access to the account to corrupt the information unless the imposter or imposters had an internal connection that could bypass this security check as I assumed they had with my bank as discussed earlier, which seemed plausible with all that was going on. This dilemma just animated concerns for identity protection on a professional level also as I take a moment to digress.

Unfortunately, health professionals are in a serious catch 22 when it comes to maintaining security of their personal and professional information. Because the office staff and hospital staff are privy to this confidential information for credentialing purposes, healthcare providers experience an inevitable transparency that places them in a very vulnerable position financially by dangerously exposing them to identity theft because this information can be misused. So the members of the staff have to be properly vetted and in good moral and ethical standing. But even with these safety and prudent measures practiced, someone can still commit a crime for the first time after being exposed to all of the sensitive information they are privy to in these circumstances. In any event, I was glad to take this step of securing a PIN number with the IRS in order to initiate greater safety precautions with the credit bureaus moving forward, and I also signed up with "LifeLock", an entity that helps to protect against identity theft and fraud. As time went by, I found out that the Florida address associated with my social security number on my Equifax report was linked to a bogus bank account in my name. This pseudo account was the same one that received the $10,000 loan that I didn't have access to because I couldn't authenticate myself due to the spurious information on this alias account representing me. I also learned that this address was real and not fictitious and represented a property someone secured in my name in Florida. How that happened without me there to sign and present proof of my identification puzzles me to this day as well. With some of the details involved in this scam that I was already aware of, it wouldn't surprise me if my credentials weren't required at all to affect this shady arrangement.

Another very interesting observation was noted with the Equifax experience after several visits were made to this facility. There appeared to be an ongoing fluctuation in my score each time I went. Sometimes, it would be very good, and other times the number would be poor with no rhyme or reason and then back to good strangely. I was disturbed by this instability observed with my credit score but realized that until I could resolve the current financial dilemma which prevented me from seeking legal help, things wouldn't be much different. Each time I visited the Equifax center, I would routinely obtain a copy of my credit report and credit score and keep it in my records. One day while reviewing my credit reports with their respective scores I viewed a discrepancy in the spelling of my name. My first name was incorrectly spelled on some - not all - of the reports. Instead of "Lilith", which is the correct spelling, some reports had my name erroneously spelled as "Lillith". Ironically, the incorrect spelling seemed to consistently have the better credit score compared to the correct spelling and this trend was confirmed on several occasions although both names were connected to the same social security number (mine). Another even more interesting fact was discovered. The loan for $10,000 was secured with this specific account that had the incorrect spelling of my name which appeared to always be associated with a good credit score. Also, this incorrect spelling of my name happened to be one of the alias names seen on my credit report. So what appeared to be happening with this revelation could only be logically attributed to someone manipulating things in order to swindle me out of my available lines of credit. When I speculated to friends and family about the possibility of suspected duplicity exercised internally within this credit bureau, I was met with the harsh renunciation that this thought process was preposterous and literally impossible. However, five years later (September 2017), this same credit bureau (Equifax) announced a security data breach that affected over 148 million American people's confidential information and the other two bureaus have had their cases of this as well. So this conclusion wasn't as absurd and far-fetched as presumed, but rather on target. It was just revealed years later in regards to my case. Nevertheless, patience would have to be something I exercised in order to get to the bottom of this mare's nest I found myself in because substantial evidence was still lacking. However, for now, the problem centered around the fact that someone else took advantage of my window of opportunity to secure funds by counterfeiting my identity with the misspelling of my name during this moment of a pecuniary advantage when the $10,000 loan was secured. This was just an eye-opener to some of the inaccurate information on the bank's fraudulent account they had for me that we addressed earlier. This deceptive arrangement left me monetarily strained as it catapulted me into a stressful and inauspicious predicament financially. So, once again, I was financially paralyzed with seeking legal assistance in this mare's nest even though I had evidence right there at my fingertips concerning this outright fraudulence. Meanwhile, I would be dutiful about gathering more data and facts on this case until its revisitation.

The experience with the forensic guys was the largest investment made during this investigation and proved to be a huge disappointment. No helpful information was gained from this intense undertaking which left an immense deficit in my financial resources with the huge expenditure sacrificed to get information. Disappointingly, I was back to square one and extremely frustrated with this forensic hiccup experienced amidst all the concomitant discoveries being made that begged for a plausible explanation, yet the forensics investigation supposedly found nothing. I realize that my gesture to secure a forensic team of experts was foiled because I still had one person working in the office who had worked with previous employees dismissed for suspicions of dishonesty. Therefore, it was reasonable to suspect that a connection was made between these disgruntled ex-employees and this remaining employee where she was potentially compromised through harassment to leak confidential information about the practice. And this could have been an avenue for someone to connect with this team of cyber investigators to threaten or compromise them. This staff member ironically was the one my husband talked with the day of his arrest for a while when he called the office collect. To this day, the content of their conversation still remains unknown. For this reason, the peace and drama-free atmosphere that transpired after her dismissal came by no surprise. Taking this initiative to start anew and remove every potentially tainted or defiled influence from the office, definitely gave me an inexplicable peace of mind and also gave the office a welcoming and refreshing new climate. And the craziness witnessed with the insurance agent earlier was also explained. The practice of cyber espionage was definitely a major problem around this time. And I was strongly convinced of some foul play with my insurance profiles and how they were originally set up during the credentialing process after I witnessed all of the discrepancies and red flags exposed after the internal audit when the staff was removed. The insurance agent's premature gestures to reach out to our office before I could even request his support and assistance, served to substantiate the suspicions of the ongoing cyber espionage in the office at the time as explained earlier. It also left me feeling apprehensive about dealing with him. I figured that he had been compromised after connecting all of the dots with this incident. When he mentioned that he had spoken to my practice manager before the meeting that morning, this information alone sufficed to corroborate my suspicions because I didn't have a practice manager at that time. With everything that had transpired, I had to replace staff and that position was not yet filled. I was wearing that hat this particular morning and he didn't speak to me. Things got murkier when I revealed this to the insurance agent and told him why I dismissed the staff. Shortly after divulging this information, this representative was suddenly evasive and ultimately was found to be missing in action. Of course this information put a halt in my moving forward at that present time with him regarding my reimbursement issues, which he now appeared to be covering up. Instead, I concentrated on analyzing the information I already had to put pieces of this puzzle together for the time being. This decision to analyze things more thoroughly with the current data already available, was prudent at the time and would address all of the eye openers mentioned in the previous chapter sufficiently. Because I was on a hiatus from the office during its investigation, I had plenty of time to implement this game plan.

Chapter 8

"Think It Not Strange"

I REALIZED THAT there was no simple or straightforward answer to explain what had gone on and what was still ongoing. Consequently, I knew that there would be no quick fix for this dilemma, so as stated before, I resolved to reassess things later and figure this enigma out then. Over the six-month period of numerous discoveries since our domestic upheaval, it felt as if much more time had elapsed than had actually transpired because of everything I had encountered. After undergoing my horrific storm from the crisis that commenced that morning which marked this journey's onset, along with tolerating everything else that ensued, my psyche was totally exhausted, confused, and wounded. With the mind-blowing findings and precarious situations that occurred, I was inundated with information and drama overload and it was about time for another mental and emotional timeout. This would entail finding more time in the day for individual devotion and getting in my secret place at home alone with God - my Refuge and Fortress extraordinaire. During this time alone with Him, I would hear Him speak words of comfort and wisdom to me. I am forever grateful that

God preserved my sanity and integrity during this mentally devastating and emotionally traumatizing time in my life. The resilience He instilled in me allowed me to weather the storm successfully and to avoid being drowned by the enormous and ominous waves of despondency and hopelessness.

As I reflect back on this time in my life, I recall initially being tempted to just throw in the towel and assume defeat due to the circumstances. There seemed to be no way out of this enormous maze. Every effort on my part to free myself from this chaos, just seemed to get me further entangled. There were so many missing pieces to this puzzle that I felt hopeless and I didn't know where to begin in finding an answer or solution. I was almost tempted to give up the fight because I was disheartened with the losing hand that I felt I was dealt by life's deck of cards during this crucial period in my life. Furthermore, I was alone because no one seemed to really understand the magnitude of what was plaguing me - not even family. And my friends and church family appeared clueless overall as well. It was just the girls, Jesus, and me. Thank God for His promise in Hebrews 13:5,6 to never leave or forsake us. And His presence made all the difference.

On the contrary, some of my friends and some relatives had a different perception of things. They suggested that my misfortune and grief were a result of the choices I had made, which they believed explained the crummy hand of cards I was compelled to deal with in my crisis. They were bold and uninhibited with sharing their unsolicited advice and evaluation of my situation, along with expressing their judgement of me as a wife, mother, and business woman. And this was done without any regard of my feelings or to what actually happened. In other words, the unsolicited opinions and advice voluntarily given to me, for the most part, were devoid of the facts and details centered around the events in my life and therefore unfounded. This should come as no surprise to you as the reader if you've lived long enough. People are quick to form opinions and concoct pseudo facts based solely from the rumor mill circulating at the time. In addition to this, you often find that the ones who give the most unsolicited advice, are the very ones who don't exercise the advice they're giving and need it the most. We have to focus on ourselves instead of others while we get the plank or beam out of our own eyes first before we can attempt to get the mote or speck out of someone else's eye. This is the paraphrased version of Matthew 7:5 and Luke 6:42 that the Bible instructs us to follow. And I say this because, interestingly enough, these same individuals who now stood in the role of judges all of a sudden, had some serious experiences in our adolescence (and even in adulthood) that only the grace of God delivered them from, but apparently they forgot. So I cautioned them not to be judgmental because the reasons for various struggles in life are not always so straightforward, but complex at times. For example, when someone is killed by a drunk driver, this misfortune in most instances did not occur because of the actions or decisions of the individual killed, but because of the actions and decisions of the drunk driver who chose to dangerously drive under the influence. That being said, we realize that some struggles and misfortunes are inevitable in the sinful world we live in no matter how cautious we try to be. Jesus forewarned us in the Bible that the just and unjust both will experience sunshine and rain from time to time, so we don't need to get bent out of shape when we go through difficult times on occasion. However, we do need to exercise Proverbs 3:5,6 where advice is given to consult God in our decision-making in order to prevent consequences that were not in His plan for us and that we didn't have to go through if we had only heeded to His guidance and instruction. Nevertheless, practically speaking, we've all made mistakes that could have taken our lives in another direction if it weren't for the grace and goodness of God. The Bible so clearly reminds us in Romans 3:23 that "ALL have sinned, and come short of the glory of God." However, Isaiah 53:6 reassures us that Christ paid the penalty for our sins through His death and justified us. Therefore, because nobody stands guiltless or perfect in God's eyes, no one is in any position to judge. Clearly, outside of the courtroom, the gavel doesn't belong in any human being's hand. Now, it's true that all mistakes and sins are not the same and this explains to some extent the different consequences. I emphasize "to some extent" because there are those who suffer for wrong they didn't do (Jesus is the perfect example). And, as aforementioned, just living in this imperfect world of sin, we are all subject to some form of misfortune in our lifetime. Whether it's financial or physical (health-related or a catastrophe of some sort), we can expect to face some challenges down here despite our lifestyles and choices because it is not heaven and we're continuously surrounded by sin. In other words, even when we make healthy choices and have healthy lifestyles for instance, we can still face a premature death by a freak accident or even get diagnosed with cancer because of genetic predisposition, which has nothing to do with our lifestyle choices. And all of this is because of the imperfect world we live in. Now, I'm not suggesting that healthy living is futile because we know that we are what we eat, so we must take care of our bodies if we want to have quality of life and optimal health - this is a given. At any rate, even though we all will face some problems in our lifetime of some sort, we do have the assurance through God's promise to us in Psalm 34:19 that He will deliver us from all of our troubles and afflictions if we ask Him to. And even in the face of the inevitable when it is our time to face death, He has promised to never leave or forsake us in Hebrews 13:5 and to comfort us with His ever abiding presence. So, as we see, events in our life are not always related to our choices, behavior, or actions. The life of Jesus is a perfect example. His life was full of anguish and suffering for our sins as our Substitute, yet He was sinless. As pointed out, we can face adversities by simply living in a corrupt and wicked world which is why we shouldn't think it is strange when we suffer as the title of this chapter states and also as 1 Peter 4:12 tells us. Another example of innocent suffering aside from the life of Christ, is in Job's case, where God chose him to suffer hardships in order to demonstrate what real faith looks like in the midst of adversity because He (God) trusted Job with the test and knew Job would serve him in spite of his great loss and suffering. In other words, God knew that Job's response in this trial would be a powerful testament of what a true soldier for Christ looks like, and thus, give Him glory.

Then there are those who suffer consequences for their obvious wrongs (e.g. homicide, theft, drugs, or any behavior in conflict with the law). But at times we witness punishment that far outweighs the wrong or misdemeanor, while others who have committed egregious crimes get off scot-free or with minimal punishment. We've all witnessed individuals who seem to be perpetually connected with folly, yet they don't appear to have suffered any consequences for the wrong they've done in their lives, and some have done some heinous acts that are unspeakable. The key word here is "appear". Even though they don't "appear" to have suffered for their unscrupulous actions because no public punishment was effected, you just never know what someone is truly going through or has gone through in their life. We all put on our social masks to hide our inner struggles during our daily interactions. So our guise is not always reflective of our emotional climate. Furthermore, these individuals that are believed to have escaped consequences or punishment for the grievous things they have done, don't escape their guilty consciences, nor do they escape their troubled lives that lack the peace and joy that only come from a clear and guilt-free conscience. As Shakespeare so eloquently stated in *Hamlet*, "to thine own self be true". In essence, we all have to realize that we can't fool ourselves as we look in the mirror and see ourselves for who we really are on a daily basis. That's when we can choose to accept Jesus and His death at calvary which paid for our sins so that now we can see a new, blood washed individual in the mirror - one who is sin-free. The acceptance of this free gift allows Him to change us so that the image reflected in the mirror revealing our carnal nature and wretchedness is eclipsed by His imputed righteousness. What an amazing God to give us a clean slate that we don't deserve because He paid a price through death that He didn't deserve. And He did it just for you and me. Oh what a love! We couldn't ask for anything better. However, He does expect that we would rectify our wrongs with those we've mistreated and ask for forgiveness. Even if someone informs you that they have already forgiven you, it is still your obligation as a christian to assume accountability and admit your wrong while you thank them for their pardon in advance. One's conscience is only clear when wrong has been acknowledged and ownership assumed for hurtful or injurious actions done against someone. And this penitent spirit is enkindled only by the new heart transplant received through Christ which exudes a meek and humble spirit. The recipient of the wrong doesn't need this gesture of forgiveness as much as the offender. However, the recipient has to manifest a spirit of forgiveness regardless if the offender has asked for pardon or not. In fact, the Bible makes it clear both ways. So, if we have aught against our brother due to any unreconciled issue, we have to reconcile things first with that brother before praying to God about anything. Otherwise, He won't hear us. The Bible is clear on this.

If the efforts are unsuccessful after following the instruction from the Bible, we have to let God deal with the individual and move on. The same with praying to God while we're mistreating someone or engaging in deception at the same time. God will not hear the prayer until things are made right. In fact, it's considered farcical to be knowingly involved in mischief or wrongdoing of any kind and praying to God as if you are innocent. This is blasphemous and blatantly sacrilegious to our omniscient God Who is already aware of our shortcomings, but asks us to confess them to Him for our benefit. Therefore, anyone living in perpetual sin with unsettled matters involving those he or she has wronged and are still wronging, cannot be happy because one is not at peace with God or themselves in this situation and God can't hear the prayers of this individual. What a miserable state to be in, as well as a dangerous one because this is where Satan often steps in to delude things. In other words, Satan will have individuals who are outright guilty believe that they are innocent and have them continually avoid dealing with the truth as well as ignore their guilty consciences. So, these individuals that appear externally to have beaten the system and be "living the life" so to speak, are internally suffering with feelings of worthlessness, misery, and stress in reality as they try to keep up their image and facade because without Jesus there is no peace, happiness, or true success. There is just perpetual internal conflict. Simply put, they need to try Jesus and be set free (John 8:32,36). Now, having said all of this to express my hurt with the ridicule and condemnation hurled at me in my time of distress, along with the fault finding that I mentioned no one is in any position to initiate because we all have our faults, I would have appreciated just a little compassion with some understanding in my seemingly hopeless situation. In any event, as we redirect back to the consequences which are sometimes incongruent with the offense, we realize that we live in an imperfect world of sin where justice is mediocre at best and that's why this world is not our home. We're simply passing through to a better place where there will be no more pain, sorrow, crying, death, poverty, or injustice. In essence, there will definitely be questions we will want to ask God about when we get to heaven, but for now we must realize that the secret things belong to God (Deuteronomy 29:29) and our finite minds cannot explain everything and we shouldn't attempt to do so. We are admonished not to judge others because we don't want anyone to judge us (Matthew 7:7) and we don't know the circumstances of others. God alone is omniscient. So this censure was hurtful and disappointing coming from christians who should have been prayerful and supportive instead of critical. Insensitive and uncompassionate gestures such as these are often responsible for individuals leaving the church. If the church family fails to express unconditional love and sympathy, then the purpose of the church is in question and individuals are left to conclude that there is no difference between the world and the church. Quite frankly, those categorized as "worldly", "unsaved", "unholy", "unrighteous", or "heathen" - you name it - are oftentimes more tenderhearted, benevolent, and amiable than our so-called nominal christians.

Meanwhile, I was left feeling very isolated and condemned by those I expected to love me and to be concerned about the well being of the girls and me. Also, oddly enough, we were being scrutinized and criticized for being wrongfully treated - not for any wrong that we had done, but instead, for the wrong done to us. Now, you go figure. If that isn't the epitome of insanity, I don't know what is. It was a real mind blower! We had nothing to do with someone else's unethical and corrupt practices directed towards us that caused us much financial hardship and suffering - not to mention the life-threatening gesture that nearly ended my life which started us on this journey. Why would we aim to sabotage ourselves as this train of thought suggested. In any event, we were just praying for God to keep us free from hatred, malice, and vengeance. It was tough enough being misunderstood and ridiculed as broken and emotionally torn victims, but to be blamed for all of our misfortune was even more disheartening. I knew that God was my Strong Tower that I could run to and be safe from all of the opposition, confusion and distress (Proverbs 18:10) and I chose to cling to Him in this distressing time.

For a brief moment, I felt compelled again to capitulate to my present adverse situation and accept whatever fate had to offer me. The despair I suffered from being misunderstood, along with the insensitivity shown by my inner circle was hurtful and revealing. This crisis unmasked individuals in my inner circle and exposed the simple fact that they really didn't know me and weren't genuinely concerned about my well being. Some were just fair-weather friends or relatives in the relationship for the ride and excitement with the pretension assumed. Thus, instead of an amicable, nurturing and symbiotic relationship, these relationships appeared to be parasitic, fake and emotionally unhealthy in nature. Unfortunately, the timing of this painful awareness couldn't have come at a worse moment in my life because my inner circle was paramount at this time. So, it was extremely painful and disappointing that they were not supportive in this time of my domestic urgency, but were fake, discouraging and indifferent instead. And then there were others in my inner circle that seemed anxious to help, but they voiced that they didn't want to take sides between my husband and me. According to them, they preferred to stay "bipartisan". Now,

I had no problem with friends and family being concerned about the both of us and offering genuine help where they could on both sides. Afterall, they were friends of my husband and me, so I didn't want them to take sides. I was not trying to have my husband ostracized during this crisis by any means - I still loved him and cared about his happiness and overall welfare. For this very reason, I informed my church not to temporarily disfellowship my husband while my TPO (Temporary Protective Order) was in effect which prohibited him from coming within so many feet of me. The church's argument was that he could temporarily go to another sister church during this period of his restraint from the girls and me to prevent any drama. However, I knew that the majority of his support systems were at this particular church where he and I attended as a family with the children when we were together. So I requested for the church's security to give him a chance to comply with the TPO before temporarily removing his presence altogether during the period of this restraint. Once again, I had no vengeful emotions towards him - I only wanted him to get the help he needed - spiritually, mentally, and emotionally. Therefore, his church home's assistance was crucial and lifesaving at this point, so I requested that the church allow him to attend during this critical time.

Reflecting back on my mainstay of friends and family, I only wanted the domestic incident to be acknowledged for the wrong that it was and hoped that this concerned network of friends and family would offer my husband and me the advice required to get the help needed. I felt my husband and I were owed this forthright gesture from an authentic inner circle who really cared about us. However, some of our close friends and family didn't match this profile. They were devoid of this authenticity required to qualify as the core people in our lives during this trial and we had no idea of this until confronted with the dilemma at hand. I also needed to be comfortable with venting all of my flabbergasting moments to someone without being considered crazy. Amazingly, people can witness these life tragedies and atrocities on television, in the movies, and even read about them in a novel, memoir, or newspaper, but to actually hear a friend or family member relay similar experiences, they have to be crazy. I guess that some believe that this doesn't happen in real life and that it's all make-believe and only for the theater or television. Then again, this act of denial may be their coping mechanism in dealing with such grief and anguish because they can't mentally or emotionally handle the real deal. Unfortunately, this denial of reality is counterproductive when one is trying to constructively deal with these issues in the cruel world we live in so that healing can take place. These disturbing accounts are not fantasized, but real. The TV and movie producers get it from somewhere - real life experiences they've either observed, endured or read about. So, individuals that have suffered some of the cruelties, atrocities, and scandals that we (my girls and I) experienced, as shared in the previous chapters of this book, are not crazy. The cruelty and injustice inflicted on these individuals who are suffering and need support is what is crazy instead. If the focus is correctly directed at the real issue - the actual problem and its offender - maybe we can start solving some real and major societal problems. How I longed for someone to understand the agony and anguish I was feeling during this impromptu confrontation with my current tragedy. While suffering during this challenging epoch, I would have settled for the merest hint of genuine sympathy or concern from my core group of friends and family, but, for the most part, I was sadly disappointed. Consequently, I was left drowning beneath all of the confusion and insensitivity that tried to crush my spirits and render me a hopeless case in my deplorable predicament. But, in spite of my disillusionment with the mess I was currently in, I trusted God to bless me with someone who possessed a compassionate ear to unload all of my frustrations, woes, and concerns on. He proved to be this Counselor Par Excellence, as well as my Confidant and Soulmate extraordinaire. I found Him to be everything that I needed as well as a husband as Isaiah 54:5 reveals. In the presence of my heavenly Daddy, I experienced a "peace that passeth all understanding" as Philippians 4:6 reminds us. And as far as companionship was concerned, to my surprise, I found my daughters to be a source of comfort and cheer that I so desperately needed despite their ages (10 and 7 years of age) and despite our surrounding environment of setbacks and uncertainty. We inevitably grew closer together with an inseverable bond and developed an amazing faith in God through it all.

This bond was one of my mainstays as my confidence in my inner circle waned due to the insight I gained from their response in my ongoing dilemma. After all, no one seemed to care that my world was falling apart all around me, hence, no lifeline was thrown to rescue me from my crisis. Instead, I was only offered harsh and insensitive criticism, along with judgemental slurs as if I was the guilty one who was responsible for my current state of affairs that exposed the corruption and fraud targeted against me long before I got married. Consequently, this inimical environment left the girls and me in an extremely ostracized sitch with essentially no one to lean on. My focus, however, was on my girls who were like babes (10 and 7 years of age) during this calamity. Despite our adversity, I prayed for God to give me the tenacity to successfully endure this trial in order that the girls may have a promising future. And fortunately, he put some prayer warriors in my path whose prayers kept me optimistic in spite of my predicament. These heartfelt and sincere prayers kept me hopeful and trusting in God as He began opening doors for me.

During the initial phase of this journey through adversity, we didn't immediately feel the aftermath of what we had been exposed to thus far. When relocating from our toxic domestic environment in the beginning, God blessed us with a lovely and serene new residence where we could heal for the first couple of years following this ordeal and emotionally regroup from the domestic turmoil and devastation we had suffered. This new home, described in earlier chapters, also afforded us the topnotch surveillance needed at the outset of our journey when the atmosphere was virulent and unstable. But, as the saying goes, "all good things must come to an end". As revenue slowed down in the office because of the fraudulence with reimbursements, resources dwindled down to naught. Sadly, I could only financially cover my business expenses with my personal funds for so long before my personal well ran dry too. Hence, I was repeatedly confronted with the realization that, financially, I was in no position at the time to initiate an investigation or to seek legal counsel concerning the exposed corruption involving mismanaged and stolen money in this fraud. Furthermore, I was dealing with insufficient information as well which crippled any legal pursuits. Eventually, all of this double dealing led to our eviction from our residence and office space marking the second major event in our journey. The first major event in this crisis was the domestic incident which destroyed our family and the long term dreams associated.

Over time, my divorce had finally been granted after completing a full year of family counseling together, which was mandated by the state of Georgia for cases like ours prior to considering a divorce. Surprisingly, I deemed the counseling to be extremely beneficial although I had my doubts at first because of all the bizarre things going on during that time. The girls seemed to benefit the most with this mandate by the family court system which proved to be a blessing. They enjoyed expressing themselves openly and freely without the threat of any repercussions. And my husband and I appreciated the opportunity to confess some concerns, share perspectives, and agree to disagree with issues concerning our relationship. It fostered a time of closure for all of us with some family matters and marital concerns in an amicable and positive way for everyone. The girls were also able to communicate with their dad safely and cordially in a protected and judgement-free environment that allowed their suppressed issues and concerns to surface while they got them off of their chests and dealt with them. This designated time of emotional unloading was liberating, empowering, and emotionally cleansing. It allowed them to do the healing that was vital for them to move on and be at peace with our new normal - or at least learn to be. Any questions, hangups, or concerns harbored in their hearts were all expressed uninhibitedly here in these sessions, which were prompted to foster an atmosphere where everybody felt unrestrained and comfortable with letting their guards down. Seeing the girls be freely transparent and candid about various family issues addressed and discussed, was refreshing to me as a concerned mom in our current domestic distress. They appeared to be handling everything amazingly well and I just praised God for answering my prayers concerning their emotional health. This opportunity they were granted to unload their burdens and express their concerns freely through counseling was a godsend that got us through the emotional maze we were currently dealing with in our difficult predicament. I expressed to the girls how blessed they were as I contrasted my upbringing with theirs where the value of family counseling - and counseling in general - was not as popular. Everything was always so hush hush which left many issues, concerns, and emotional wounds unaddressed, which was the norm back then. Communication was lacking which resulted in unstable and unhealthy family bonds being established that were devoid of compassion, intimacy, authenticity, and transparency. This practice led to an overwhelming load and burden of unresolved, unreconciled and broken relationships. Consequently, many family and friendship bonds, along with marital bonds, were indefinitely destroyed. I remember my husband and I mentioning that we wished we were granted this privilege to express our troubles, concerns, and burdens to our parents so freely and respectfully during our childhood and adolescence as the girls were allowed in these counseling sessions. In essence, we wished that our voices were heard during our childhood and adolescence. Nevertheless, we realized that we were living in a different era back then where counseling had a negative connotation. But thank God that the stigma with counseling, and behavioral health overall is changing in our current society in comparison to four to five decades ago. And where we used to only hear of psychiatrists, psychologists and licensed professional counselors, we now have life coaches and motivational speakers in addition to these much needed professionals to encourage, inspire, and provide direction for many individuals in today's society. Overall, benefits of counseling are now being realized and where counseling formerly carried a negative stigma, it now has become faddish. This appreciation for the mental health field, however, must now extend to the government and health insurance companies so that proper funding and reimbursement can be established to support these much needed services. In any event, everyone was happy for our family counseling that allowed all of us to embark upon a new beginning and to heal in the process.

As time went on, the girls and I had more interesting experiences to encounter as we continued to face misguided disdain directed at us from clueless and confused church members, family and friends. Support from the church and legal system during this difficult crisis, as well as from our family and friends, was definitely lacking and I found it terribly disturbing that I was so callously and wrongfully censored for something that someone else had spitefully done to me. Afterall, it was my family that was destroyed in this fraudulent fiasco when someone decided to illegally manipulate my sensitive business information and PII (personal identifiable information) for financial gain leaving the girls and me in a critical financial bind that caused us much hardship, suffering and grief. My character and reputation were attacked as well. Yet I was absurdly viewed to be mentally and emotionally disturbed and the one with the problem.

Because of the misconstrued perceptions and beliefs of some of our friends and family, we were deprived of the support and love we so desperately needed. These were real lonely times for us where we learned to just lean on each other and more importantly, on Jesus. We realized that during this time, all we really had was each other because no one truly understood our plight but us. And from the looks of things in this crisis at the time, we were clearly not batting a thousand. We had no support from the judicial system, no consistent support from the church and no solid support from our inner circle of close friends and family, which was painful. This was a time we gained strength and comfort from the biblical promise in Psalm 27:10 that essentially says when we are forsaken by mother and father (as well as others in our village - family and friends), God will be there for us. Some of my church members repeatedly questioned my story and insinuated doubt with its credibility. Some of our family and friends criticized and denied our story behind our backs also while trying to appear supportive in our faces. Then other family and friends ironically felt the need to remain neutral taking no sides at all and thus, offered no support. However, to their defense, so many things were happening all at once and coming from so many different angles that nobody knew what to believe or what to do, or just where to make sense of things. Because this storm was multifactorial in its attack where several aspects of my life were targeted (finances; career; family; reputation and character; spirituality; and sanity), everything almost seemed to be a farce and totally incredible. The multiple angles this storm came from also served to be a puzzling factor. Not only were multiple areas of my life attacked, but the attacks came from multiple angles and sources. So we (the girls and I, along with bystanders in our storm) were all bewildered, and the isolation we experienced was real. However, despite the dismal outlook, God - the Omniscient One - sustained us through it all. The formidable overcast hovering over our situation couldn't eclipse the silver lining that God encouraged us to see. We learned to appreciate the common expression that "every dark cloud has a silver lining". And this saying is in sync with the biblical teaching revealed in the life of Joseph that showed how God turned what was meant for Joseph's evil into something good (Genesis 50:20). As christians, we know that all things work together for our good as Romans 8:28 reminds us. So, with this gleam of hope, we pressed on in spite of our situation confidently knowing that our lives were in God's hands and He would bring us through these hard times victoriously in His time.

Because people felt we didn't look like what we were going through at the time, some people were less sympathetic and supportive. They felt that we were embellishing our difficult times, which left me baffled because I couldn't imagine anyone bragging about personal suffering that had potential to cause public shame and humiliation. For anyone

SILENT TOO LONG

to exaggerate details in this scenario would be absurd. This was the furthest thing from my mind during these times and totally out of character for me. I had enough going on already and, consequently, didn't have to dramatize or magnify things any more than they already were. But maybe they thought we were trying to draw unnecessary attention to ourselves and get the sympathy we craved from our loved ones during this misfortune. Whatever the case may have been, it didn't dismiss the fact that at times we felt isolated, abandoned, and alone because of the insensitivity, apathy, and indifference shown to us by some who professed to be our friends. Some close family members exuded this same behavior towards us causing us much distress and heartache as well. I want to stop here and caution anyone who assumes that individuals who are economically strained have a certain appearance that conveys their real picture. Afterall, many of us live from paycheck to paycheck and hide it well. For clarity, let's examine some assumptions made about homeless people that are occasionally inaccurate. Some view homelessness to mean that one is devoid of anything valuable so that if a homeless person is seen to possess assets of any kind (e.g. a car, electronic device, nice clothes, even a job, etc), they are considered a fraud. Sometimes we're tempted to view them as scammers when they don't fit our "homeless profile" and we assume that they are just hustling for money when they could be just a couple of days away from losing everything. They may have lost their home at the moment, but have not yet lost their other possessions at the time you encounter them. When people are evicted, they are forced to leave their home, but they can take their possessions with them which may be expensive and costly making their current situation look unbelievable. And oftentimes because we have our own preconceived ideas of how someone homeless should look, we feel these individuals with expensive visible assets are committing fraud when they really need help before all is lost. Besides, they could be living above their means. These individuals are the ones you find sleeping in their cars, which may be the only possession they have at the moment. I know that our society is saturated with a flood of bogus solicitation and for this very reason, it is prudent that you consult God for the best response in these situations so that you don't get bamboozled, or worse, you don't mistakenly assume that a soul sincerely in need of help is a finagler. It's like the warning from the old adage, "don't judge a book by its cover". Many serious situations are overlooked because of this, which causes people who are in desperate need to be robbed of the vital help they need. This help can include money, food, lodging, or whatever succor one can give at the time. But, the help is limited when done individually, which is why ministries that provide resources, support, mentorship, education, and safe environments (for those in need and those rendering help) are needed. Through these ministries, individuals can conquer their addictions and learn to manage their resources wisely. Otherwise, what they receive is squandered. A deprived individual can be given one million dollars, but if they don't know how to use it wisely because they've never been taught or just don't have the resolve to make prudent decisions, it will be dissipated on the pleasures of this life or on addictions that need to be broken. This is similar to the story of the prodial son in the Bible (Luke 15), which is why there is wisdom in the adage: "Give someone a fish and they eat for a day, teach someone to fish and they eat for a lifetime". However, as I mentioned earlier, one can't judge someone's situation by their outer appearance. Even those who look well kept are often in dire straits unbeknownst to the observer. My daughters and I were repeatedly told that we didn't look like what we had gone through and what we were currently going through when we shared our story, which is why people found it hard to believe us, and thus, were reluctant to help us. And after two to three years into this journey with all of the theft and fraud we experienced, our finances were significantly depleted and we would have appreciated any help. However, there were those who felt that I was fabricating our situation, so unfortunately, we weren't taken seriously.

I want to take a moment to shed some light on the concept of homelessness that I discovered throughout the course of this experience of mine. When my daughters and I permanently left our home after the domestic incident that severed some immediate and extended family bonds, we never initially thought that technically we were considered homeless during this brief transition because we weren't destitute of finances and God saw to it that all of our needs were met. Because of the urgency we faced that compelled us to immdediately relocate to a safe place, there was no time for planning to secure a home prior to leaving. And no relatives lived in our state which left us essentially on our own. This scenario serves as an example of homelessness due to safety issues and not financial issues at all. Finances for us were stable at this stage of our journey and our brief state of homelessness was only because of safety concerns requiring us to uproot ourselves and to relocate immediately without a warning. It is clear then that some cases of homelessness have nothing at all to do with finances, but can involve transitioning suddenly and temporarily when someone is in a precarious position. Nonetheless, we still needed help even though we weren't lacking monetarily. The challenge we faced was finding an undisclosed location quickly due to the high-risk circumstances involved. Sadly, because we weren't viewed to be suffering economically, people weren't aware of the seriousness of our predicament and chose not to be supportive or helpful. Therefore, this serves as an example of temporary homelessness due to a brief transition that warranted help that would have been life-saving and had nothing to do with monetary resources at all.

On the other hand, the residential transitioning that occurred years later in the story involved serious financial instabililty as a consequence of the longstanding fraud and theft that we suffered. This placed us in a financially precarious condition where the support and assistance from family, friends, and church members would have been gladly welcomed. However, because we didn't look like what we were going through, once again, we were not taken seriously and consequently, not helped. So, because we didn't outwardly depict someone's picture of being in need of some help and assistance, our condition was not viewed to be urgent or genuine. On the other hand, God knew the difficulty we faced and was aware of the shams that entrapped us and that tempted us to feel hopeless and broken. And He never once left or forsook us as He promised in His Word (Hebrews 13:4-6). He showered us with His abiding presence and love that were sufficient to sustain us through this emotional and financial cyclone.

I remember another unwelcome incident that served as an opportunity for God to show His omnipotence and His watchcare over me as I learned to trust Him no matter what. It was very early one week day morning around 3:30 a.m. while I was sleeping that I heard my phone buzzing on vibrate. Now, I was in hiatus mode from delivering babies (obstetrics) and taking GYN (gynecology) call at the time, so phone calls at this time of day were anomalous for me. Feeling as if I was dreaming because it was way before the crack of dawn, I continued to sleep until two hours later when I began getting ready for an appointment scheduled for later that morning. The interview was forty to fifty minutes away and I knew that I would have to leave early in order to be punctual. I was interviewing for a job to cover an OB/GYN's practice during her maternity leave, which was two to three months away or so. My name was given as a referral to her for this position from a mutual colleague who knew I was on a temporary hiatus and available. This OB/GYN (obstetrics and gynecology) practice informed me that I already had the job because of this referral and that this interview would only serve to allow us to formally meet while this particular OB/GYN (obstetrician and gynecologist) acclimated me to the office, the staff, and the hospital. Subsequent visits would be arranged for me to familiarize myself with her EMR/EHR (Electronic Medical Records/ Electronic Health Records) system used in her office. The knowledge of my acceptance for the job prior to the interview eliminated much of the stress and anxiety I initially had concerning this new venture and allowed me to simply relax and just focus on meeting the doctor and her staff. While I continued to get ready, I decided to see what the buzzing of my phone earlier that morning was all about. Surprisingly,

I saw that someone had called me three times in the wee hours of the morning, but because the number wasn't recognizable, I didn't attempt to call it back right away. Suddenly, an eerie feeling came all over me, but I dismissed it as just nervousness coming on all of a sudden as the time for the interview drew near. By this time, I noticed that time was on my side and that it was a lot earlier than I thought. However, I maintained my same momentum in getting ready considering the rush hour traffic I would encounter and the unfamiliarity with the destination. As I prepared to leave for my interview that morning, I noticed that I could not find my car in this huge open parking lot in the apartment complex we were staying in at the time. The fact that it was very early in the morning before anyone left for work didn't help things either because this left me multiple cars to browse through as I searched. Because I wasn't one hundred percent sure of where I parked and there were no designated parking spaces, I realized that I was destined for an unwanted treasure hunt at this point. I was concerned about being on schedule with my interview and making a good impression, so I begrudgingly took on this unpleasant task to quickly find my car. While diligently searching for my car, I sensed a voice in my head all of a sudden telling me to adopt a plan B because my car had been repossessed. At that instant, I decided to curtail my search and follow this advice that I believed to be from God. The thought that my car could have been repossessed was foreign to me because I had never experienced this before, so I felt awkward with this thought. However, in this situation, I had been forewarned through letters over the last few months that my car note payments were overdue and the next step would be car repossession. So, I wasn't totally in shock with this potential explanation for the inability to find my car that morning. Nonetheless, because I had never experienced car repossession, I was taken by surprise when I realized that it actually happened that day. I was already in a pickle financially around this time because of the ongoing fraud that had left me financially depleted, and now this car repossession at this inopportune time with no apparent recourse was all the more inundating. Knowing that this financial mess I was experiencing all stemmed from the chicanery aforementioned, and that any legal pursuit was too premature at this point because of the lack of finances, as well as the lack of information to connect all of the dots, was extremely frustrating.

Nevertheless, in retrospect, I realized that I had been given warning after warning, but because it had been weeks with no action taken, I was led to believe that God was going to work things out in my favor. Needless to say, that morning I was sadly mistaken as I realized that God had other plans in this situation. I was just left feeling boxed in at that moment, to say the least, because of my impending interview that morning with no obvious or viable solution to meet my immediate need in this dilemma. I found it to be briefly traumatizing as well because it was a new experience for me and happened at the most inopportune time in my life leaving me without a clue of what to do briefly in this defining moment. All I could think about was making sure my girls were okay and not lacking in any way. Therefore, I didn't want to blow this financial opportunity where I could get on my feet again. I was literally at my wits end. Glancing at the time on my cell phone, I realized that I was supposed to be leaving for the interview in just a few minutes in order to be punctual, so this pickle of a situation was definitely unwelcoming. With all that the girls and I had already suffered, we definitely were in no position emotionally, mentally, or physically to take on anything else. All we could think of that morning was, "what next"! It also didn't help that I was offered this great opportunity to financially resuscitate at this crucial time in my life and now this! Obviously, at this time in my life, I was learning to get very accustomed or immune to these life-altering setbacks while navigating through my current journey of misfortune. Clearly, I seemed to be on a roll with first time life-changing events in my life. Meanwhile, I was waiting for my tax refund check which would have allowed me to satisfy my car-note payments, but it was extremely delayed. In any event, I couldn't dismiss the thoughts racing in my head reminding me that the illegal manipulation and exploitation of my PII and BII was responsible for this financial hiccup that I was now facing. It was most upsetting and hurtful. But, in my anguish and uncertainty, I asked God for His wisdom and guidance. During this time, it had not been long since I experienced the eviction from our home that occurred because of this same fraudulence that exhausted my monetary resources. The fraudulence had left us in a financial pickle that was irreparable at the time because more pieces of the puzzle were still forthcoming that were essential to help elucidate the unknowns necessary to crack this case. However, for now, substantial evidence to do anything was insufficient, so legal assistance was consequently still on hold temporarily. With my hands tied for the moment, I was compelled to take a raincheck on rectifying this pecuniary corruption and to innocently suffer this hardship with no recourse as stated earlier. More information was needed to connect the dots and to iron out this financial conundrum, which was going to take time and money. Patience was literally going to become my best friend as I would learn just how much of a virtue it truly is. I could hear the promise in Isaiah 40:31 promising renewed strength in waiting on the Lord and I resolved to wait and to be patient because I trusted God to fix things in His time. So, I put things on the altar and left them there.

Realizing that this timely insight I was afforded that morning while searching for my car in the parking lot was a "God moment" for my direction and discernment, I immediately yielded to God's guidance. And it was at this moment of yielding that a paradoxical peace came over me that allowed me to exhale and keep a level head while working through this temporary crisis. When I returned the missed calls from earlier that morning, I discovered that the calls were made to give me the opportunity to clean out my car before it was repossessed which confirmed my divine insight. God had given me the answer before I asked (Isaiah 65:24). Therefore, I was able to get the address to the lot where my car was taken and retrieve my essentials after the interview. What happened next shocked me when recalling this distressing life event. After verifying things with the gentleman on the line and obtaining the address to the car lot where I could recoup my essentials later when time permitted, I simply and calmly called a rental car agency nearby and made a reservation for one week. I started with one week to see what God's plans would be for my transportation thereafter. My next step involved contacting Uber for transportation there. Now at that moment, I was definitely exercising the faith God so mercifully gave me that morning in my dilemma because my financial profile was a muddle with my credit history looking bleak at its best because of all the double-dealing with my PII (personal identifiable information) and BII (business identifiable information). Clearly, this was not an opportune time to initiate any transaction that would involve a credit inquiry due to the fraud involved that mercilessly tainted my credit and had me in this predicament in the first place. The recent discoveries involving identity and financial fraud that were yet to be completely resolved, would only serve to expose a very precarious financial platform for me that I knew would render my case to be impracticable. So, I definitely recognized this to be a faith move that God helped me to execute as I took my focus off of the circumstances at hand, and instead, focused on my omnipotent God and His resume'. His resume' discloses His sovereignty and authority that He wields over the entire universe and His specialty in executing the impossible! Also, Uber was still relatively new in Georgia around this time and my use of its services that day involved some desperation and faith as well considering the circumstances. As a single mom in my current challenging plight who was unfamiliar with even using Georgia's transit system, my faith that day was strong. Nowadays, information about the driver can be obtained prior to the service being rendered, but this was not so then. Nonetheless, the calmness and level headedness that I exuded in this urgency is what shocked me, but I knew the Source of my even-tempered composure. It was the awesome influence of the Holy Spirit. Even in this no-win situation with seemingly nowhere to turn, I was amazingly at peace. The Holy Spirit had given me a sweet, supernatural, and inexplicable peace in my present extremity that assured me that God had already worked out my present financial fiasco in advance in my favor. This reminded me of the familiar saying, "man's extremity is God's opportunity". It sounds illogical from a secular standpoint I know, but when you know Jesus, it makes all the sense in the world because spiritual things are spiritually discerned (1 Corinthians 2:14). I could perceive that God was using this perfect opportunity to manifest His power and reveal just how capable He was of taking care of me. I was claiming Philippians 4:19 on this occasion that promises that God would supply all my needs according to His riches in glory. Therefore, I didn't hesitate to move forward with solidifying a car as I called Uber that morning for transportation despite my financial and credit crunch. I refused to feel boxed in with no hope in this despairing predicament that I had unjustly inherited from the current financial corruption I suffered when I was the child of the world's Owner of everything. I was just going to do my part in the partnership and move forward (or shall I say, I resolved that morning to put the rod out over my "Red Sea" experience as Moses did in Exodus 14:15 and watch God part my sea of difficulty). This was going to be my Exodus.

As I mentally rehearsed the fact that the cattle on a thousand hills and every beast of the forest are my heavenly Daddy's, along with the world and the "fulness thereof" (Psalms 50:10-12), I quickly regained the confidence and authority as a child of God to go into that rental car facility and claim what was mine because my heavenly Daddy owned it all. I was there to get my blessing and nothing in heaven (smile) was going to stop me. Ironically, I had no anxiety or worry. God had given me a sweet peace in the midst of this storm and it permitted me to think prudently and rationally as He taught me that partnering with Him is the solution to every problem - great or small. Even today, as I reminisce on this situation, I see how God allowed me to face this challenging time without being mentally and emotionally ruffled to the point of defeat before I could even initiate a response because of all the apparent hopelessness. Instead, He gave me the fortitude and confidence needed to work through this setback as I leaned on Him. When

I walked into the lobby of the rental car agency, I noticed that I was the only customer there and I immediately got a good feeling because I saw God orchestrating everything perfectly as He set the scenario in my favor. With this setting, I anticipated getting the time and attention that I needed in my desperate situation, and that's just what happened. Prior to my arrival, I informed the gentleman about my credit issue to see if the reservation would still be viable there as I was prepared to go elsewhere if it wasn't because I knew that my God had an open door for me somewhere that morning and I was determined to find it (Matthew 7:7,8)! This reminds me of a favorite song by Mary Mary, "Go Get It" that encourages individuals to go get their blessing. Sitting back and waiting on it isn't enough. We have to partner with God and go get it sometimes. In any event, my plan that morning was to give my information ahead of time to get the ball rolling and to find out if this was the open door arranged by God or not in the essence of time. I shared some details about the identity and financial theft in advance to explain the unfavorable credit score he would discover during the credit check and told him that I would see him shortly. So upon my arrival, I waited to see how God would work things out because I was determined to be optimistic recognizing that I was partnered with God Who can do the impossible - the impossible is His specialty. Well, at this point in the story, I'm sure that all of my prayer and faith warriors already know the outcome. The gentleman calmly looked at me as he informed me that I was approved for the reservation and that he could extend it for however long I would need it, never mentioning anything about the credit issue at all. But wait before you get your "hallelujah" on. There is more to the story. In addition to the sweet sounding music heard regarding the approval of my reservation, God blessed me with a luxury car at an extremely affordable and significantly reasonable rate despite my tainted and abused credit score from the preexisting and ongoing corruption. The gentleman also found all the discounts he could possibly apply to my reservation despite my precarious financial portrait to lower the costs even more, and there were no credit issues to hinder the transaction, which was yet another major praise report. My emotions at that moment were stirred up inside of me with so much gratitude that I thought I would explode. I immediately sent up a heartfelt praise thanking God for taking care of me yet again. And because He always orchestrates everything perfectly and timely, I was able to walk into my interview early and unflustered. The meeting went well and I felt positive vibes with the physician and her office staff, as well as with the hospital personnel after spending the entire work day with everyone. She was the chairman of the Obstetrics and Gynecology department of this hospital which was located just outside of the major city and I found her to be exceptionally warm and amiable. I observed the office staff to be the same. I also noted that the office was well-organized and ran smoothly, so I looked forward to covering her during her maternity leave which was just a couple of months away. We scheduled another appointment for a week later so that I could train on her EMR/EHS (Electronic Medical Records System/Electronic Health System) and acclimate to the office and the staff. We planned for at least four visits or more to allow me to feel comfortable with her office setting and its flow, but her little precious one had other plans. These plans involved this little bundle of joy delivering prematurely to our surprise. I can still remember getting that call one morning informing me of the exciting news and the request to start several weeks earlier than planned, so our other scheduled meetings for training never took place. I was taken aback, but once again, God works in mysterious ways because now that I had the rental car to fit into my weekly budget, starting work earlier would only work in my favor with satisfying this new expense. This praise report served as another opportunity to apply the promise of Romans 8:28 that reassures us as christians that God will always have things work out for His children. On the first day, I anticipated some awkwardness and some adjusting that I figured would be initially uncomfortable, but to my surprise, it wasn't as difficult as I initially expected after having my training curtailed by this doctor's premature delivery of her little one. Instead, I found the staff to be remarkably accommodating which helped me to navigate smoothly through the challenges, complexities, and uncertainties I faced from time to time adapting to their office's electronic medical records system and overall flow of things. The hospital setting mirrored the same affability observed at the office, and this just made my experience all the warmer. I truly missed everyone when my assignment was complete and strongly considered the offer to join the practice. But God had other plans for me that I was still figuring out, so I said my good-byes begrudgingly and set out to see just what these plans entailed. I was confident that God knew what was best for me and had my best interest at heart; therefore, I unreservedly put my complete trust in Him for my next steps along this journey. This was just another anecdote conveying God's protective care and providence for the girls and me while letting us know we were in good hands - His hands.

Throughout all of our hard times, we always had a praise report in the midst of the storm and a lesson learned. It was these vicissitudes in life that made us stronger and taught us how to wholeheartedly rely on God. Looking back on these difficult times, we surprisingly don't have any regrets overall because these times were actually some of the most memorable, tender, and cohesive times for the girls and me that not only made us stronger, but connected us at our hips, as well as our hearts. Instead of the "dynamic duo", we became the "tried and true trio". Through these challenges, we grew closer together as we grew closer to God. And, instead of allowing pessimism, victimization, hopelessness and defeat to take over us and dampen our spirits, we chose to thank God for the trials realizing that they were opportunities for us to magnify His name in spite of our misfortune and for Him to show Himself strong. He definitely held us up through it all and made a way out of no way. For this, we are eternally grateful.

To this day, we laugh about these redolent times that evoke strong emotions that are amusing, inspiring, encouraging, and empowering. Oftentimes, we just sit, relax, and reflect on God's goodness and how we made it over only because of Him. These afternoons or evenings where we recapture these memories are spiritually nourishing for the soul as they remind us that God is truly our Jehovah Jireh (Provider), Jehovah Nissi (Protector and Deliverer), Jehovah Rapha (Healer), and Jehovah Shalom (Peacegiver) in this sinful and wicked world. We're constantly reminded that this is not our home. And these reflections are firsthand encounters that serve to show God's awesome love for us and to testify of His ability to do more than we can ask or imagine (Ephesians 3:20). It is important to me that the girls and I never forget how God miraculously intervened on our behalf and delivered us from the malicious and diabolical attacks that confronted us that epic morning and throughout our journey since that day. The powers of darkness tried to annihilate any memory of us, ...but God! As we recount our powerful testimonies of deliverance during our walk of faith amidst the strong and fierce opposition, along with the troublesome times, we can be confident that what God did before, He can do again. Knowing this, the girls can be confident that whatever they face in life, God is more than able to bring them through. Hence, testimonies serve as encouragement and reminders of God's power as we navigate through the challenges and difficulties in life. These stories then become paradigms and templates for others experiencing similar struggles. The Bible is full of stories of deliverance, liberation, and restoration. There are also stories that teach essential life lessons giving the positive or negative consequences of our decisions and actions. God knew that these stories and life lessons would be helpful, ennobling, and uplifting to us and our children as we recount them and share them - the blessings and the trials. Before there were books, this sharing of information down throughout the generations was practiced to provide wisdom, knowledge, and history. The Bible says that we will overcome as christians in the end by the blood of the Lamb and the word of our testimony (Revelation 12:11 KJV), hence, I share mine. So, recounting and telling your testimony is liberating and encouraging for others going through difficult times. Never let anyone discourage you from sharing what God has done for you. Remember the tests we encounter are so we can have a **test**imony - it's all about God. Our lives are lived out for His glory. As we lift Him up through our lives - in the good and bad times - all people will be drawn to Him - the Source of life, strength, peace, and happiness (John 12:32). He is the Way, the Truth, and the Life. Also, sharing our life lessons with our children and others, which includes our victories as well as our mistakes (those that can edify or inspire), makes us more relatable and allows us to win their trust to direct them on the right path. This rapport built through transparency creates life-changing experiences that are life-saving. So, join history and tell your story (instead of just **his**tory, there will also be **her**story). Afterall, history is compiled of stories, experiences and accounts that give us purpose, direction, and insight into the past. It serves as the foundation for our existence and also as a reminder that God can deliver us from any trouble currently as He did in the past lest we forget. So, as slavery, the Holocaust (or Shoah), the Passover, the Exodus, Calvary, and even the more recent 9/11 terrorist attacks are all commemorated for their various reasons, my daughters and I choose to commemorate our experience that commenced on April 26, 2012 when God trusted us with the trial that he allowed us to endure. He also manifested His power on our behalf and saw us through our difficult times giving us a powerful testimony to share with others. These reflections serve to validate and authenticate God in our lives and give us credibility when sharing Him with others as we commemorate our "Breakthrough".

As I reflect back on the title of this chapter, I am reminded in the Bible that the devil comes to steal, kill, and destroy (John 10:10), so I tell the girls that hard times and misfortunes are inevitable in this world, so we shouldn't think of these circumstances as "strange" or surprising. Instead, we are to anticipate them and fret not because we have an advocate in God Who will always see us through these hard times. I also stress to them the importance of being vigilant about recognizing the enemy with all of his schemes, shenanigans, and lies to avoid falling as prey to him. However, they are encouraged not to fear him because they are aware that "greater is He (the Holy Spirit) that is in us than he (the devil) that is in the world" (1 John 4:4). God left us this gift of the Holy Spirit after Jesus resurrected and went back home to heaven (John 14:16-18, 26-27). With this gift, all power in heaven and earth is at our disposal to be used for His glory and to protect us from the arch enemy - Satan (Mark 16:17,18). And to think that we hype the Transformers, Star Wars, the superheroes and other science fiction movies when all of them pale in comparison to the power we have access to and can possess as the inherited legacy of God - His off-spring. We have a lineage of royalty and therefore, we have all power and authority in heaven and earth through the Holy Spirit's presence in us (Acts 1:5,8). We just have to access it and ask for it (Luke 11:9-13). Essentially, we have to know who we are. Although I'm no supporter of science fiction, I am reminded of the movie, *The Matrix*, where Keanu Reeves spent the entire movie weak and defeated against his antagonists until he recognized just who he was - *The Matrix*. His power came with his awareness of who he was. Similarly, our power as christians is activated when we become aware that we are God's children and allow Him to live in us. When we do this, we become invested with all power through Him and thus are invincible (Romans 8:31 KJV). Reflecting on this biblical truth reminds me of a specific encounter I had with my husband right after the expiration of our one-year TPO when I decided to execute this God-given authority and power. I still chuckle recounting this memory. Amazingly, I had experienced some powerful supernatural experiences during this time that gave me a God-confidence that transformed me into a force to reckon with as I look back. Now, let me clarify things a bit. My first glimpse into the supernatural arena as a christian was not during this time in my life. I had been fortunate to testify of some supernatural events long before this difficult time in my life that allowed me to reinforce my spiritual relationship with God. So, I was no novice in this area because He had allowed me to see and communicate with Him on more than one occasion up close and personal. And during this trial, I experienced some more supernatural encounters that were amazing and empowering as well. As I reflect on one such occasion where I decided to exercise my God-given authority as His child, I remember a conversation I had with my husband in the parking lot as I prepared to leave with the girls after a church program. We were getting in the car and preparing to leave when he appeared in the parking lot and began to approach the window to tell the girls farewell for the night. Recognizing his hesitancy and awkwardness because of the previous one-year restriction with the TPO which had just expired, I welcomed him to approach our car and tell the girls goodnight as I informed him that he didn't have to worry about us being afraid of him. I assured him that although the TPO had just expired, he could relax and communicate with them freely in my presence because we weren't scared of him. As he gave me a bewildered look and then came closer to the car to tell the girls goodbye, I chuckled in a joking manner and informed him that I would catch bullets with my teeth if necessary. Although this was said jokingly, the message to him hit home conveying that I realized Whose child I was and knew the power I possessed as God's child. Therefore, I anticipated no hanky panky with his gesture as I warned him appropriately. Through our experiences that year, I felt like David when he shared how God had enabled him to "run through a troop" and to "leap over a wall" in Psalm 18:29. We truly could empathize with this as we reflected on all that we had undergone that past year and yet, still came through victoriously.

Nonetheless, I repeatedly reminded the girls as the title of this chapter states, that we should not be surprised when we suffer hardships and strife on occasion. It comes with the territory in this world of sin (Acts 14:22). Some sufferings will be consequences of sins we have committed in our lives (have mercy on us heavenly Father) and some will just be inevitable from our existence in this wicked world. In both cases, the answer is Jesus. And, we must remember that God instructs us to rejoice in our trials because this makes us partakers of His afflictions when He came to die for our sins as He faced all of this and worse for our sake - no fault of His own. He reminds us that as participants in His sufferings, we will also be participants with Him in all of His glory when it is revealed in the end and we joyfully live with Him forever (1 Peter 4:12,13). Through this difficult journey, we were also able to testify to the promises cited in Psalm 34:17-22. As we cried out to the Lord in our anguish and disappointments, He heard our cry and delivered us from all the snares and traps set on our path. Not once did He leave us to battle this storm alone. He was there right by our side leading, protecting, strengthening, and sustaining us all along the way. It was comforting knowing that He understood just what we were going through and became our Confidant and best Friend.

Oftentimes, I would encourage them to steal away with me as I pondered Calvary and the great sacrifice made for us. I would explain to them that even though we must shoulder our cross as christians, we will never have to go through what He endured to save us when He died on the cross for our transgressions. In love, He took the painful and fierce blows for us as they beat and buffeted Him. He was disrespected as they spat in His face and ridiculed Him by stripping His clothes off and clothing Him in a robe and a crown of thorns in mockery doubting His Lordship. Finally, they pierced His hands and feet with nails to hang Him naked on the cross and then pierced Him in His side as they left Him to die. What an ignominious death for the Creator and Savior of the universe Who came and suffered this cruel and heinous treatment merely to save us! And amidst all of the utter wickedness he faced, His concern before He took His last breath was that God would forgive His murderers who He came to save despite their bitter rejection of Him. When I ponder this scene, I get overwhelmed and tearful as I consider the unconditional love manifested for me. So, in view of this great sacrifice, our suffering in this life can't even begin to be comparable or noteworthy. And His life on earth before His death wasn't a bed of roses either. He was misunderstood, envied, hated, disrespected and ostracized by family and friends. As the scriptures say, He walked the winepress alone (Isaiah 63:3) and there was no one to accompany Him. I recall referencing the life of Christ when responding to individuals relaying to me that some friends, family and church members were calling me crazy during this storm. My response always focused on Matthew 10:25 (in KJV & MSG) where Jesus informed His disciples that if they called Him cruel names and He is the King of kings and Lord of lords, then they were not to be surprised at the cruel treatment they too would suffer as His disciples. So I rested in the fact that I was in good company (Hallelujah!). I still chuckle even today when I remember the troubled and disconcerted responses as I voiced this rebuttal - that if they called Jesus crazy, the King of kings and Lord of lords, then I was in good company with people calling me crazy. Besides leaving a discombobulated expression on their faces, they were also left stupefied and speechless. God always gave me an answer in times like these to confound the apparent foolishness circulating at the time. I often encouraged the girls that to suffer for Christ's sake was better than to suffer from a life without Him because a life without Him would be miserable and devoid of happiness and peace. I stressed to them that, one way or another, all will suffer strife and misfortune in this sinful world - it's inevitable. But we are reminded as christians that we don't have to suffer alone (Hebrews 13:5) and we should glorify God in our suffering knowing that in the end we will experience the glory He has in store for us - eternal life. The nonchristian, on the other hand, will suffer alone when experiencing the pain, misery, strife, and injustices in this unjust world and then be lost in the end - what a tragedy! The choice is ours and God won't compel us in either direction. He wants for us always to be free moral agents serving Him out of love - not automation or compulsion.

When we think about the fraternities, sororities, and other social organizations and causes that we choose to experience distress and difficulty for without something eternal promised in return and without Someone to bear the brunt for us as Christ did on calvary, it becomes crystal clear that heaven is cheap enough with the inconceivable price paid for us by a loving Savior Who died a criminal's death for us. Reflecting on Christ's life and death definitely empowers us to face our trials and tribulations with fortitude and to have a forgiving spirit in face of cruelty and injustice. When the girls and I have heart to heart talks on occasion, I always inform them that being a christian is analogous to enlisting into the army of God, and as soldiers we need training for the anticipated adversity. This training bootcamp comes in the form of trials and tests that strengthen our faith muscles and mature us spiritually. These trials also allow us to empathize with others and to help them in their crises. I have explained to them that when we surrender our lives to God daily, we are giving Him permission (because He does not coerce us) to use us as He chooses, and this will often be done by allowing us to experience calamities in our lives so that He can show Himself strong to us and to the bystanders that He orchestrates to observe us while we're weathering our storm. A good case in point that I've shared with them is when God hardened Pharaoh's heart to resist freeing the children of Israel as He wielded His signs and plagues manifesting His power to Pharaoh and to the surrounding nations looking on. The Israelites, themselves, were even blessed as they witnessed God moving on their behalf. God's Sovereignty was ratified as these manifestations and wonders endorsed His monopoly when it comes to omnipotence which ultimately led to the deliverance of the Israelites and the memorable "Exodus" experience. Other illustrations I've shared with them where God exhibited some of His wonders, were in the lives of Job as a Restorer (Our Divine Resource Center) and Lazarus as a Resurrector (The Source of Life). In Job's devastating and comprehensive loss, God evinced His ability to restore in a way that far exceeded Job's loss. In Lazarus' death, God revealed His divine monopoly on being the sole Life Source and Creator by resurrecting Lazarus and thus validating His sovereign credentials. So, I remind them over and over that we have signed up as followers of Christ to be used for His glory in any way He chooses. I also remind them that it is a privilege to be used by Him because He uses those whom He trusts with the various tests and trials that He allows to occur. He knows that their response in the tribulation will glorify Him. So I often express that we were chosen for the storm that disrupted our lives that day. Through our tests and trials in this situation, our aim has become to remain loyal to Him with unwavering faith in the midst of our misfortunes that we are still going through even today to empower others in similar adversities to stay strong and do the same. So, I stress to the girls over and over again that He handpicked us for our current trial to be the soldiers He can use to reveal His omnipotence, protection, providence, and omniscience as this trial is not yet over. Through our trial and testimony, others will be able to see how real faith looks and functions. I also explained that He trusts us to manifest His agape (unconditional) love and forgiveness throughout this test in spite of the cruelty, fraud and injustice suffered. With this positive perspective on things, the girls and I were more motivated to pass this test successfully that God entrusted us with as we leaned on Him to carry us all the way through to our victory. Recounting the story of Esther in the Bible, I encouraged the girls that we should view ourselves in this trial as "Esthers" for "such a time as this". I also would remind them of Jeremiah 12:5 - one of my favorite Bible verses. The paraphrased message here happens to be a favorite spiritual mantra of mine, stating that if I can't run with the footman now (because of fatigue), how on earth do I expect to run with the horses later.

Chapter 9

My Perspective

Going back to the beginning again, I felt as if my life was swept up suddenly by a vicious domestic and emotional tornado that unleashed devastation in my household that morning destroying my marriage and family. This violent and disruptive storm tried to destroy my life as it shattered my stability by causing significant losses that left me confused, isolated, and broken. As I witnessed this horrific event that day, I felt as if someone had literally torn my heart into pieces and then threw these pieces, along with my hopes and dreams, out of the window. The inseverable family bond I had envisioned and prayed for was ruined now and I was left to pick up the broken pieces and move on as if nothing happened. I struggled just trying to mentally grasp what had occurred and to figure out how things escalated to this magnitude. The emotional and physical intensity was so surreal that morning that I wrestled with trying to find answers to this catastrophic mayhem. In that moment, I suffered an inexplicable disorientation as I watched unrestrained emotions surface and evil forces bear sway. Observing this negative energy in operation that morning was mentally, emotionally, and physically inundating as I witnessed the diabolical current that engulfed my household in that moment seek to end my life ...., "but God" (my mantra always)!

My perspective in that epic moment as I reflect back is liberating because I witnessed God's omnipotence first hand as He delivered me from Satan's snare exposing his inferiority and weakness compared to God's matchless power and authority over everything. As He said in His Word concerning Himself, "All power is given unto me in heaven and in earth" (Matthew 28:18 KJV). He possesses all power in heaven and on Earth. All I had to do was call on Him for help, and although this call was inaudible due to the circumstances, He heard my heartfelt and despairing cry and responded less than a second later. In fact, He was already there because I'm reminded in Hebrews 13:5,6 (KJV) that He never leaves us or forsakes us. I just needed to simply give Him permission to move on my behalf because He does not intrude or force Himself on anyone. Therefore, I had to simply let Him know that I wanted to live. It is here where I get emotionally overwhelmed because I think of those individuals in similar dilemmas who were so deeply distraught and exhausted that they gave up the fight and threw in the towel choosing rather to rest in peace until that great family reunion (1Thessalonians 4:16,17 - KJV). Now, I don't fault anyone who made a decision like this in a dire situation because I found myself in this same mindset briefly in my vulnerable moment as the first chapter of this book describes, but it is here where the perspective of my life abruptly changed and my relationship with God made all the difference. In that unpropitious moment, God redirected my focus back to Him - the God of all hope. He also let me get a glimpse of my daughter Kelly who happened to be in the room absorbing everything. From her appearance, she looked to be praying and internally fighting all at once. At that moment, Kelly not only represented my precious baby girl who I realized I had to fight and live for in this fierce struggle for my life, but she also represented all those in similar circumstances who needed hope and a story of deliverance. My survival story would be just that!

In this defining moment, the conception for the ministry God was preparing me for was underway, and it would involve reconciling broken relationships and comforting the troubled at heart, along with providing help for the hopeless and financially strained. Along this journey's walk, I would be growing and nurturing this ministry internally until its birth at God's appointed time.

In the meantime, I had a rude awakening from this incident while reflecting later during my time of solitude. I realized that the girls had a close call of prematurely memorializing their mom that morning when I had a face to face encounter with death leaving them and me momentarily stunned. Reflecting on the gravity of this reality is spine-chilling, and attests to God's miraculous intervention being even more compelling that morning. Out of all my testimonies, this is one of the major ones that I find to be most empowering and life-changing when I share it on occasion as God leads me. In these instances, I become more relatable in my profession as an obstetrician and gynecologist (OB/GYN) through my transparency, and consequently, patients feel more comfortable and uninhibited sharing their problems and concerns. This established rapport allows me to help them even more as I not only minister to their physical needs, but to their emotional and spiritual needs as well as a holistic healthcare provider.

Unfortunately, I am aware that there are some individuals who have had to memorialize their loved ones in similar settings and it deeply disturbs me that their loved ones saw no recourse in dealing with the conflict and toxicity in their relationship. I sympathize and empathize with those who have experienced this and I ask God to comfort the hearts of these individuals while they await their reunion with loved ones when God comes to take us all home. As I contemplate the different outcomes that could have very well been my story in the perilous state I found myself in that morning, I have a heart of gratitude to God for allowing my spiritual breakthrough April 26, 2012 right at the focal point of the chaos and confusion. His message was clear to me that morning leaving no room for any ambiguity or doubt. He was not finished with project Lilith yet (a borrowed expression from one of my favorite pastors - Pastor Henry Wright). Consequently, my life was spared and I accepted the calling God had for my life through this new ministry that He impregnated me with that morning at my crossroad. As time went by and God unfolded the ministry He planned for me to launch in more detail, I resolved in my heart to fulfill this God-driven mission no matter what the cost. I just never imagined how painful the cost would be to execute this task; nor did I anticipate the strong opposition I would encounter. And, I definitely didn't expect this antagonism to come from individuals I loved and trusted. But then again, what should I have expected as I contemplated the life of Jesus where he was ridiculed by His brothers and His own family who didn't understand His mission. In fact, Luke 4:24 and John 4:44 tell us that He wasn't even accepted in His own hometown. I've since then learned that whenever something profitable and fruitful is about to flourish, the enemy viciously wields his deceptive and destructive tactics to impede progress. So as God shared with me what He envisioned for my life ministry, Satan employed those closest to me to distract and discourage me from fulfilling this vision from God. Because of this, there were many times I felt lonely, dejected, and downright hopeless with no one to talk to. This provided the perfect platform for me to experience God like David expounded in Psalm 23:1 (KJV - King James Version). It afforded me the opportunity to get up close and personal with God where I not only humbly beheld His omnipotence and glory in awe, but I also experienced His compassion, gentleness, peace and inexplicable joy. Reminiscing on this time in my life, I can attest to the song Donny McClurken and Marvin Winans sing entitled, "Who Would've Thought". I shared the same sentiments while going through this arduous journey. I never new that I'd get to know the Lord the way I did and I don't have any regrets. My experience with God during this season in my life was truly amazing and I wouldn't trade this time in my life for anything.

It was intriguing to see how my domestic squabble on that

morning transmogrified into something altogether different from what was initially thought to be the only concern - the domestic incident. Mysteriously, pandora's box exploded following this incident exposing all of the unimaginable fraudulence over time. The inconceivable financial corruption uncovered in the aforesaid flabbergasting accounts was downright unthinkable and left me dumbfounded with what to do next. By God's grace I kept my sanity through it all and managed to maintain my peace of mind in this conundrum although at times this was very difficult. However, I claimed His promise for peace as I looked to Him in lieu of this disheartening bewilderment (Isaiah 26:3) surrounding me, and I decided to trust God to see me through all of this. Looking back, I surprised myself with the unshakable faith I had in God and the relentless determination I demonstrated during these times of hardship that the girls and I faced. But as I intimated in the first chapter of this book, the maternal instinct of a mother is powerful when it comes to protecting and providing for her child and it is this inherent trait that God gifts mothers with that motivates them to go to any length to achieve this goal. This invaluable attribute is what makes a mother (and a parent in general - biological or nonbiological) ensure the welfare of the child. At the onset of this emotional and domestic turmoil in our lives, I knew I had to be strong because I realized that I was the sole guardian and advocate for the girls because we were devoid of all local family support. Most of our relatives were out of state and supporting us was not an option. Later on in this challenging journey, I found this to be true with relatives who were close by as well because of the confusion and dissension that arose after the traumatic breakup with my husband that seemed to cause some family and friends to distance themselves from us. Because we were misunderstood by family as well as friends and church members in our domestic ordeal, we were not supported. Many felt we were overreacting and being insensitive to the needs of my husband who they felt needed us then. They failed to see the danger involved during and after the incident because they maintained their skepticism concerning the details of the occurrence that severed bonds that morning. It seemed as if no one wanted to believe that the domestic incident had actually happened. I guess it was too emotionally overbearing for those who knew us as a married couple and as friends. I tried to sympathize with them as I gave them the benefit of the doubt because I too was having difficulty accepting the reality of things even though it was my marriage and family that was ruined, along with my financial stability, career and relationships with some of my family and friends. Even my character was in jeopardy because of the detestable lies and accusations that were falsely hurled against me for no apparent reason. I was informed of rumors circulating that blamed me for the insurance fraud that I was discovering in this scandal where my sensitive information was being manipulated. This literally made no sense because the girls and I suffered great losses because of this double-dealing that placed us in the most unfavorable position financially and overall. Sadly, I recognized over time that no one really knew the degree of suffering and loss that the girls and I experienced because of this ongoing duplicity. It was at this time in my life that I felt humbled and overwhelmed as I reflected on the life of Jesus and tried to imagine what He must have felt as the Creator of the universe coming to subject Himself to a heinous death by the very ones He created and came to save from their sins despite their ingratitude for this awesome and selfless sacrifice. It was His silent acquiescence to die for our faults although He was faultless that speaks volumes. The brutal and heinous treatment He suffered for you and me is heart-wrenching as well, yet He never stopped loving us. And to think that the Creator allowed Himself to suffer at the hands of his creatures just to save them is unfathomable. But what's more difficult to believe, is the unappreciative attitude for the great sacrifice He made. Pondering this, I resolved to follow the perfect example of Jesus manifested through His life here on Earth and to keep a loving and forgiving heart in spite of all the adversity I faced. My desire was to be used by Him in this trial. I could hear the words in Romans 8:31 that reminded me that if God is for me, I don't need to worry about who would even try to stand against me because my favor, my deliverance, and my victory is a "done deal" with God as my Advocate. I just simply had to sit down on the right side of God and allow Him to make my enemies my footstool as He promised in Psalm 110:1 KJV. The challenge was realizing that even though God's promises are sure, the timing for resolution and breakthrough is totally up to Him and we had no idea that there would be several years from the onset of this crisis to its completion. It is not fully resolved even now.

Our faith and trust muscles were in for an intense boot camp as they would be worked to their maximum potential while awaiting our breakthrough. And we planned to give no less than one hundred percent by standing strong during this interlude just before our quantum leap into our greater that we knew God had for us. This perspective kept a fire going in my spirit despite the doomy overcast the enemy sought to keep ever before me concerning my current condition. I strove to remain optimistic, however, although things appeared seemingly foreboding. With this positive frame of mind, I was able to dance in the rain and experience many sunbursts where God showed me the sun in the middle of the pouring rain. From a little child, I learned the power and influence of a buoyant mindset and adapted a light-hearted and cheerful spirit even in the midst of overwhelming misfortunes. I later realized that this was a gift from God. Whenever circumstances were strained or tension was evident in the atmosphere, I was always finding a way to make someone relax, laugh, and smile. I just enjoyed making people happy. Because of this character trait I possessed, my personality type was viewed to be sanguine when in fact, I learned later that I am more strongly phlegmatic than sanguine. That may come as a surprise to some childhood friends and some family who may find this hard to believe, but I did realize this fact as I experienced life independently in my young adulthood. I've always said that the ones who actually know you the most are your college friends who see you independently make decisions and respond the way you would respond to certain life events or challenges in lieu of following suit to your parents' leading when at home or just acting the way your family would expect you to act. This also applies to those who have gone to boarding school for high school. Case in point, because of my enthusiastic and vibrant personality, many view me as a social butterfly when in fact most of my time is spent alone, in small groups or one on one. I enjoy people as I shared earlier, and although I enjoy social events and gatherings on occasion, surprisingly I spend most of my time alone with my girls, close friends or family and I'm content. In fact, I love my time alone and tend to gravitate to more intimate settings (e.g. prayer groups, small group teen talks, one on one time with a loved one or friend, etc.) from time to time. In any event, the coping mechanism of laughter that I acquired as a child really helped me weather life's storms and see the cup half full instead of half empty throughout my life. This habit tremendously helped me with my present conflict and gave me a brighter outlook on what appeared to be an unbearable storm. It also revealed how the principles of Philippians 4:8 are truly beneficial. Consequently, the girls and I had many laughs and good times in the middle of the confusion and distress as we implemented Proverbs 17:22 KJV in our lives at the time. With this positive attitude, we were able to welcome the rain of heartaches and misfortunes as a refresher, cleanser, and nourisher right before the beautiful rainbow of promise. Learning of Jesus' love as a child also perfumed my surroundings with much love amidst the struggles and challenges that all families face. With this knowledge, I was led to believe that I was living in my very own little fairytale world. This fairytale world of mine that I had accepted as my reality was often disrupted by injustices and challenges witnessed and experienced while growing up. However, overall, my atmosphere exuded love and I felt that my childhood was peaches and cream because of the cheerful attitude I was determined to nurture despite some disappointments I faced as most do in this imperfect world with all of its inequities. Reminiscing back to my grade school years, I can still hear my third grade class singing, *"Everything Is Beautiful"* by Ray Stevens and H.R. Ragsdale. Not only is the melody of this song beautiful, but the message is even more beautiful. The message declares that there is beauty in diversity and that everyone is beautiful in their own unique way. It also sends the message that the inner self is of more value than the outer self. Another favorite song that inspired and uplifted me during my younger years with a beautiful message was *"Reach Out and Touch Somebody's Hand"* sung by Diana Ross. Other favorite songs of mine that lifted my spirits were: *"Sing"* by the Carpenters (and really all of their songs); *"You Light Up My Life"* by Debbie Boone; *"Caravan of Love"* by The Isley Brothers; and *"Wind Beneath My Wings"* by Bette Midler just to name a few other songs with positive messages. In the Bible, music is seen to be a mood modulator that is capable of infusing peace into the atmosphere as illustrated in the story of King Saul when he often besought David to play his harp for him to bring peace to his spirit when he was troubled or disturbed. Through the messages in these songs that were popular during my earlier days, love permeated the atmosphere and brightened many dark days for me as I purposed to maintain optimism no matter what I faced and to always focus primarily on the positive. It's no wonder that I was intrigued with the late motivational speaker Dr. Leonardo Buscaglia known as Dr. Love, who was a professor at the University of Southern California in the Department of Special Education in the seventies and eighties. I was introduced to Dr. Buscaglia through his book, *Living, Loving and Learning* while in high school and pleasantly surprised with his vitality and transparency. It was refreshing to read a book so liberating, motivating, and transparent. It restored my belief in love after being so bitterly disappointed with the disparities and corruption of this life. I also started reading books written by the author Ellen G. White in high school, and her book entitled "Desire of Ages" radically changed my life giving me a new outlook and perspective on life as it solidified my purpose as well. During my upbringing, I was sheltered from some of the atrocities and scandals in our society that I'm now getting a 101 course in through this ongoing trial in my adulthood. Nevertheless, I know it's equipping me for the vision God gave me concerning my ministry, so I'm determined to withstand the test come what may.

Although I kept a promising outlook on things by habit from this storm's outset, the facts that were surfacing revealing the constant discoveries of deception within the practice were difficult pills to swallow. And the fact that we were misunderstood and ridiculed because of the adversity we suffered was even more hurtful. This was an emotionally draining time for the girls and me, and to say that I was totally hurt and frustrated would have been an understatement. Thankfully, the optimism of my youth, along with my relationship with God in my adolescence allowed me to see brighter days in spite of the gloomy overcast I was experiencing at the time. I'll reiterate here again that there is nothing comparable to alone time with God in your secret place away from the noise, excitement, and distraction of this world where you can truly experience the blessing of just resting in His presence and hearing His words of comfort, peace, wisdom and direction (Psalm 46:10 KJV). There is no substitute for these treasurable moments where you can refuel, refresh, renew, and rededicate your will to His purpose for your life. Recounting the life of Christ, I read how He often withdrew Himself from the crowd to escape and spend quiet time communing with God in prayer. Just as He recognized that His continual connection with God was His sustaining power and grace, we should do likewise.

During this time, there would always be a lot of queries concerning my whereabouts as I withdrew from my usual day to day activities in order to achieve my goal of stealing away from everything for some alone and quiet time with God. Of course, the rumor mill was ignited as inquiries were raised questioning my occasional short-term absences away from my usual scene. Nevertheless, the girls and I appreciated this time to reset and recharge away from all of the confusion. However, this time of respite for us was viewed by others as being odd and questionable in terms of our emotional stability because I also chose to take a social moratorium briefly during this time as well where my phone was completely shut off. I was in hiatus mode with my career at this time so I didn't have to worry about receiving any calls from the hospital. With no one to trust, God was my sole Confidant and Counselor and I wanted to block out all distractions as I listened for His voice alone. Because those in my inner circle disappointed me by suggesting their skepticism with my story and questioning my stance in my marital dilemma, along with offering little to no support overall, our situation was made all the more difficult to bear. So taking this hiatus for emotional and spiritual healing was paramount at this time to allow God to restore our hope and joy that was waning under the circumstances. During this social break, I was able to think clearly and exhale from all of the flabbergasting incidents that I was confronted with around this time. However, the rumor mill was ignited with vicious rumors circulating on social media and in my social circles questioning my mental health because of my choice to take a social moratorium from all of the chaos. It was during this hiatus that I asked for God's healing and guidance as I spiritually recharged during this difficult time in my life. Nevertheless, because I am not easily bothered or influenced by gossip or by ill-intentioned criticism coupled with disparaging comments from misguided sources, I was neither flustered nor fazed. I viewed all humans to be in the same predicament - in need of a Savior, so there was no room for anyone to judge. My philosophy underscored the reality that because no one has a heaven or hell to give me but God, He alone is the rightful Judge and His view and assessment of my actions is always my sole concern as it was then and always has been. In addition, we all stand in need of a Savior, so there is really no room to judge. What I did find unsettling, however, was the disturbing news that those closest to me were the very culprits circulating the disturbing news that I was acting strange and crazy as if they weren't aware of all of the stress and trauma I had endured due to my turbulent domestic situation which could have very well left me more than crazy - I could have been dead. They even entertained casting doubt on my story as if it were fabricated and embellished when they were aware that my youngest sister was with me the day it happened and could attest to its validity. But thankfully, God kept me in perfect peace through it all as He promised in Isaiah 26:3 because I kept my mind on Him and not the circumstances. However, the knowledge of this betrayal from some individuals in my inner circle only served to complicate matters more for me because it led me to build up walls in relationships from that point on. If I couldn't trust those closest to me, who could I trust was the question.

Nonetheless, I used this precious time of solitude to meditate and commune with God as I claimed His promises to fulfill my emotional, spiritual, and physical needs. When this hiatus was over, I resumed my usual activities and social interactions while I also focused on what posture I would assume in this dilemma moving forward. Now I don't claim clairvoyance by any means, however, I purposed to use the God-ordained gift of discernment that was sharpened by God in this ongoing travesty as I recategorized some people in my life, along with some prior interests. Through the enlightenment I was given in these trials that I faced, I realized that some individuals I classified as "ride or die" friends, or just friends in general, didn't fit this profile and needed to be reclassified as acquaintances, associates, or even frenemies. Other insight gained through this misfortune involved accepting the rude awakening that one's village or inner circle is not always as supportive as one would anticipate. Dealing with the crude reality that sometimes those who are closest to you can be painfully indifferent and uncompassionate when you are facing hardship is hurtful and difficult to accept, but nonetheless factual. Hence, I determined at the time to exercise caution when dealing with these indifferent individuals recognizing the inconsistencies and vacillations with their fidelity in our relationship. This was a tough decision and one that caused me much anguish as I was compelled to detach from some of those I thought to be my core. Unfortunately, I was sadly mistaken concerning their genuine fidelity as a true friend and consequently had to reclassify our relationship.

This heartbreaking awareness left me feeling isolated and despondent at times, but once again I was reminded where my help comes from and I was comforted. In the paraphrased words of David in the book of Psalms in chapter 121, I looked to the hills for my help at this time, which I knew to be from the Lord Who is the Creator of everything and Who sleeplessly watches over me protecting me from all harm or danger. This knowledge sustained me along this journey of misfortune and gave me a serenity despite this turbulent chapter in my life. However, I still suffered the loneliness and heartbreak on occasion from the unfaithfulness shown by the very ones I considered close. These were some emotionally tough times for the girls and me, but God sustained us through it all as He never once forsook us - not even for a moment, but kept us safe under His protective wings while He comforted us. Reflecting on these times, we can't help but to be eternally grateful for God's presence and sustenance.

As things became more clear with all of the troubling and distressing discoveries made, we knew that we were only able to stand in our right mind with our emotional, spiritual and physical health intact because of God. These were truly some rainy days in our lives that tried to severely dampen our spirits and wash away any ray of hope. If I didn't have a relationship with God during this difficult time, I would have surely lost all hope as well as my mind. When close friends or family complimented me on my strength and fortitude in this crisis, I unreservedly declared my sanity to be sound only because of God's omnipotent hand upholding me through it all. Recognizing this battle to be supernatural in nature, I knew that my strength alone was insufficient and that I was in need of an Ally and Advocate who possessed preeminent power. Therefore, I called on God - my Rock and Fortress. God had taught me from previous trials that my faith would be severely tried as a christian and that my weaknesses would be exposed in these onerous times. Oftentimes, we can be unaware of our shortcomings or defects that are still under construction until we go through some hard times. The awareness thus gained from these vicissitudes in life allow us to pray more specifically and intentionally as we realize our weaknesses and ask God to rid us of them. Also, when we are praying for specific character strengths like patience for example, God will send various challenges and problems our way that will help us acquire this attribute that we desire. Therefore, we have to be mindful of what we are praying for always.

In any event, as I tried to wrap my mind around this unscrupulous situation that I was entangled in, I became even more frustrated as I tried to understand what was really going on. My biggest struggle was dealing with the denial I harbored inside concerning everything that was going on. I suppose that this was just a coping mechanism I employed to prevent suffering from the emotional devastation that was inevitable after facing the cruel reality of things. The naked truth revealed behind all of these discoveries left me momentarily speechless, distraught and crestfallen. My heart never felt so wounded and heavy laden as I felt at that memorable moment when the truth surfaced and I was left to deal with it alone. The weight of this burden was almost unbearable as it nearly crushed the very life out of me. I recall the laborious breathing I experienced as I fought to hold back the tears that flooded my face suddenly in that moment of realization.

The culprits had to be someone I did business with or someone who knew me personally. The question that continuously bombarded my thoughts was, "What had I done to cause this?" To this day, there is no rational rhyme or reason for what I innocently suffered at the hands of those I trusted and loved. The only explanation was greed and hidden personal agendas that were far from civilized and good natured. These inhumane and self-centered motives that were manipulated to defraud me knew no boundaries as they destroyed my family, negatively impacted my career, and attempted to tarnish my reputation as a mother, wife, christian, and businesswoman, but God! And although I was the innocent bystander, or nonparticipant in this fraudulent snafu, I eventually became everyone's Aunt Sally as if I was the guilty party when, in fact, I was the one defrauded. My credentials were compromised, my credit score was tainted, my financial stability was wrecked, and my reputation was attacked in this shady predicament where I was made the scapegoat. In any event, I didn't lose hope but just continued to trust God to see me through everything according to His will and in His timing.

As stated before, this was the hard part - waiting. Not knowing how long the wait would be or how things would finally pan out was the challenge. In essence, living in the unknown was difficult and uncomfortable for me because as humans, we are curious by nature. Also, because I don't possess a badge of honor for patience, immediate gratification is always tempting as my usual way out as it is for most of us spoiled by this "on demand" society that we live in. So, this was definitely going to be a grueling process of perseverance until my breakthrough, but I was determined to get to the light at the end of this tunnel when God would see fit to culminate things in His time. In the meantime, I had to exercise my faith and endurance muscles to strengthen them for this test and not give up. Oftentimes, we succumb right before the victory because of our exhaustion and loss of all hope. I didn't want this to be my plight, so I was intentional about maintaining an optimistic attitude in spite of the current menacing atmosphere of gloom and doom. But I also had to learn that I could not push my personal agenda or my proposed deadline for these shenanigans on God. My exhaustion and frustration with everything was just the beginning of my bootcamp in my course of "Learning to Trust God 101", and this I foresaw as being a long and arduous process - not a speedy quick fix. I was reminded that God's ways and thoughts are not like mine (Isaiah 55:8,9). Even though I so desperately wanted to get speedy vindication for everything wrongfully done to me, I knew that vengeance belongs to God and He would settle things when He saw fit. Knowing this, it behooved me to avoid wasting time sitting around waiting for something to happen that had no appointed time or date. In other words, I could look up one day and a whole decade (or a year more realistically) could have escaped me while I was inclined to put my life on pause, so to speak, awaiting my breakthrough. So, instead of coming to a standstill in this moment of grief and hopelessness as if I was in a coma of despair from my current crisis and just left to vegetate while awaiting my breakthrough (cause I was certain it would happen), I chose to live in the present and to germinate and be fruitful where I was at the time. Afterall, I realized tomorrow wasn't promised and therefore, wasting time pondering over it was futile and nonproductive because there was enough to deal with in the present (Matthew 6:35).

However, telling the girls this was another ball game altogether. Their little innocent and naive spirits were eager to get their breakthrough that we repeatedly mentioned in our "taylor-made" devotions everyday, and this meant soon - if not tomorrow - to them. In our devotions, we focused on the promises of God for protecting and delivering His people from all of their troubles (Isaiah 54:17 and Psalm 34:19). We also discussed God's vindication for those wronged (Psalm 37) and the promised restoration to those robbed and defrauded (Joel 2:23-27). Other biblical strongholds for us were Psalm 23, Psalm 91, and Psalm 121. My intent was to empower and shower my babies with immeasurable hope and encouragement in this time of difficulty. And I realized that my mission was accomplished because there wasn't a day that the girls didn't talk about our breakthrough in anticipation of it coming to fruition. What I didn't focus on was teaching them the importance of patience and how God rewards those who patiently wait on Him. I had to begin inculcating Bible verses in our devotions that conveyed the value of this Fruit of the Spirit like Galatians 6:9; Romans 12:12; Romans 8:25; and Isaiah 40:1.

Upon retiring one particular evening, I observed the girls' spirits to look a bit downcast and I inquired about this change in their attitudes. Their response troubled me and aroused the maternal instinct in me when I learned that a family member teased them about the breakthrough they talked about and had the audacity to tell them it was nonsense considering their current situation. They went on to sneer and ridicule them concerning this mindset because of the length of time this supposed breakthrough was taking. Needless to say, my "mother bear" vibes were heightened after hearing such insensitivity, and in that moment I planned to confront this individual. However, because of the potential for this gesture to result in an inflammatory exchange that would potentially cause more damage than good and risk permanently impairing family relationships, I decided to ignore it and assure that the girls were not adversely affected. It was more important to me that I avoided creating a hostile environment for them among loved ones during this critical and vulnerable time where they needed to interact on occasion with family.

Despite my intentions to remain optimistic with the girls in our struggle, it registered to me that being pragmatic was necessary - especially to keep them emotionally balanced. Now, by no means did this mean giving up on God and doubting His promises to deliver and restore us in our crisis. I just had to inform them that God's ways, thoughts, and timing are not like ours (Isaiah 55:8,9) and we would have to let go and let Him have His way in our lives and be Who He is - God. We would also have to be content with how He chose to handle our situation even if we didn't quite agree with it. We were challenged to trust that He knew what was best for us and for the situation at large. Claiming all of the biblical promises concerning deliverance and restoration was easy. But claiming the biblical promises dealing with the blessing in waiting was another story. This would be our challenge. And the hard part was conveying this to the girls and helping these two youngsters (along with myself) to understand the blessing of delayed gratification. With their spiritually naive mindsets, their expectations were immediate because they believed God would do what He said He would do right then and there. And, quite frankly, that was exactly what I found myself guilty of doing too on occasion - expecting God to rescue me right away from the overbearing and trying circumstances causing me so much woe. So, it was no small task for me to attempt to change their point of view about waiting patiently on God to fulfill His promises because I had to change my viewpoint too. Some popular biblical stories I would typically use for our devotions to illustrate the blessing in waiting on God in our trials were the stories of Job and Joseph. The outcome for these two stories was great, but there was a grueling process to endure to get to the happy ending for both Job and Joseph. As I impressed this upon their minds in our devotions and leisure time, I knew that it would not be a concept they would grasp overnight. But over time I believed that they would come to understand and appreciate the waiting process while learning to trust God. As I stated earlier, I also would be learning the blessing of patiently waiting on God while my faith and trust in Him were tested. Through this dilemma with its delayed resolution, I would undergo a faith and trust bootcamp where I would acquire attributes in my christian character that I believed God was equipping me with for the ministry He was ordaining me to do. This delay would also allow time for those who wronged us to reconcile and make matters right. So it would be a potential win-win situation for everyone.

While in the waiting process, however, I decided to delve into the issues and problems implicated in domestic violence or intimate partner violence. Because this was one of the issues I envisioned dealing with in my future ministry, I saw the importance of learning as much as I could about it. Even though I had suffered a one time experience with this toxic physical behavior that awful morning and had received some seminars on this topic that were optional during my residency in Gynecology long before I was married, I didn't dare consider myself to be an expert on this subject. I had also witnessed this societal plague on more than one occasion while growing up through the experience of a friend, a family member or just being an innocent bystander observing a public altercation with individuals I didn't even know. Now, these cases referenced above were not exclusive to physical abuse alone, but included verbal and emotional abuse as well. Other recognized types of domestic violence deal not only with physical, verbal, and emotional abuse, but sexual abuse, isolation, control, and economic abuse. These forms of abuse are often overlooked because they're not usually addressed when discussing this topic and they are not as obvious.

Nevertheless, I recognized that there was so much more to learn beyond what I had witnessed first-hand and experienced through the accounts of others. However, this misfortune of mine provided great insight that I was willing to share, and also motivated me to research this subject more in depth. I also realized that many individuals aren't aware that they have experienced or been guilty of one or more of these forms of abuse in a relationship before or currently. Oftentimes because things haven't become severe or toxic, they aren't recognized as significant until they become toxic, and then at other times, they are not recognized at all. As mentioned earlier on, however, we are imperfect people living in an imperfect world and every relationship can glean from learning new ways to express love better and more appropriately. One thing that I consider top priority and apparent in these touch and go cases, is providing a safe haven for the individuals endangered (male or female). There are shelters in place to solve this problem, however, some are exclusive to men while others cater to women and then there are those that are open to both. Individuals with children may run into a common impediment where some shelters don't allow children, and those that do allow children don't always have provisions for children when the adult has to go to work or school. So, if the children are in school, they will not require any provision during the day from the shelter because they will be at school when the parent is at work and can stay in aftercare until the parent picks them up after work. Of course aftercare is only an option for the parent that can afford it. On the other hand, if the children are not school age yet, or if the need for a shelter is during the summer months when the children are out of school, this can pose a problem for the parent trying to make arrangements for them during the day because some shelters don't have lodging arrangements or daycare during the day. Most shelters just provide a place to get a good night's rest at best because their rules involve checking out in the morning and returning at the end of the day. So if an individual has no where to go during the day, waiting until the evening for the shelter to reopen can be real challenging. Finding daycare services for children during the day can also be challenging especially when one is financially strained or depleted. Safety concerns also exist for most shelters where adequate security is a problem. Either the shelter has security that is inadequate or they don't have security at all. Experiencing rape or theft in a shelter is not uncommon. Shelters specific for just women and children help prevent this in most instances, however, these shelters are few. Also, shelters usually operate on a first come first serve basis, so an individual is never guaranteed a spot. Hence, each day the process of standing in line at the end of the day to hopefully secure an available bed to sleep in overnight is repeated. There are usually no reservations or secured spots in most shelters. It is a day to day ordeal.

The next essential in these particular cases involves restorative counseling for the perpetrator which entails working through anger management issues, addiction, and self-worth issues in efforts to rehabilitate this individual back to sound mental, emotional, spiritual and physical health. This step is the sine qua non of achieving successful outcomes with intimate partner violence because it is the root of the problem. This societal problem exists because of the offender's behavior. Therefore, resolution of the problem resides in this individual's successful rehabilitation. Oddly enough and unfortunately, this step is often overlooked because the immediate need to secure a safe environment for the abused individual overshadows this pivotal measure. But both are necessary to constructively resolve this crisis and effect change. If the victim successfully escapes, the perpetrator will just find someone else to lash out on and the cycle will live on. Therefore, to achieve optimal and effective treatment for both parties involved in this ubiquitous social problem, the help cannot be one-sided. Both individuals need help and attention.

Another important area of focus is the self-esteem of both the perpetrator and the recipient. Low self-esteem usually plagues both individuals and perpetuates the destructive behavior that is in question. This distorted and pessimistic concept of oneself often leads to self-hatred, which leads to hatred of others as well. There's some wisdom in the old familiar saying that suggests that it is difficult to love others if you don't love yourself. In this case, the malefactor who feels worthless treats the recipient the way he feels about himself - valueless. With a hollow emotional foundation, there is nothing beneficial to give. In other words, nothing in is nothing out. This void must be filled with worthwhile substance in order to interact constructively. So the way the offender interacts socially just manifests his or her self-perception. They treat others without value because they don't value themselves. The recipient's mindset is manifested in the choice of a significant other. If the self-concept of the recipient is poor, then the choices will follow suit. Partners will be chosen who don't have a genuine interest in the recipient, or who don't treat the recipient respectfully. This cycle will be ongoing until thought processes are changed through intervention and counseling, along with behavior modification. Recapping these well known problem areas in disruptive - and sometimes toxic - relationships, one can see the benefit for the intervention plan just mentioned so that the cycle will be broken in this current generation in efforts to prevent its perpetuation in future generations.

During this particular journey of mine, I saw ways to do just this through the divine forethought I was given. As I mentioned earlier, this is not the only social issue I would like to address in the ministry God has given me. The vision God gave me during this storm encompasses overall brokenness from unreconciled relationships (parental, marital, social, and familial) and aims to heal these relationships through the powerful ministry of restorative reconciliation. In addition to ministering to broken individuals, this vision also aims to address the needs of the deprived and less fortunate, along with anyone who has been subject to mistreatment of some kind. With the ubiquitous nature of these societal issues, there will never be too many resources to address the overwhelming demand for help in these areas. There is no such thing as too many shelters or halfway houses or crisis centers with the outlandish need we see daily (as well as the hidden need that we don't see). There is already an overwhelming deficiency in this area and there are other needs where resources are lacking in a major way also. The same for counseling - it definitely has its value and is currently underutilized. These glaring social exigencies outweigh the current available resources unfortunately, and I envision my nonprofit to be another source of help as it lessens the burden for the existing facilities that are currently inundated dealing with these overwhelming societal problems.

As I reflect on my marriage then, I see how it would have proven beneficial and life saving if counseling had been pursued on a biannual or annual basis at the least. A quarterly wellness check in a marriage appears to be the best way to go if not more frequent. Also, open and effective communication with transparency fosters healthy relationships. However, when a marriage is plagued with substance abuse, communication and conflict resolution can be difficult and potentially inflammatory. The vision would address these issues of substance abuse as well and provide classes with counseling to nurture and promote healthier habits and relationships.

As I continue reflecting on this turbulent time in my life, I remember my disappointment with the strongholds that failed me terribly in this dire time of need. I would have never expected such frustration and disappointment from some individuals in my inner circle, along with some of my church family and the legal system during this distressing time in our lives. The lack of support we faced when we were in dire straits, along with the false accusations and unkind words were extremely hurtful. And, to add insult to injury, the deception discovered along the journey just intensified the pain even more. From childhood, I believed my village included my family first, then friends and church family next with the legal system following close behind. I remember participating in the Officer Friendly program in grade school and feeling safe and protected when accompanied by these friendly police officers. This love for law enforcement was rekindled the day of my epic moment when the APD (Atlanta Police Department) officer came to my rescue and made sure things were safe. However, reflecting on another memorable moment during this time in my life, I didn't quite feel the love from the police officer who was assigned to my domestic case from its onset. It had been several weeks or more from the incident when this situation arose and I didn't find this officer to be supportive or sensitive to my needs and concerns at the time. On the contrary, I found him to be very dismissive and apathetic with my situation. I vividly recall the frustration I experienced that night while desperately looking for a place to go after abruptly leaving the hotel in the middle of the night because of my eerie experience described earlier where the door latch of my hotel room appeared mysteriously broken. This officer's unavailability and nonchalance in the midst of this conundrum left me feeling unimportant and devalued. Although he was on visitation with his son that weekend, I was disappointed that he didn't have another officer on backup for him for any emergencies like the one I was facing that night. Equally disturbing was the fact that this was the one and only time I had ever reached out to him for help since he was assigned to my case as my advocate several weeks ago when this case opened, and sadly, he wasn't available and wasn't the least bit concerned. Although I had been given his number earlier on in my domestic dilemma for security reasons and assistance if needed, I never used it until that night, and after that night, I never used it again. Interestingly, this officer never followed up with me after the weekend and I essentially never heard from him again. In addition to this discouraging incident, I was disenchanted further when I observed several breaches with the TPO that were essentially ignored by the legal system without any apparent concern for the safety of the girls and me. So, I deduced from all of this that the girls and I would not be able to rely solely on the legal system for their support, advocacy, and protection. Our current trial had lifted the curtain on the stage revealing the feelings, opinions, and overall infidelity of individuals in our inner circle who we once thought were our village. The skepticism conveyed by those who doubted my story concerning my domestic incident was painfully upsetting. This doubt led to disparaging comments and a lack of optimal support from some of those I trusted.

Recognizing that not one, not two, but every "earthly" support and stronghold assumed in this life (the legal system, the church, and our village) failed us, we were tempted to feel hopeless. We were in a desperate situation from a human standpoint and this letdown was untimely because we were in dire straits with options that were scarce to nonexistent. The temptation to just succumb to what appeared to be sure defeat was strong. Thoughts raced through my head about the potential outcomes from our unfavorable situation and also the possibility of the girls and I being separated. This latter thought entered my mind because I recalled the court hearings with my husband where my lawyer had to prove my competency and capability to take care of the girls financially when things became strained secondary to the theft and fraud suffered by my business. I remember being shocked after the expiration of the TPO (temporary protection order) when the option for the girls to possibly stay with their dad temporarily was raised by his legal counsel. I objected on the grounds that the girls were stable under my guardianship and their well-being was not in question. Thankfully, the court agreed and that is when family counseling was mandated instead. Nonetheless, we felt isolated and unloved in this predicament that we found ourselves in, and being misunderstood and unjustly criticized about our current situation that we had nothing to do with at the time, made us even more frustrated. We were the victims of this foul play just trying to survive from the fraud, yet we were condemned because the blame was wrongfully shifted on us. We were in a no-win situation and we didn't know how to break free. Awakening some gleam of hope in what appeared to be a bleak future for us was paramount at this point in our journey. We had to keep hope alive and find a reason to go on. We were aware of the opinions of those looking on and observing us during the trial because they voiced them freely to either mutual friends and family or posted them on the various social media platforms. Questions were raised and criticism voiced in these posts that were circulated at our expense with no consideration for our feelings and privacy. The question now was what were we going to do in our dismal bind.

Situations like these often cause one to contemplate one's self-worth and reason for existence. Satan uses these circumstances of distress to overwhelm and frustrate individuals to the point of despair where there is no confidence in things turning around for the better. His aim is to eclipse the silver lining behind the dark cloud and leave no room for any glimmer of hope. Oftentimes, individuals come to the conclusion that there is no reason for living because they feel that their life is meaningless and too painful to continue. With the lack of support from our village, one may even lose the desire to live. This, of course, is a precarious place to be in emotionally, mentally, spiritually, and physically. And unfortunately, resources are still lacking to provide the help needed for the many individuals who find themselves in this dilemma. Thank God we didn't entertain this thought process during this trial.

As I began to get inundated with all of the confusion and unanswered questions in my present enigma, I turned to God and asked Him for strength, wisdom, and the perseverance to press on no matter what. I was determined to go all the way with God and persevere through all of the opposition, isolation, derision, betrayal and heartbreak.

Chapter 10

RAYS OF HOPE

IN SOME OF our most dire moments, God intervened and not only showed His awesome presence, but His amazing love also. Besides His timely supernatural appearance the day of the incident that completely changed the entire scenario in my favor, He also revealed Himself to the girls and me on many other occasions throughout this journey of adversity. The experiences I'm referencing that were most memorable were the ones where God used complete strangers and some friends to let us know just how much He cares and to encourage us in all of the turmoil and confusion we were encountering at the time. These were some awe-inspiring and amazing times where we were privileged to behold the miracles of God up close and personal. When our support was lacking from our village, God compensated by using individuals who were willing to be used by Him to offer a ray of hope to three despondent young ladies who were terribly broken by a severed family bond and hurt by the unscrupulous and disheartening ordeal they were facing.

As I reminisce on this one particular occasion, I was in line at the

Equifax Center to obtain an updated copy of my credit score and report. The lines were never long as I mentioned before, but this time there were two people ahead of me - a gentleman at the window and a mother with her teenage daughter in front of me in this short line. The girls accompanied me there and I was glad that the wait wasn't long at all. Anyhow, while we were there waiting in the line, the mother and her daughter standing in front of us turned around and engaged in conversation with us while the gentleman was being helped at the window. Before long, the mother was sharing how God had blessed her as a single parent financially, emotionally, spiritually, and physically while raising her daughter due to the father's negligence and now absence altogether. She testified how God was her Jehovah Jireh (Provider) through it all in spite of her circumstances. Her face beamed as she recounted numerous times God stepped in right on time and blessed her daughter and her in some situations that appeared insurmountable.

As she openly and freely shared how God sustained the two of them through all of their financial challenges, she paused and asked if I would be offended if she prayed for my daughters and me. Surprised by this offer in the setting we were currently in, I paused for a moment to mentally absorb what I was hearing. During this time, she didn't hesitate to search her purse and pull out a bottle that I learned later had olive oil in it. Realizing what she was preparing to do, I expressed that I would appreciate this gesture very much and she requested for me to get on my knees right there in the line where I was and to have the girls stand beside me. Without hesitation, I knelt down with my daughters right beside me and she placed a dabb of olive oil on our foreheads with her finger to anoint us as she and her daughter encircled us in prayer. What an incredible and phenomenal moment this was for us! We literally witnessed a metamorphosis firsthand in this Equifax Center that afternoon as we watched this lobby mutate into a sanctuary where this mother-daughter duo of prayer warriors petitioned the throne on our behalf. We were being anointed for our journey and purpose through God's chosen conduits that day and this was definitely a powerful and unforgettable moment that I recognized as God's way of assuring us that He had not forgotten or forsaken us. He wanted to make sure that we knew that He had His protective Hand on us and we need not fret or fear. After the prayer, we noticed that the young man was gone and the attendant at the window apparently had gone to the back momentarily. As the girls and I got up after the prayer, we all embraced each other forming a "group hug" as we affirmed each other. By this time, the female attendant had returned and asked the mother and daughter who were next in line to approach the window. This mother and her daughter, along with the girls and me were the only ones in the lobby at the time and strangely enough, the female attendant at the window evinced an unstirred demeanor as if she wasn't aware of what had just taken place in the lobby. Her attitude was indifferent as she helped them, which led me to believe that she must have missed the extraordinary anointing that had just transpired right there in the open space of her work environment. She was most likely dealing with tasks in the back at the time. It was as if God had things strategically arranged so that we could enjoy our own little prayer service in one of the most unforeseen places. This precious occurrence was a memory worth treasuring for a lifetime as it spoke to our hearts and reminded us that God has innumerable ways to bless us tangibly and intangibly. This represented an intangible way - through inspiration, empowerment and transparency. A cathartic wave permeated the atmosphere that day and refueled the girls and me with strength to endure the rocky road ahead of us.

On a subsequent visit to the Equifax Center, the girls and I experienced another similar situation where God used someone to encourage us. This time it was the attendant at the window when we just happened to be the only ones in the center that day. While obtaining yet another credit report and score, the attendant present that day who I had never seen before suddenly took my hands in hers and asked me if I would mind if she prayed for me. I assumed that she read the frustration on my face as I reviewed the report that revealed more corruption despite my multiple calls to the credit bureaus alerting them of the identity theft and fraud. My account was supposed to be locked and only accessible with a security pin that I had created. I was discouraged as I witnessed the persistent aliases and unfamiliar addresses associated with my social security number and personal identifiable information (PII) even after I informed the credit bureaus that I was not familiar with this information and that it was fraudulent. I had even obtained a security pin to block such mendacious actions, but apparently, this was to no avail. Upon contacting them later, they informed me that they did remove this false data when I alerted them, but the information reappeared. I realized later that because these falsified identities with unfamiliar addresses were apparently associated with viable accounts executing fraudulent transactions with my sensitive information, this forgery and deception would continue to be an ongoing problem until I got to the bottom of things and cut this chicanery at its root - closed these fraudulent accounts. But first, I had to find these unscrupulous accounts in order to close them. And, I was aware that this would be no small task and it would definitely warrant legal services, which was even more disgruntling because I was still financially paralyzed at the time during this sour, pecuniary pickle and, consequently, hiring a lawyer was temporarily out of the question. Also, until I found out how I would be exonerated in this fraudulence using my PII and BII, I knew I would have to wait on God because there was potential that I would be indicted for these heinous charges although I was innocent. You see, because everything in this mess used my sensitive information, it all traced back to me. My identity and sensitive information were being exploited when I had nothing to do with the corruption exercised. It would look as if I created these other entities for my financial gain when I had nothing to do with these businesses or their profits. In fact, these entities were not legitimate businesses, but shams instead. So, once again, a raincheck for these services was my only viable option at the time, but meanwhile I planned to gather more information that would help assist the lawyer with getting to the root of things when the time was right. In other words, this unwelcome postponement would not be wasted with sulking and complaining, but with productive efforts to obtain more helpful information to provide to legal services when the time was right. I was confident that God would deliver the girls and me from this mess in His divine timing, and until then, He would sustain us in this conundrum. We were claiming our deliverance as we stood on God's promise in Psalm 34:19 that says God will deliver us from all of our afflictions.

Focusing back on this attendant after briefly digressing, I realized that she discerned my frustration and troubled spirit from my countenance that day and sought to be of some encouragement. Reflecting on this scene even today, I recognize that God used this willing female to demonstrate His love, watchcare, and presence during this challenging time. He was reminding the girls and me that He had not forgotten us and for us to hold on and not let go of His omnipotent hand. As this attendant, who I didn't even know, took my hands and prayed for me right there at the help desk with such compassion and sensitivity, it felt like she was a personal friend who was aware of my struggle as she mentioned all of my unexpressed concerns and prayer requests as if I had shared them with her at one time or another. At that instant, an inexplicable peace rested upon my spirit as I saw God orchestrate another occasion where He manifested His love and concern for the girls and me by using a perfect stranger. It was a tender moment that encouraged and strengthened me just when I was tempted to be hopelessly overwhelmed with discouragement. So, as I left the center that day feeling refueled and emotionally replenished, I stumbled upon yet another blessing as I walked to my car with plans to head home and retire for the afternoon. It was my intention to take time when I got home to meditate upon what had just occurred and allow this demonstration of God's love to marinate upon my spirit to inspire and motivate me in my current dilemma. During this alone time, I would also seek direction and wisdom from God for the next step to pursue in my current situation. However, while walking to my car, I noticed two individuals standing by their cars that were next to each other engaged in an intense conversation. As I got closer to my car, which was next to their cars, I overheard the gentleman giving advice to the young lady he was talking to as he watched me walking to my car. Before I reached my vehicle, he turned to me and asked me if I had ever experienced identity theft or fraud. Stunned with his bold question to me as a complete stranger, I was speechless momentarily as I attempted to regain my composure. I was also taken aback that his inquiry was spot on with my current predicament and, once again, I didn't even know him. Interested to see how this would pan out, I told him that I had in fact experienced this and he immediately began sharing his story of how he was a victim of tax fraud. Someone had filed his tax returns and received his refund the previous tax year and he was relaying his story to this young lady who had suffered the same ordeal. Fortunately, he was able to acquire a lawyer who recouped his money and resolved his identity theft case. He informed the young lady and me that he gathered as much information as he could before seeking the assistance from legal services, which saved him a lot of money and time, and advised us to do the same. I thanked him for his advice and then went home. On the drive home, I realized that God used this encounter to speak to me through this gentleman and guide me in my dilemma at hand. He wanted to relieve my frustrations concerning my current financial impediment with seeking legal services by conveying the message through this gentleman that it wasn't the time to acquire legal help yet anyway. God was allowing me to see through this gentleman's experience that I needed to gather more information and, in essence, lay the groundwork for the rest of the evidence prior to involving legal services in order to give the investigation direction. This would also save a lot of money and time. So, here again, before I could even go home and meditate on that prayer for the girls and me by the Equifax attendant, God was giving me yet another message out in the parking lot on my way home. I could definitely attest that day to the promise in Isaiah 65:24 that says that before we call, He answers and while we are yet speaking, He hears. That day God made His message clear to me through the willing conduits He chose to use that day - the female attendant at Equifax and the gentleman in the parking lot. Through the prayer of the female attendant in Equifax, we were reminded of God's love and care for us, along with our value in His eyes. In addition to this positive reassurance, He used this gesture to also remind us of His omnipresence with us always - even in the midst of our current dilemma. Through the wisdom and instruction of the gentleman in the parking lot we were encouraged and at peace knowing that God was in control and would orchestrate things in our favor in His time. In the meantime, I just needed to wait on Him and continue to praise Him for His omnipotence, omnipresence, and omniscience.

Reminiscing still on incidents that served to uplift our spirits and renew hope, I remember when we were being evicted from our condo as mentioned in one of the chapters earlier. God showed Himself strong in this calamity also. Because of the ongoing fraud and theft involving our finances during this time, this outcome was inevitable although we were still caught by surprise. I guess we were expecting God to perform a miracle and rescue us from this awful plight, but our thoughts and plans were evidently not in sync with God's thoughts and plans (Isaiah 55:8,9) for our lives once again and instead, He allowed us to have a Job-like experience in this scenario. Apparently, this misfortune was part of His plan for our journey and He gave us the strength to weather this storm. Although this storm was the direct consequence of the duplicity and theft of these perpetrators with our money and sensitive information, God allowed us to gracefully endure and persevere in spite of the evil done without repining and without harboring bitterness or hatred in our hearts against those who wronged us. I can still remember the troubled and defeated looks on my baby girls' faces as the tears welled up in their eyes during our preparation to leave as the policemen at the door firmly and insensitively instructed us to do in this process. At this point the girls were devastated as they felt that God had disappointed us because we were being evicted. They wondered where the miracle we prayed about in our devotions was and why God had let us down. In essence, they wondered where our breakthrough was. Seeing them look to me for answers and help in their despair, devastation and confusion, I immediately told them to lift up their heads and to wipe their weeping eyes because their heavenly Daddy owned the very building our condo was in, as well as the universe, so if He wanted us to stay, He would have prevented this eviction. I told them that we couldn't question how God works, we just had to trust Him even in this difficult time - especially while we were suffering because someone was stealing from us through fraud. Knowing that the mischievous deeds of someone else had put us in this treacherous condition, was extremely disturbing and hurtful. Nonetheless, I instructed the girls to throw some of their things in a bag while we were being rushed out during this eviction process. I assured them that everything would be alright. My focus was on packing up the important documents that I was able to obtain during my investigation that would be helpful when it was time to seek legal services. In addition to this, I had to control Ruby (our dog) and put her leash on to prevent her from taking care of her business while we were taking care of ours. With this impromptu visit, her protective instinct was heightened and she was in her no tolerance mode as she was prepared to demonstrate who was the boss in what she considered to be her territory. Taking care of business was her middle name - especially when it came to protecting the three ladies who were the love of her life. I immediately recognized the issue at hand and worked to placate her stance by assuring her that we were alright as I calmly talked to her and gave her much tangible love in this moment. However, this was short-lived in the essence of time because we were forced to quickly vacate the premises. Thankfully, my efforts to pacify her were successful. Meanwhile, the police decided to leave and allow us time to get our things together to leave. During this time, the concierges on duty called up and expressed their sympathy about the situation. They asked me if we needed any help with transporting things and I explained that unfortunately, in our predicament, I would be compelled to leave a lot of things because of the uncertainty of our next move. Because storage was not an option in our financial condition, transporting things was not an option either. Hearing this, the concierges immediately began making claims on the furniture and other objects of their interest while thanking us profusely which felt strange and awkward due to the circumstances. However, I was thankful that I could brighten someone's day in the midst of our sudden misfortune. As I look back on this particular scene, I am amazed how God kept our minds focused on what was more important - our lives and God's promise to sustain us in our quandary at that time. Not once did we think about the things we were leaving behind that were quite valuable. Not once did we mourn these things. We mourned the situation instead that left us in this bind we were in. We realized that the God who blessed us once with valuable things was able to do it again in time.

Meanwhile, we concentrated on getting our things that could fit in the SUV as we prepared to leave and stay over a young lady's house that I had recently met that worked for a colleague of mine. I met her when we were evicted from the office space several months or so prior to this incident. She was the practice manager for one of my colleagues who bought my office furniture and used some of my equipment during my hiatus. From that time, we became friends, so we chose to call her that evening and ask to stay overnight as we planned to make arrangements in the morning for relocating to a new residence. Because she wasn't in our social circle, it was convenient for us not to have to explain ourselves or fear having our business circulated.

After getting everything packed up and situated in the car, I said a prayer right before pulling off to exit the garage of the condo when I suddenly saw two police officers walking towards my SUV. As they got closer, I saw a book in the hand of one of the officers. It was a Bible that we left while quickly evacuating and, apparently, they felt intentional about getting it to us as the condo was being emptied of all the things that we left. As the officers approached the window, I thanked them for being so kind, but asked them to keep the Bible because it was one of many that we had. I had three Bibles of different sizes at the time. One small enough to carry in my purse, another one to carry to church, and then my home study Bible that I made notes in and highlighted. The girls had two Bibles of their own as well. Besides buying nice Bibles for the girls and myself, we also received them as popular gifts from friends and family on special occasions (baptism, graduation, etc.), so we had room to share. Therefore, we were moved to donate this one to the officers that day and to be a source of positivity in the midst of the present hostility. Puzzled by this gesture in the current situation, they were embarrassingly taken off guard but complied with our offer and kept the Bible. We then proceeded to leave when all of a sudden, this gentleman came out of nowhere and ran up to my car window. He appeared to be striving to remain inconspicuous while approaching the car, which made me very leery and hesitant about rolling down my window to see what he wanted. As I made eye contact with him to question his intent with my startled facial expression and body language, he reached in his pocket while I cautiously rolled the window down and immediately pulled out a folded stash of cash that he handed to me. I was speechless for all of a second or two and then began to thank him profusely as he wished us well and then departed hurriedly. He apparently had been observing the situation and wanted to help. Our things were being left outside on the ground right in front of the lobby of our designated parking garage level and everything from our condo was being removed. At this point, anyone was free to take whatever we couldn't take with us at the time, which happened to be the majority of our belongings. Witnessing this heart wrenching scene involving a single mother and her two daughters losing what appeared to be everything, compelled this gentleman to perform this act of benevolence. The fact that this scene alone prompted him to extend himself as he did that day touched my heart when reflecting back. I could only imagine what depth of sacrifice he would have made if he were privy to all that we had suffered and were still suffering as victims of identity theft and fraud with the ongoing chicanery we faced. Glancing down at my hand in curiosity to see what he had given me, I was flabbergasted as I counted his monetary gift of love in the form of five one hundred dollar bills that were gifted to us just like that, without hesitation. God had blessed the girls and me with five hundred dollars from a perfect stranger. The despondency that tried to creep in and overtake us emotionally just when we were about to leave everything behind us that couldn't fit into our SUV, was utterly squelched by this compassionate deed. Now, I must digress a bit as I mention that our "things and stuff" never once competed with our Ruby when packing the SUV. Her seat was secured before any piece of luggage was placed in the SUV. Whatever didn't fit after Ruby, the girls, and I were situated, didn't come along with us. We had become the "Ferocious Four" and our bond was inseverable. But getting back to our aha moment with the generous gift by the unknown gentleman, we realized that we had once again witnessed our God show up and show out on our behalf. This awareness inspired us even more with hope and reason to go on. It also assured us of God's presence, which made all the difference in the world. With Him right there by our side as He had just demonstrated, we were confident that we could weather our current storm. Our half-full spiritual gas tanks due to the current crisis, immediately were refueled to full after this act of kindness. We were refueled, recharged and ready to face what would come next.

Leaving the place we had once called home that evening, along with everything we were unable to transport that day, was a solemn moment for the girls and me as we fought to stay emotionally strong. It was truly a struggle for me to be optimistic and resilient for the sake of the girls in this scenario, but God gave me the strength and fortitude to do just that. I must say that this was an "Abraham moment" for me where I just had to trust God to relocate the girls and me safely to a new home because we had no idea where to go next or where we would end up. And even though we were compelled to leave in our situation which was unlike Abraham's story where he was given a choice, we still had no idea where to go and what would be our outcome when the journey began, which was similar to Abraham's story. For now, my next move, which was temporary, was to stay overnight at this friend's house until God revealed my next step in the morning. I was learning the faith walk depicted in the first part of Psalm 119:105 (KJV), which states that God's Word is a "lamp unto my feet and a light unto my path". At this stage of my journey, God was focusing on the lamp for my feet where I would only take one step at a time because the next step would be all that I would see in this faith bootcamp in lieu of the entire path. With this limited vision allowed, I would have to trust God implicitly to direct me. Of note, I later learned that we did have a choice after being evicted. We could have gone home to my family in Chicago where all of the current difficulties and financial struggles would have presumably been circumvented, but this was not God's plan and He made that crystal clear to me so that there would be no doubt.

Nevertheless, I was aware that being pragmatic in our entanglement was equally important and served as a teaching moment for the girls. Observing their disappointment and confusion with God for how things panned out, moved me to take the opportunity on the ride to my girlfriend's house to remind them how hardships and trials are inevitable in the sinful world we live in and that God is not to blame for sin. I told them that Satan is the author of sin and God allows some trials and misfortunes to make us aware of the consequences of sin so that we will make heaven our goal by choice because there will be no more sin there. I also reminded them that trials serve to exercise our faith muscles and teach us to trust God in spite of our circumstances. This was an awkward time to learn these essential life lessons, but addressing their concerns in the middle of this complexity helped them to shape healthier perspectives on life and its adversities and to initiate the development of constructive coping mechanisms. Therefore, I explained to them that just because God did not choose to deliver us from this unfortunate event didn't mean He didn't love us. He was allowing us to go through our faith bootcamp in order to develop the required fruits of the spirit for our christian journey. I also reminded them that He had specifically chosen us for this test because He trusted us with it and knew that with His help, we would glorify His name in spite of our circumstances. So, during our ride, we were able to praise Him in spite of what appeared to be hopeless because we witnessed His loving care for us through this gentleman's act of kindness. This act assured us that He was orchestrating things and there was no need for us to worry. So, I encouraged the girls that no matter how hurt and loss we felt in the midst of this misfortune, God had not forsaken us and would open doors for us during our temporary transition as He had done in the past and was currently doing. With our recently refueled spiritual gas tanks, we just chose to praise Him anyhow in this moment and learn to rejoice in Him always - no matter what the situation - as advised in Philippians 4:4 (KJV - King James Version).

As I stated earlier, it was very important for me to be brave and strong for the girls in our present crisis, but over time, I realized that I needed to point them to Christ for that. He is the authentic source of all strength and everything they would ever need. Instilling this principle in them would be the greatest legacy that I could ever give them and the one thing with eternal promise. I knew at their ages that this concept would probably be nothing more than a nebulous thought until they began to mature cognitively and spiritually. However, I also realized that their current life experiences, along with the life lessons that God was teaching them in this trial, would accelerate their understanding of this particular principle at an early age compared to their peers and allow them to mature spiritually beyond their years. From time to time, I would remind them over and over again that they were like Esther in the Bible - chosen by God for "such a time as this". Esther manifested an extraordinary measure of faith and courage in God despite the peril surrounding her and despite her young age, and I encouraged them that they could do the same. Other Bible characters that were spiritually mature at a young age and exercised God's will at these tender ages were Samuel, Josiah, and Jeremiah among others. Samuel was just a child when God spoke to him and gave him a message of warning for Eli, the priest, concerning his sons. Josiah was eight years of age when he became king and Jeremiah was a teenager when he became a prophet. So, I stressed to them that there is no age limit when it comes to being a vessel for God to use, and that they were chosen along with me to be used as vessels for God's glory in our current crisis. Although everything seemed vague to them at the time because of their tender ages, I trusted God implicitly to reveal things to them over time. For now, however, I strove to exemplify fortitude and patience to them in our current struggle no matter what we encountered. It was also equally important to me to exude a spirit of forgiveness and unconditional love in spite of the wrong done to us in the current financial fiasco as this is the greatest attribute of an authentic christian. I explained that this is the true litmus test for a Christian when seeing where someone truly stands with Christ. And I would often recite to the girls how Jesus epitomized this love throughout His life and by his death on the cross.

In any event, I repeatedly consoled and comforted them on the way to my girlfriend's house in efforts to dispel any sign of fear or grief that could potentially dampen their mood. We repeatedly recounted God's demonstration of love revealed through our blessing that evening on our ride to my friend's house in order to keep our spirits uplifted. Other manifestations of His love were contemplated as well to serve as sources of encouragement. When we arrived at her house, she warmly welcomed not only the girls and me, but our Ruby Duby. And surprisingly, Ruby was not defensive or apprehensive, but rather mild and submissive. She behaved that evening as if she realized our situation and was thanking my friend for her hospitality that night. My friend was surprisingly shocked that Ruby's appearance and visible constitution didn't match the gentle spirit she exuded that evening. On the contrary, she found Ruby to be a rather large teddy bear and a very affectionate bulldog just as we did. Well, I knew that God had orchestrated everything perfectly because we all needed somewhere we felt comfortable and welcome to stay that night and we weren't disappointed.

The next day God ordered our steps and we were able to find a place where we stayed a short while before transitioning to our new home. This new home afforded us a hiatus from the chaos for a while, but unbeknownst to us, the comfort of this house was orchestrated by God to be only for a season. After a couple of years, we were divinely instructed to move on to the next phase of our trial, which dealt with uprooting from our current residence and relocating to another state where I had a job opportunity to start all over again. Our journey was definitely an adventure that had no monotony for sure because it was ever changing. The girls and I started feeling a nomadic vibe overtaking our new norm with this transitioning, especially with God's plan of relocating us to another state altogether. This came as a surprise, but I acquiesced realizing God knew what was best for me during that time and always. However, for the purposes of this book, our journey in Georgia is the focus for now and the experience after the relocation is for the sequel to this book.

Another occurrence where I saw the hand of God move in my favor in a miraculous way centered around the unanticipated cancellation of my malpractice insurance. This event took place about a year or so before the domestic incident that catapulted the girls and I into the chaos and instability we were navigating through at the time. In retrospect, I see now how this complexity concerning my malpractice cancellation was one among others that led to the beginning of the exposure of this double dealing we were experiencing at the time and how someone was fixated on ruining me and my career. This occurrence, along with other situations we faced prior to the domestic mishap, actually served to usher in the domestic whirlwind that confronted us that morning and lift the veil to eventually expose this duplicity that had been ongoing for some time. It all began when I received this notice of cancellation while relaxing at home one early afternoon after work one day. This notification left me bemused and speechless for several seconds while I struggled to mentally and emotionally process this appalling news. It was as if my livelihood was being balled up and thrown into the trash can right there before my eyes as I read the letter. Without liability coverage, I would not be able to safely practice medicine. Practicing under these circumstances would put my career and me in financial jeopardy and most - if not all - hospitals required malpractice coverage for physicians to be on staff. So I would not be able to use the hospital facilities for surgery and hospitalization of my patients without malpractice coverage. When I finally recovered from my bewilderment from this startling news, I recalled a clinical case where I intervened to prevent an obstetric fatality involving another doctor's negligence with her patient. This negligence resulted in an unfavoraable outcome of the pregnancy. However, this still didn't explain how I got into this conundrum because this was not uncommon - covering for someone else in an emergency - and I was left perplexed as I pondered what to do next. Things just didn't add up. At any rate, I began rummaging through some mail on the kitchen counter and noticed an invitation. After opening the invitation and calling the number on the card, I learned that my daughter's invite to this party was a mistake. Nevertheless, as I talked on the phone with the grandfather of the child soon to be celebrating his granddaughter's birthday, we became very acquainted and I realized that he was a neighbor I had not met before. We were both shocked by this revelation because I had lived in this neighborhood for five years at the time of this conversation and he had lived in the neighborhood most of his life, yet we never crossed paths. This phone call that initially was simply an inquiry concerning an invitation, blossomed into a warm and enjoyable conversation as two neighbors got to know each other. I discovered that he was a retired medical doctor and lawyer who was now employing his credentials in corporate America where he was working with some health or disability insurance company that I can't recall. As I shared my occupation as an obstetrician/gynecologist with him, it dawned on me just who I was conversing with and how God had once again orchestrated everything perfectly. I not only had a seasoned and experienced professional colleague to obtain wisdom from in my dilemma at that present moment, but a lawyer as well. All of a sudden a feeling of timidity came over me and tried to block my blessing that God had placed right before me, but I whispered up a brief unspoken prayer during our conversation for the tenacity to seek this gentleman's wisdom and advice in this window of opportunity even though he was a complete stranger. At that moment, I felt that I was undergoing an outer body experience as I heard my voice sharing my recent unfortunate news about my malpractice insurance policy and how it had been cancelled without my knowledge. I was extremely apprehensive about my transparency with this total stranger as if he would even care about my dilemma at all. Unexpectedly, his voice changed from a jovial tone to one of a more serious and grave nature as he instructed me to call my malpractice carrier right then and inquire why this decision was made. He advised me further to be prepared to challenge the response by requesting a meeting with the board to discuss in more detail how this conclusion was reached. Exercising his legal degree, he stated that I had the right to due process in this case and that I needed to utilize it. What I wasn't prepared for was the response I received from the insurance company when I followed through with everything the neighbor recommended for me to do. The receptionist placed me on a brief hold and then returned asking me if I was available that afternoon to meet with the board in an impromptu meeting around 4:00 p.m. Apparently, there was already a scheduled board meeting for 2:00 p.m. that day and mine would be scheduled to follow. The participants of the first meeting would be asked to stay for my impromptu meeting later that afternoon. It was already 1:00 pm, so I only had a few hours to prepare for this meeting that would significantly influence my career's future. Realizing this was an avenue to immediately rectify the matter at hand, I didn't mull over this proposal long because I recognized this to be a Godsent open door, so I promptly consented and began to quickly get ready as I didn't have long to prepare. For a moment, I was tempted to be defeated by my fear and nervousness with the unknown proceedings to be expected in this meeting. However, I encouraged myself as Donald Lawrence (a gospel artist) says in his song, and I stayed the course. Sometimes when there is no one else to encourage you in an uncertain or troubling situation, you have to encourage yourself like David did in 1 Samuel 30:6 (KJV - King James Version). I was determined to address this hiccup and any others that were threatening my career at the time.

Arriving thirty minutes prior to my scheduled appointment, I waited patiently in the lobby for what I anticipated to be a successful and succinct meeting. Seeing how God had orchestrated things that day in my favor, I was confident that the outcome of this meeting would be positive and my insurance reinstated. Also, because this meeting was only called to address my concerns with this new development concerning my malpractice insurance, I foresaw it as being very direct and straightforward and thus, not taking a lot of time that evening. Shortly before the appointed time, I looked for someone to come and escort me to the room in efforts to begin promptly. As minutes passed by, I began to reason that the impromptu nature of this meeting was responsible for the delay that was thirty minutes by this time. Believing this to be the case, I remained unruffled and quietly waited. The receptionist asked me if I wanted something to drink and I declined because I didn't want any bladder emergencies to arise when the meeting began. I decided to occupy my time with a magazine displayed in the lobby since I was uncertain about the length of this delay. After a while, I looked at the time and realized that an hour had gone by and still no peep from anyone concerning the meeting. By this time, the receptionist had a puzzled look on her face and informed me that she would go and see the reason for the delay. Oddly enough, this took ten minutes when I thought it would be much shorter, but she informed me when she returned that they were waiting for one other individual to meet their quorum for the forum and the individual's estimated time of arrival was quoted to be somewhere between ten to fifteen minutes.

Taking a deep breath, I sighed from exhaustion as I mentally and emotionally fought to maintain the tenacity I had when I first arrived for the meeting. It was difficult because I hadn't eaten since breakfast and it was close to 5:00 p.m. then. With the unexpected news that day, along with the phone conversation that occurred by happenstance, I had missed lunch and was unaware until my stomach reminded me. I struggled to mask the audible gas bubbles traversing my stomach and intestinal walls due to severe hunger pains during this prolonged wait. It was tough enough withstanding the uncomfortable air conditioned climate in the lobby that had me freezing while waiting, and now this disturbingly long wait. Just when I thought that I couldn't take it any longer, a gentleman came out and requested that I follow him. Looking at my cell phone, I noticed that it was now 6:00 p.m. - two hours later than the scheduled meeting time of 4:00 p.m. I had literally been waiting there for over two hours for this meeting to take place. And, to be exact, my wait was actually two and a half hours because I arrived thirty minutes prior to the scheduled time, which made my wait even more frustrating and exhausting. Although I was extremely relieved to be transitioning to the next phase of this mission, I felt myself becoming slightly nervous as I followed this gentleman to a door that he instructed me to open and enter first. When I opened the door to enter this conference room, I saw that I was immediately at my seat, which happened to be at the head of a long conference table filled with many people that I quickly learned were physicians on this malpractice insurance company's board. The insurance company's lawyers were in attendance as well and were seated in chairs positioned alongside this long conference table. So, one can only imagine how intimidating this was to walk into this room as the last person to join this meeting and with all eyes on me as I was strategically placed at the head of the table. After walking in, I immediately became frozen in my footsteps from the serious intimidation I felt with all these eyes glaring at me in anticipation. As I finally took my seat, I felt like assuming defeat before I could even begin my appeal. What seemed like 100 menacing faces all fixed on me was really more like 30 or so faces intently waiting to hear what I had to say. I remember plopping down in my seat and wondering what I had gotten myself into that evening. The unnerving feeling that came over me in that instant, paralyzed me momentarily and I almost relinquished the task I came there for that evening. Just in that instant, I whispered up an inward prayer as I did by habit in times of trouble and instantaneously an assurance came over me that I knew was God's presence. I sensed the Holy Spirit prodding me to get it together, sit upright, and be confident because this was my moment to allow God to use me to vindicate my cause. Following suit to this divine directive, I immediately straightened my back and leaned forward resting my arms and elbows on the table with folded hands to convey the message of expectancy with the outcome of this meeting. The meeting then started with an attorney at the far end of the room introducing the meeting's agenda after introducing himself and everyone else present. After this, he quickly turned his attention to me as he questioned my involvement with the case he briefly summarized. As all eyes intently gazed at me, I calmly and emphatically repeated the scenario in question, but this time with all of the details concerning the case, which included mentioning those individuals specifically and primarily involved in this case other than myself. After summarizing things with clarity and filling in the loopholes in this case, I then stated that this was obviously an inherited case that occurred because of my availability and choice to intervene on someone else's behalf to save a life. I explained how my focus and attention at that time were not on the consequences or cost of being involved in someone else's negligence when someone's life was at risk, but rather on saving a life - in this case two lives (the pregnant mother and fetus). As I looked around the table and then at the lawyers in the periphery, I transparently stated that most of us - if not all of us - as providers and professionals have faced situations where we got entangled in someone else's mishap and sometimes even blamed for someone else's oversight all because we made the decision to help at whatever cost. When making this declaration, I noticed that the body language of the attendees in the room changed and I read empathy in their expressions because I knew they could relate. Finishing my remarks that served to illuminate the significant particulars in this case, I concluded that there was no breach in the standard of care on my part in this case. In contrast, I exercised my humanitarian rights as a person and employed the Good Samaritan law in medicine as a physician to help someone in need when their provider was unavailable. Therefore, this cancellation of my malpractice insurance policy was unfounded. After I made this closing statement, the lawyers in the periphery questioned who represented me because my role in this case unquestionably mirrored more of an altruist than that of a culprit. The real clincher for them apparently was the fact that I was not this patient's provider and essentially had nothing to do with this patient's admission, management, or hospital course that day. I simply was the available provider who didn't mind responding to someone else's negligence and patient mismanagement when it became an emergency, which was apparently overlooked in the settlement of this case. Evidently, the nurses had notified this physician of the unfavorable test results that she ordered when she admitted this patient, which was over 24 hours prior to the emergency that later ensued. However, the provider chose not to intervene then when there were signs of fetal compromise and this patient went into labor later that day around midnight. While I was at the hospital evaluating a patient of mine, I was confronted by the nursing staff with this provider's patient whose case had become an emergency by then. Being the only available provider who was willing to intervene in that instant, I performed the necessary emergency cesarean section which revealed a baby that should have been delivered long before my involvement, which was not surprising. In fact, this patient's delivery should have occurred shortly after her admission when the tests that were ordered by her physician revealed evidence of fetal compromise. This would have most likely prevented this emergency and offered a more favorable outcome. At any rate, if I had not intervened, this case would have resulted in a fetal death with maternal morbidity and mortality as well. Avoiding a fetal death, as well as a maternal death, was more important to me than avoiding my name being wrongfully documented as this patient's primary doctor accepting all responsibility for this unfavorable outcome. The truth is, I was the only willing doctor available at the time who agreed to cover in this doctor's absence to save two lives. Saving these two lives in this instance was paramount. Although I realized that my intervention as the delivering doctor in this medical mismanagement could potentially denigrate my professional reputation when I had nothing to do with the care and outcome of this patient's delivery, I consented because it was lifesaving, and I have never regretted it. I later learned that this case represented two areas out of the five that my current storm intended to attack - my character and career. From the morning of the domestic incident when I was blindsided by this storm, I realized that its intent was to disrupt and attack five areas of my life; hence, I reference it as a "five-tier" storm. These five areas involved my marriage, my finances, my character, my career, and my spirituality. And this was demonstrated by the discoveries made and those that were forthcoming. Later two cases came up where I covered a colleague for less than an hour, yet I was mentioned in an investigation concerning the labor management that I was not involved in. However, the outcomes of these cases were seen to be genetic and not related to medical management at all. Therefore, my colleague was exonerated and I was dismissed from the cases altogether because I didn't have anything to do with the management. Interestingly, the medical board declared that these cases should have been dismissed from their onset beause they viewed them as frivolous and unfounded. Oddly enough, the plaintiff in both of these cases was not the patient, but the state. And the charges focused on the significant medical costs absorbed by the state that led them to pursue legal assistance in these cases. It appeared as if someone was trying to cause me undue anxiety because I was mailed court papers with actual trial dates for both cases, but the dates came and went with no trial and no explanation. They just mysteriously settled outside of court despite my preference for a trial, which prompted the investigation by the medical state board mentioned earlier. And strangely enough, not one of these court dates could be found on record. Someone was obviously playing games while attempting to besmirch my reputation and destroy my career, but God.

In any event, as I switch gears back to this impromptu meeting concerning my malpractice insurance, I remember being baffled with the question from the lawyers concerning my representation. I was shocked that they were unaware that their company had represented me. I guess they saw that it was a no brainer that my involvement in this case was not in question or at fault, and that the standard of care was exercised appropriately. So, at this point, they were trying to see why their lawyers had a problem vindicating my role in this case when things were pretty straightforward from their standpoint. I simply compensated for another doctor's dereliction of duty as this patient's healthcare provider, yet my legal council failed to advocate on my behalf and exonerate me, which would have removed my name from this case. The patient's doctor would have been seen to be the sole physician responsible for this clinical delinquency. Nevertheless, I informed the legal team present at this meeting that this malpractice company had represented me, which I assumed they were already aware of prior to this meeting. My response triggered mumbling among the attorneys in the room and I saw them grouping together in private conversation when all of a sudden the leader in the group said that I was dismissed and they would be calling me in the next couple of days with their decision. This decision was whether or not to resume my malpractice insurance coverage. I surprisingly got up and left the room as if I was in a trance. I was dumbfounded with how quickly this meeting ended after taking forever to start. It literally lasted only a matter of a few minutes. From the time the lawyer opened the meeting with his three minute introduction to the time of my response, which was no more than five to six minutes or less, the meeting had ended. This whole occasion was befuddling and left me bemused as I drove home. I didn't anticipate a long meeting as I mentioned prior to the start of it, but I definitely didn't think that it would be this abrupt. The brevity of it left me in a state of shock that evening as I drove home. When I arrived home, I snapped out of my delirium and hurried to find my husband to celebrate and boast on God's intervention on my behalf that evening. I was so grateful for God seeing me through what looked like a painful and grueling process initially that surprisingly worked out in my favor in the end. One would have thought that I had already received the verdict from the meeting to reinstate my insurance the way I was celebrating. I was exercising my faith at this point and claiming the victory in advance. The Bible promise in Mark 11:23, 24 was high on my radar.

Well, not long after briefing my husband about the meeting, I received a phone call from a gentleman from the insurance company that same evening. He was calling to inform me that my malpractice insurance had been renewed and there would be no lapse because the cancellation was their error. He also offered me an apology on behalf of the company for this mistake and thanked me for my patience and understanding during the rectification process. After he finished his comments, there was a long silence on the phone as I took the time to process what I was hearing before responding. Sitting there stupefied for about thirty seconds or so, my husband nudged me to arouse me out of my daze so that I could respond to the gentleman who was patiently awaiting my response. Realizing this, I quickly thanked the gentleman and expressed my gratefulness to the board for granting me the opportunity to appeal this apparent mishap earlier. After hanging the phone up, I just fell on my knees overwhelmed with gratitude to God as I praised Him for doing it once again. From earlier that day when I opened the mail, to later that evening, I thanked God for resolving this nightmare quickly - before the end of the day. In essence, God had answered my prayer before I even knew there was a problem because as you recall, the neighbor's invitation was in the mailbox with the letter from the insurance company that notified me of my insurance termination. And it was this invitation that connected me with the neighbor who turned out to be a godsend that day. So, just to reiterate, God had already divinely orchestrated everything before I even recognized a problem, because as you recall, the cancellation notice and the invitation were in the mailbox that morning at the same time. In other words, after I opened the cancellation notice of my insurance, the invitation for this neighbor's granddaughter's birthday party was there for me to open next, which connected me with my solution for the unwarranted cancellation of my malpractice insurance. Once again, God had arranged for the solution to my problem before I knew it existed and had me open the mail in the right order - the problem first, then the solution (Isaiah 65:24!!). Meeting this neighbor proved to be a blessing because God used him and his credentials as a doctor and lawyer to give me the wisdom and instruction that encouraged me to appeal this unfavorable and fallacious decision by calling this meeting that ultimately turned around in my favor. That evening and throughout that night, I reflected on just how awesome God is and I thanked my neighbor profusely as I notified him of the meeting's outcome. That weekend I shared this testimony in an early morning prayer service at church and praised God for His favor and vindication on my behalf. What if I had never exercised faith in this situation?

This next blessing I recall occurred when we had to leave the condo and all of our things along with it. Reminiscing on that occurrence, I remember being called later that week by a young lady who was a resident there and who I had met briefly with her son a couple of months before the day we left. She apparently got wind of what was going on and decided to gather what she could of our things and store them in her condo. She decided to store as much of our belongings as her condo could accommodate to prevent a huge loss. And, surprisingly, she was able to store a significant amount of our valuables in her condo and contacted us later to make us aware of it. She was even kind enough to inform us that she didn't mind storing our things until we stabilized free of charge. What a tremendous blessing.

Although we weren't able to recoup everything we lost, we were extremely grateful to regain what this angel of a young lady was able to recover, which was a lot. So, after stabilizing, we were able to go and get our things that she was able to store and thank her for her kindness. Over the days that followed, she and I got to know each other better and enjoyed getting together just to exhale. We shared a common struggle as single parents and often talked about the goodness of the Lord and how He saw us through many troubles and hard times. As I think about her now, I regret having lost contact with her because she was truly a genuine individual who proved to be a blessing in our dilemma. With all that the girls and I faced ahead that included more residential and financial instability that revisited us down the road because of this fraudulence, this friend's information was lost and I regretted it terribly. I pray to see her in heaven if our paths don't cross again down here, but until then, I pray that she and her son will be covered under God's protective hedge until that day.

Reminiscing on another memorable event that occurred in the beginning of our journey, I remember a gentleman who came to visit me at my office to bring me a monetary gift of love during the time the office was transitioning right after the incident with my husband. To my astonishment, this gift of love that day was one thousand dollars cash! This moment almost seemed unbelievable as I opened the envelope he gave me and saw the ten one hundred dollar bills inside. Although we were not financially strained at that time, this blessing was greatly appreciated. It occurred in the beginning of our trial and the fraud had not yet caused the financial crisis that it caused later on by redirecting nearly all of my reimbursements to a fraudulent bank account leaving me financially destitute and without any way to prove it at the time. Anyhow, I learned that this gentleman that blessed me that day was a family member of several patients of mine and also a medical student who shadowed me at one time during his clinical training in medical school. While shadowing, he was able to assist in the delivery of his niece, which he still talks about to this day. His monetary gift of love that day was his way of thanking me for caring for his family and for being a mentor and blessing to him and his family during his clinical training. I also learned that this was a collaborative act of kindness from all of the family when they became aware of the domestic incident I had suffered, along with all that the girls and I were going through as far as adjusting and transitioning to a new residence. This gesture communicated to me that my patients cared about me and that I was special to them, which went a long way during this difficult time while the girls and I were trying to adjust to our new norm along with everything else going on. This family that consisted of patients of mine ultimately became my second family and we were truly blessed by this relationship. I can say today that I truly love them and appreciate them for being there for the girls and me during that phase of our journey in this trial.

As I reminisce further about all the love God showered on the girls and me through complete strangers and then some friends during this trying time, I get emotionally stirred. One particular friend from Maryland flew down to Georgia to ensure that the girls and I were fine and to be supportive. Because of her, the girls were given the opportunity to have safe visitation arranged with their dad during his TPO as I mentioned in an earlier chapter. She sacrificed her time and money as she flew down on a couple of occasions to orchestrate things, support us, and ensure that we were fine, and for this, I am eternally grateful. And because I know that behind every amazing friend that is married, there stands an amazing spouse, I also thank her husband profusely for lending her to us. Another girlfriend of mine who happened to be my church choir director when I was living in Maryland, made sure to show her love and support also during this tough time for the girls and me. She made sure that she stopped by my office in Georgia to encourage me and shower love on me through her prayers and hugs while visiting her family in Georgia - where I resided at the time. This gesture gave me just what I needed in this difficult time to persevere and to trust God in spite of my circumstances. Her husband also was willing to offer free legal advice, along with his expert opinion earlier on when the flabbergasting discoveries were just surfacing and we needed legal counsel. He recommended revisiting things when we had more information and we could make more sense of things as we connected the dots. I love and appreciate these two couples more than they'll ever know. And, by the way, these two couples know each other and are very close friends.

I'm also reminded of an undergraduate classmate who was kind enough to homeschool my baby girls with her children during our time of transitioning, and for her love and support during this time, I am forever grateful. The following year I took a hiatus from work so that I could homeschool my girls their second and final year of home-schooling. I was aware that my baby girls needed just a little bit more of mommy during this emotionally challenging time and now we would spend our entire days together. What a treat! The fond and treasurable memories that we made were affectionately cherished then and now. There were other kind gestures that we truly appreciated during this difficult time as well that left us feeling encouraged and uplifted, and for all of these acts of kindness, we are truly grateful.

Another cherishable memory I recall occurred at the onset of our journey shortly after our domestic incident when the girls and I de-cided to return to church after being absent for one month while we were waiting for things to settle down from our tragedy. Immediately following our domestic misfortune, the girls and I were intentionally absent from our church home as we emotionally adjusted during this difficult time. I felt it was prudent to avoid any familiar gatherings and events that could possibly lead to an unpleasant encounter with my husband while there was still tension between us and our court hearing was still pending. So, our absence from the church scene lasted a little over a month during this period of caution. Thoughts of his potential to stalk us and follow us home to discover our new location weighed heavily on my mind and influenced my decision to be wise and inconspicuous while restless emotions prevailed. Our low profile during this time alleviated a lot of drama that would have only served to escalate things even more.

In any event, on this particular Sabbath, which happened to be the first Sabbath back for the girls and me since our family turmoil, we were warmly greeted by this matriarch in the church who embraced us and let us know that our absence was strongly felt. This kind act instantly removed the trepidation and insecurity that initially plagued me as I prepared to face my church family and to answer their anticipated inquiries from the rumor mill circulating at the time. We were still trying to figure things out ourselves, so I dreaded trying to answer all of the questions that I was still puzzled about and had no earthly clue concerning what was really going on. Nevertheless, this deaconess in the church who was several years my senior, made it her business to take us under her wings this first Sabbath back to church since the incident. Having some knowledge of our story, she openly shared her story with me and offered consolation and advice as she reassured me that the girls and I would be fine as long as we trusted God to take care of us and lead us in this difficult time. Her transparency blessed, encouraged, and empowered me in the most meaningful way. God divinely arranged for me to cross paths with this deaconess on this first Sabbath back to church. After being absent for a while, church members expressed how glad they were to see the girls and me this particular Sabbath after missing us for nearly over a month. And, as I mentioned, God orchestrated things perfectly that day by letting one of my first encounters be with this inspiring woman who could relate with me because she was a survivor of domestic violence. It didn't matter that I had suffered only a single incident of physical abuse by being nearly choked to death that memorable morning while this woman shared that she had been physically abused for most of her marriage. The fact still remained that we could relate with each other after being survivors who experienced some form of physical abuse - whether it was once or multiple times, it didn't matter. This similar experience of being subject to some form of cruel behavior at some point in our lives was sufficient for us to be able to empathize with each other no matter how many times we suffered this cruelty and no matter how different our experiences had been. Having her support that first day back to church after my brief hiatus meant more than words could ever express. On my first day back to church that Sabbath after being away so long (one month), I was concomitantly excited and anxious. It was exciting for me because I missed my church family and friends and longed to reconnect after being away so long due to my circumstances. However, I was equally anxious and nervous to return to church with my new norm as a single parent who was currently experiencing a marital crisis and was separated from my husband at the time. I realized that this new norm would be uncomfortable for my friends and church family who knew my husband, the children, and me as a family who interacted and fellowshipped with them on numerous occasions. Witnessing the remnants of this family bond on the day of my return, due to the circumstances, I knew would be uncomfortable for them. I would also have the unenviable burden of disclosing to them my current situation, which would probably clear up some misinformation derived from the active rumor mill circulating during that time. They would be able to get their story from the horse's mouth. I knew that I would be asked why I chose to stay away from the church for a month or so from the onset of our family crisis and I was prepared to explain my safety concerns for the girls and me at that time, which involved protection from the stalking with the potential harm involved. Also, as expressed earlier, we wanted to prevent the possibility of our safe haven being discovered. In addition to all of this, we just needed a "time out" where we could mentally and emotionally recover from this sudden domiciliary disruption that caused abrupt marital, familial, and residential instability.

In any event, the support I received from this deaconess will always be a treasurable memory for me. As I reminisce on that day, I remember entering the church apprehensively and feeling as if I was being gawked at and made the topic of discussion as I overheard whispering by fellow church members while walking down the church aisle. While we were warmly greeted by some church members, there definitely was an unwelcoming vibe in the air exuded by others towards us that day when we desperately needed an overdose of tender loving care and encouragement. Oh how our hearts craved for love and advocacy in our situation, along with someone who truly understood our quandary. However, being optimistic, I attributed this paucity of solicitude we felt that day to be a reaction from the shock that our church family endured when they heard the news of my immediate family's sudden disturbance resulting in severing of family ties and pending divorce. The abruptness of things hit everyone like a bombshell, and on this particular day we were facing some of the reactions. But it was this woman who saw me and immediately embraced me as she warmly welcomed me back overlooking all of the other particulars as she saw my desperate need for love and emotional support that day. She inquired how I was doing, and when I hesitated with what to say, she acknowledged that she had heard of my misfortune. She then led me away from the crowd as she shared her story with me and expressed how unfortunate it is that this issue (domestic violence) barely receives attention - if any at all - in the church, and how this refusal to address this crisis prevents individuals from getting the help they desperately need. We both agreed that this help is crucial for the perpetrator as well as for the victim.

She shared her story with me as a survivor in a chronic environment of domestic violence and how the church was reluctant to intervene on her behalf because her husband was a respected elder in the church. They felt that her story was somewhat embellished and advised her to submit to her husband and to pray. Referencing Ephesians 5:22-28, they felt that it wasn't their place to intervene because her husband was the head of the household and she should submit to his leadership in the home. What was not said to her was that although the Bible admonishes the woman to submit to her husband as the head of the household, she is only to do this as he (the husband) submits to the Lord. The husband's submission to the Lord would enable him to treat his wife with respect and love - not cruelty. This biblical text referenced in Ephesians 5:22-28 supports a healthy and happy relationship where both individuals are loved and respected - not abused and misused by dominance in any way. Unfortunately, this was not her case, and because of the church's distortion of the biblical advice in Ephesions referenced above and their refusal to help, her voice was not heard and she found no help in her miserable quagmire. The problem was never addressed, just perpetuated. And, to add insult to injury, her story was doubted over time and the church's attitude towards her changed. She eventually was treated as the villain who was supposedly disparaging her husband's name with fabricated stories when all that she desperately wanted was to be heard and her story validated. Maybe then she would get the help she so greatly needed.

Despite her sad ending, she saw promise in my situation and wanted to offer hope. What a beautiful spirit from someone so broken and scarred. Because she recognized that the help from the church was still suboptimal due to their discomfort with these domestic issues, she pointed me to social services where they could be of help and provide other resources needed. I informed her that I had employed these services and had secured my TPO prior to returning to the church scene for safety reasons as stressed earlier and she applauded this gesture, as well as the decision on my part to leave my toxic environment and relocate with the intention to start over. She encouraged me to keep trusting God to see me through the turbulence in my life at the time and to wait for Him to open doors for the girls and me along this journey. She also committed to help me in any way that she could and left me her phone number. This act of kindness that showed belief in my story along with a genuine concern to help, inspired me in this initial phase of my journey as no other act of kindness did at the time and will always be remembered and treasured. Oftentimes, the intangible gifts of goodwill, support, encouragement, empowerment, quality time, and forgiveness are overlooked when compared to the tangible gifts of money, clothing, food, and material things although both are equally important and essential. The encounter that day illustrated the powerful impact that intangible gifts can positively have on one's life. This encounter gave me the fight and motivation to go on in face of the unexpected adversity I received from some fellow church members and friends who reacted negatively to my tragic story and new norm. It also propelled me forward and strengthened me as I anticipated what was bound to come as I realized that this was just the beginning of this journey of misfortune.

As I continue reminiscing, I recall God placing this specific pastor along my path right after the incident who encouraged me not to divert from my course of relocating to a safer place for the girls and me. I can still remember his exact words to me that day saying to "stay the course", and I've been intentional about doing just that ever since. Although I received mixed messages from fellow church members and friends who were unclear of what was really going on, I maintained my focus and direction to move forward and move on despite the uncertainty of just where this new path would lead. I knew that it was paramount for the girls and me to leave the virulent environment we had faced that day when the incident occurred and I was glad to have our decision endorsed by this pastor. I was also happy to have his assistance when we were relocating right after the incident. His support and encouragement meant more than he'll ever know.

Another family friend who I love dearly accompanied this pastor while we were securing things in a storage space during our transitioning to find a safe place. He was someone I trusted and called on in this dilemma as well who willingly helped us and showed us love. I will always remember his loving support in our time of crisis. As I continue to reminisce, I remember another family friend who is like a second mom to me who came to the rescue for the girls and me in our dilemma as well and made sure we were safe and prepared in the area of self-defense. I chuckle as I recall this memory and she only will know why. She reached out to us in the very beginning of our journey when the incident had just occurred and things were pretty tense. She assured us that we had her full support and I marveled at her striking fortitude and tenacity in her early eighties at that time. Today I still fondly remember her counsel, compassion, and strong support. She is truly a feisty matriarch who I still glean insight and sagacity from even today now that she is in her nineties. Her words of wisdom and advice have been truly appreciated down through the years and I consider her to be a godsend and second mom who I respect and treasure dearly. This is just another example of the benefit of bridging the generational gap and how rewarding it can be. Because learning by one's own experience is not always the best method for acquiring knowledge in life, it behooves an individual to learn from someone else's experience instead. This is the less painful route to pursue. Therefore, because life is a cycle that repeats itself for the most part, it would be prudent to seek guidance and instruction from someone who has walked some of these paths before and to learn from their mistakes to prevent some avoidable regrets and unpleasant repercussions. I still adore this individual today.

Another warm memory I recall occurred while I was preparing for my maintenance of certification in my specialty of obstetrics and gynecology. This annual task involved reading multiple articles and maintaining a high percentage of correct answers while answering multiple questions about the articles. This particular year was especially challenging for me as I recall because of the financial instability, which threatened my ability to maintain membership with my specialty organization as well as to keep my board certification status up to date because of the costs involved. However, after explaining my situation to my specialty board (ABOG) and my professional membership organization (ACOG), I found them to be extremely accommodating. Consequently, I had no problem completing my requirements for board recertification that year. ABOG is the acronym for "The American Board of Obstetrics and Gynecology" that is a non-profit organization that provides board certification for practicing obstetricians and gynecologists in the United States and Canada keeping us up-to-date with the latest advances in our field. ACOG stands for: "The American College of Obstetricians and Gynecologists, which is a professional association for OB/GYN's (obstetrician/gynecologists), and it shares the same goal as ABOG. The support that I received from these two institutions during this process was phenomenal - especially during the time of my financial instability due to the identity theft and fraud. I will always remember and be forever grateful for their assistance and support during my recertification this particular year while going through this difficult time.

I also found this next experience to be touching and soul stirring as it completely caught me off guard. Shortly after the domestic incident, I got a call from my sons and their biological mom. They referenced their call as a wellness check to inquire how the girls and I were doing. These were my two precious sons that God blessed me with when I married their dad. During that time - right after I married their dad, the oldest was five years old and the youngest was two years old and they both were totally adorbs, which contributed to the immediate heart-bond that developed among the three of us that was unbreakable. In fact, meeting them sealed the deal with my decision to marry their dad. Our bond was inseverable and only grew stronger after their dad and I married. I was ecstatic about being their bonus mom and even more proud to claim them as my bonus sons. A year or two after I married, I birthed their first sister and then two years later their younger sister joined the family. Raising this Brady bunch of a clan (from the American sitcom I watched faithfully as a child) was challenging, yet filled with many days of laughter and fond memories. Not long before the domestic hiccup between their dad and me, however, they decided to live with their biological mom who was moving to another state at the time, so we said our goodbyes and planned to reconnect soon. So they were not with us the day of the incident. At any rate, when I received their call that day, I was happily surprised and let them know that they were terribly missed. They expressed the same feelings and we enjoyed just catching up over the next several minutes. They expressed their concern when they heard of the mishap and wanted to call to confirm that we were okay. I relieved their worries and told them that we were fine and just taking time to heal. Soon after all of the updating, their other mom got on the phone and thanked me for being a part of the boys' lives. As she continued to open up, I was taken aback when she thanked me for my involvement with raising the boys and coparenting with her. She went on to tell me some of the stories they shared with her that were special - some comical and some inspirational. This was a heartwarming moment for me as I felt as if I was getting my flowers before my funeral. It was definitely a special moment, and from that day forward, I viewed her as an exceptional mom - one who didn't feel threatened to share her sons with me - their second mom. I know that it's been a while since we were all together due to current circumstances - those mentioned and then those unmentioned - but I look forward to reconnecting when that time comes. Until then, I pray for God to keep us all safe under His protective hedge.

This next person holds a dear place in my heart as he will always be very special to me. This person is none other than my Uncle Gerald, who is the prayer warrior extraordinaire. He has been an intercessor for my family for as long as I can remember and though our connection is not biological, we have a spiritual and love connection that surpasses any bloodline. Anytime my parents, siblings, or I had a problem, he was our go-to prayer warrior as he still is today. Since my father's death, he has now become like a second dad as well. I can always count on him for sound, spiritual advice and any support that I may need. I recall one holiday season around Christmas time when he drove all the way from Indiana to Georgia alone to get us and bring us home to Illinois to celebrate the holidays with the family because it wasn't in our budget that year after the financial fraud that we had suffered. Amazingly, he made this venture during the time of the year when the winter weather was most severe for the midwest. His eyesight was also suboptimal during this time with his eye surgery pending and I recall his glasses being broken. I'll never forget the sacrifice he made for us that Christmas to allow us to see our family and to have a good Christmas. As I ponder this sacrifice, I can still see him pulling into our driveway in Atlanta, Georgia with his broken eyeglasses held together with lots of tape resting crooked on his nose as he got out to hug us and rest for the night before turning around in the morning to take us back with him to Chicago, Illinois. Just processing that he was the sole driver as he took this trip alone in inclement weather with very limited vision in his early 70's, brings tears to my eyes. This strong determination and love shown towards us that day in this selfless act of kindness, still moves me emotionally today. He was determined in spite of his vulnerability to ensure that the girls and I had a merry Christmas and we did. It was his Christmas gift to us and we were overwhelmingly surprised. During this difficult time in our lives, the girls and I could not have asked the Lord for a more devoted and dependable prayer warrior and true "Ride or Die" than our Uncle Gerald. As I stated before, I thought of him as my second father because my father had died before this setback in my life, and it was in this misfortune that God fulfilled the promise of Psalm 27:10. My uncle stood in the gap for me during this time of grief and provided the counsel, comfort, support, and spiritual direction I so desperately needed as he assumed the role of a father figure for me in my time of loss. Even though God manifested Himself as my dependable, omnipotent and omnipresent heavenly Father in a mighty way, He still provided an earthly substitute through this uncle, and for that I am forever thankful. I could always expect a word from the Lord, along with authentic godly counsel from this uncle that would be just what was needed for the given situation. During my childhood, I remember the Bible stories that my parents read to me concerning the prophets that served as spiritual guides, counselors, and intercessors for God's people. Uncle Gerald definitely fit this description for the girls and me in this crisis and for my family throughout my life as I shared earlier. Consequently, I consider him to be a prophet in his own right in this 21st century and I thank God for our relationship, along with his continual support and encouragement even to this day. Then there was my Detroit brother and sister with their sons who were similar in age to my baby girls who showed us much support and love. From the time they learned about our misfortune, they showed compassion, concern, and encouragement. Not once did they doubt or question our story as if we were embellishing things in efforts to receive undeserved sympathy, but they prayed for us instead. They prayed for God's favor, restoration and protection to cover the girls and me, and unbeknownst to them, this gesture of love acknowledging our pain and brokenness was immensely appreciated then and even now when reflecting. I also can't forget my girlfriend who came to lay eyes on me and spend time with me showing me much love and support. Her sacrifice she made leaving her family temporarily to make sure I was fine meant so much. She also invited the girls and me to her home in North Carolina for Thanksgiving that year assuring we were doing well emotionally. She too was going through a difficult time as a healthcare provider and we comforted and supported each other during this difficult time. Another girlfriend who is like a sister was out of the country at the time and made a special trip back home just to see about the girls and me. Then there was my sister from another mister who grew up around the block from me as a child. From the time she discovered what happened, she immediately assumed the role of my physical and spiritual bodyguard. She connected me with the friend who arranged my supervised visitation mentioned earlier and made sure we were safe. And then she gave me one of the most inspiring devotionals ever written by Sarah Young titled *Jesus Calling*. No matter the distance between us or the time that elapses before we reconnect, this friend and I have supported each other in difficult times since our childhood and continue to do so. I'll also never forget the love I felt when some married friends of mine visited my church from Florida during this difficult time. The hug, concern, and love they showered on me in this difficult time meant the world to me. Another couple who were friends of mine as well as my husband, blessed me with a monetary gift of love during this difficult time. And then there was my childhood friend who made it her business to find me and place the powerful book, Circle Maker by Mark Batterson, in my hand to encourage me during this difficult time in my life. This book was inspirational, life-changing, and empowering. I appreciated this act of love. For all of these kindnesses and more, I am forever grateful. It was in these moments that the girls and I saw the hand of God showering us with His favor and blessings in spite of the misfortune we were undergoing at the time. I thank every individual who allowed God to use them to be a blessing to us during this difficult time.

Chapter 11

TIME TO PROCESS

As I TOOK time to process all that had gone on, as well as all that I had learned over the two years or more from the onset of this incident, I saw that this was more than a snippet from a "me too" narrative. This experience of mine dealt with a whole lot more than a domestic issue when considering the revelations that followed the incident. In fact, the domestic episode was secondary to what was really going on. It actually could have been viewed as tertiary in the scope of everything discovered. I had no idea what the magnitude and extent of this dilemma was that I found myself in on that morning of the domestic occurrence until much later. With the revelations that surfaced over the several months following this mishap, I began to connect the dots in order to make sense of all that had transpired. Things started out hazy from the beginning, but became more lucid shortly thereafter as I sought wisdom through prayer during this time of uncertainty and also as things began to surface. Because I recognized God's omniscience, I looked to Him to shed light on the situation over time, which He did. I claimed the Bible promise that assures us that all those that follow Him will not walk in darkness, but will walk in light instead because He is the Light of the world. Consequently, I discerned that what started as an enigma turned out to be a lengthy and complicated saga instead that threw me for a loop.

This ordeal was quite complex and complicated and left me feeling totally confused initially as I wrestled with trying to digest everything that I was bombarded with from time to time. It seemed that every week a new discovery was made and I was baffled by the findings that came from so many different angles. Some of these revelations were untimely and overwhelming in nature and mandated that I take a social moratorium away from the scene temporarily so that I could catch my breath and appropriately digest everything mentally and emotionally. Some of this unanticipated news was most discouraging and disappointing and caused me to develop a new perspective on things. It became clear that this was no minor snafu concocted overnight, but a well-devised and nefarious ruse contrived over time instead. As I pondered this corrupt conspiracy that was ongoing with my sensitive personal and business information, I was left feeling emotionally and physically out of sorts. This washed out and exhausted state that I found myself in was magnified even more by the fact that I couldn't do anything about the discoveries that flooded me because more information was needed to connect all of the dots in order to make sense of anything. Initially, I saw things coming together, but as more revelations were manifested, I concluded that I was right back to square one and just as confused as I was in the beginning. I had no real idea of what was going on just yet, so, without any other options in these frustrating moments, I resolved to wait patiently on God to manifest things in His appointed time. The question for me at this point was how long. Of course I was anxious to resolve things speedily, but God had another plan. Once again I had to remember and resort to Isaiah 55:8,9. My thoughts were obviously not in sync with God's thoughts because nothing was resolved speedily, and overtime, I realized that expediting this process was not His plan. Another Bible verse that came to mind then was Proverbs 19:21

(KJV and MSG translations) that essentially says that although we as humans make plans, it is God's plan that prevails. So I was content to simply wait on God because I trusted that He knew what was best for the girls and me.

As the weeks passed by, I redirected my attention to assuring that the girls were settled with school and their other activities and I submerged myself in my work at the time. At this particular time, I recall working at a school for children and adolescents with high risk behavior during my respite from my obstetrics and gynecology practice. I enjoyed interacting and talking with the students as a consultant on different topics dealing with sex education, safe and appropriate dating, peer pressure, bullying, self-esteem, substance usage or abuse and other issues of interests to them. These memories are still fond to me as I remember some endearing and precious bonds formed during my time there. In addition to this, I worked with a group home where teenagers with substance abuse issues and other high risk behaviors lived temporarily while in rehabilitation for their drug usage and high risk behavior. In this capacity, I worked alongside the licensed professional counselor as the medical consultant and physician on duty. While the counselor was implementing behavior modifications and constructive coping mechanisms for these teens, I focused on discussing the harmful and adverse effects of various recreational drugs they were experimenting with at the time. In addition to this, I enjoyed sharing sound advice, along with life proverbs in our rap sessions where I saw my role as a life coach. While working in the school and group home, I was exposed to many troubling social and domestic issues up close and personal. I also witnessed many challenges adolescents face in today's society and how they perceive different societal issues and concerns. Many of these adolescents were from financially strained environments and underprivileged homes, which just exasperated their ongoing issues. And the peer pressure they encountered was inundating. I viewed this as yet another experience orchestrated by God preparing me for the calling He had on my life.

At the end of my hiatus, I began contracting with this OB/GYN practice doing office gynecology solely, and I must say that I truly enjoyed the staff and my time there. I took this time to slowly reacclimate back to my career norm that I had been away from for a couple of years. The transition back to my role in the office went smoothly although I had only partially resumed my duties. I waited to resume gynecologic surgery in the hospital at that time so that I wouldn't have any ER call or any surgical emergencies that could arise, but exclusively stayed in the office where I performed office gynecologic procedures for the time being. I also delayed jumping back into obstetric deliveries (vaginal and cesarean) because I still wanted to be available for the girls with their extracurricular activities and overall milestones at this sensitive time in their lives while there was still ongoing drama and while I was still learning to master the art of single parenting. They were still very young and needed to see their mommy's face often. Because I was single parenting, my face would be the only face they would see on a consistent basis anyway. My passion to maintain this availability while single parenting was further motivated by the fact that our extended family lived out of town and this absence of local support left everything on me during this time. Therefore, I assumed this temporary employment position that was strictly a nine to five job because of the flexibility it afforded me as a single parent until the Lord directed me elsewhere.

Later on that year, through God's leading, the girls and I relocated to another state as God opened another door. This opportunity allowed me to start afresh and open my new practice that currently exists today - The Image of Eve Restored, Inc. I chose this name because Eve was the first woman God created, and in her perfect state before she sinned, her original design serves as the perfect template for all females. So, I found this name to be felicitous for the holistic mission I had in mind for my practice - to restore God's image and original design in women physically, mentally, emotionally, and spiritually. On the other hand, while this name was suitable for the practice and its mission, it presented some curiosity as to how it was chosen when one considers my name. I remember asking my mom where she got my name from and learning that she named me after a lady that she admired. I was content with this answer for some time until I stumbled upon some descriptions and definitions of my name that left me dumbfounded. One of the descriptions I found was that scientifically and according to Jewish medieval folklore, Lilith was Adam's first wife who was later supplanted by Eve and became an evil spirit. So, the irony in the name of my medical practice (The Image of Eve Restored, Inc.) and my name (Lilith - Eve's rival) as the healthcare provider leaves many people who are familiar with this belief amused. When I chose this name for my practice, I was not thinking about the association involved until a patient raised the question. I recall chuckling during our conversation and confessing that I did not support this belief.

Nonetheless, I was happy once again to assume another entrepreneurial platform with this new opportunity as I had experienced in my previous practice in Atlanta which afforded me the flexibility to participate in my children's activities and balance my lifestyle to be the involved mommy that I desired to be. This versatility would also accommodate my role as a single parent. However, I'll confess that initially I had no desire to relocate to a totally new state and the girls shared these same sentiments. It was the spring of 2016 when I received this offer and I had a few months to either accept or reject this offer. During my second interview, which was prior to this deadline, God showed signs that answered my prayers for guidance and revealed this move to be His leading. So, I broke the news to the girls and they begrudgingly consented to accompany me on this new journey leaving all of their friends and what they called home behind. Because they had no intention of being separated from me, they had a change of heart and decided to venture out with me into our new beginning. Once our relocation was complete and we had settled in, the girls were the first ones to express how glad they were that we moved. Needless to say, I was astounded and happily surprised with this unexpected acknowledgment from them. Their attitude validated my decision to take this leap of faith and make the move to accept this new opportunity. Equally surprising, was the fact that my daughters declared their agreement with this move even before developing their new social circles because school hadn't started yet. So, this positive and content spirit that they exuded had nothing to do with new friends made, because they hadn't developed any friendships yet. I was just witnessing my prayers being answered concerning their peace with our new home in another state.

I remember so vividly the day we drove up to our new home this particular night and how the girls proclaimed almost immediately how beautiful the sky appeared with the visible constellation of stars. They couldn't believe that they could see so many sparkling stars and with such clarity and brightness. Being raised in an urban environment, the girls weren't accustomed to seeing many starry nights - especially not as lucid and dazzling as we witnessed that night. With the pollution and tall buildings that surrounded them in their citified upbringing, they weren't able to appreciate the wonders of the heavens like they did that night. Earlier on along our drive to our new home, they also repeatedly commented on the captivating panoramic view of nature. As we viewed the lush greenery of the meadows and hills and the breathtaking blue sky with the scattered clouds appearing like cotton balls or cotton candy, we were mesmerized with this little taste of heaven we appreciated along the drive to our new home. It didn't dawn on us right away that we would be fascinated with these awe-inspiring and scenic views daily while traveling to and from our destinations because we lived here now.

As we adjusted and settled into our new home, we were extremely content with the peace and tranquility of our new surroundings in comparison to our previous home. It definitely rendered the calm and serenity that we desperately needed after weathering such a horrific domestic storm with all of its eye openers. After all we had endured - from the life threatening domestic incident that severed family bonds and ended in divorce, to the fraud and identity theft that left us financially paralyzed - we welcomed this quietude in lieu of the hustle and bustle from the big city's rat race that we felt ourselves caught up in while living in our previous more urbanized setting. Over time we found this move to be therapeutic and refreshing as it provided a more relaxing environment for us where we could let our hair down, so to speak, and rest from the trauma we had suffered. We were excited to start anew and push our reset buttons as we walked into this open door of new beginnings that God had provided for us that proved to truly be a blessing. Eagerly we anticipated all that God had in store for us now that we were in our new norm with a fresh start.

Besides experiencing nature up close and personal in all of its splendor and beauty on a daily basis in our new environment, we were also able to appreciate the slower and more relaxed pace with less traffic and commotion as well. Additionally, we found the spiritual atmosphere to be exuberant with a strong church community. There were several options for finding a church home, and all of them were alive and vibrant with a strong emphasis on youth ministries and community outreach. Their youth programs were very active and robust and the girls were immediately interested in participating in them. They found them to be interesting and encouraging. These programs afforded them the opportunity to get acquainted with their peers and develop some strong friendship bonds that they still cherish today. With this electrifying spiritual wave permeating the atmosphere, we were on a spiritual high and believed that we were experiencing a little taste of heaven on earth in our new environment. Compared to our former environment with its prevalent corruption and crime from the surrounding city life, this new environment exuded a more celestial vibe. Consequently, our spiritual relationship was recharged and revived in this spiritually nurturing climate.

Reflecting on this leap of faith exerted with this decision to relocate and start over, I thank God for this opportunity and for giving me the motivation and fortitude to uproot myself from my comfort zone and venture out with Him in faith not knowing what to expect, but trusting that He knows what is best for me. I haven't regretted it yet as I look back and see how God was preparing me for the vision that He gave me, as well as restoring me day by day. I'm claiming the restoration promised in the Bible for everything taken and stolen during this overwhelming experience with fraud and identity theft (Joel 2:25,26 - KJV), and I see the process of restoration that God is taking me through even today. Similar to the story in the book of Job where God doubly restored Job with everything that he lost in his ordeal, I'm claiming that same promise for the girls and me today and see God doing it in His timing and His way. Even though we suffered great material and financial loss from the fraud and theft, we also suffered considerable emotional loss as we witnessed Satan destroy our family and compromise some of our core relationships with some of our friends and family through this perfidious ordeal. The lack of genuine and optimal support from some of these individuals was equally disturbing and painful as well. Nevertheless, God was restoring us emotionally, socially, mentally, and spiritually in our new environment and He truly proved to be my strong tower that I could run to and be safe from the malicious climate the girls and I faced from time to time. Amidst the distressing circumstances we weathered along with the embarrassment we withstood in certain situations from the lies and fraud, I came to know God like David in Psalm 3:3 as the "lifter up of my head". As a child of God, I am reminded in Joel 2:26, Romans 10:11, Isaiah 54:4, and Isaiah 45:17 (just to name a few) that I need not ever feel humiliated or ashamed because my God is always working on my behalf and I will come out exonerated and the victor in the end. Although the process of waiting to be vindicated can be grueling and seem like foever, the suffering is noted to be well worth the wait in the end when we recount the stories of Joseph and Job (two of the best examples in the Bible where two individuals innocently suffered, but were remarkably vindicated in the end after waiting patiently for their deliverance).

During this waiting period, character is built, faith is strengthened and patience is developed. It is in this interval of waiting on God that one learns the importance of just ceasing from all activity and freeing oneself of all distractions to acknowledge God's presence (Psalm 46:10). The confusion and noise of society is arrested momentarily as one transitions and escapes to a place of placidity. This moment of meditation and repose allows one to recalibrate mentally, emotionally, spiritually, and physically. This recalibration allows one to meet the day's tasks recharged and rejuvenated so that productivity is optimal. I must confess that I'm still mastering this waiting process, but I will say that I'm shocking myself at times while under this character reconstruction as I see some of the positive changes in me that God is maneuvering as He forms me into the masterpiece He desires. This reminds me of the song by Danny Gokey (another favorite artist) - ***Masterpiece.***

In this interval of waiting, I also learned that my frustrations from being at a standstill with seeking legal assistance in my current entanglement were all a part of God's design as I reflect on Exodus 14:14. Because of all the missing pieces in the current fraudulent puzzle I was in, it was almost impossible to find a starting point to even begin a legal pursuit in order to get some direction in this case. But I see now that God was telling me to just be still because He was going to fight for me. Therefore, any headway in this dilemma was going to be His doing anyway; I just didn't know if He was going to move independently or through me. Nevertheless, the standstill I found myself in at the time confirmed that this was a time to halt from all of my efforts (at least at this time) and to wait on God and only move when He instructed me to do so. He would fight for me as He had been doing all along. And, because He is the Captain Who has never lost a battle, I was in the best hands with a sure victory anticipated in His timing. Now that I've digressed for a moment as I shared our new location, we'll go back to the scene for this book's storyline - Atlanta, GA, and we'll discuss the relocation to Huntsville, AL later on in the sequel.

Chapter 12

~~~

AUTHENTIC MINISTRY

Now I know this title is puzzling to some, but all ministry doesn't stem from a genuine desire to solely meet someone's needs and be a blessing. The motivation is skewed at times and often contingent on receiving recognition and acclaim, or in some instances, financial gain. In some cases, all three of these are sought after when engaging in a ministry of some kind. In terms of financial gain, some individuals may establish a nonprofit as their job and be more interested in the business aspect than the ministry aspect. You might be tempted to say that this distinction is pointless because as long as someone is doing something good, it really doesn't matter how they truly feel or what their motivation is because, at the end of the day, needs are being met and, therefore, the mission is being accomplished so everything is co-pacetic. However, God has something different to say in 1 Corinthians 13 where He informs us that any deed - no matter how big or small - done devoid of love is meaningless. In other words, just because we can check this task off of our "to-do" list of good deeds done on occasion doesn't mean we're batting one thousand or that it's acceptable by

God as a genuinely good deed. Our motivation for doing the deed is what counts. If recognition and acclaim are the motivation when participating in community outreach and ministry, it is not genuine and this mindset, which tends to suggest a merit system for one's spirituality, is spiritually precarious. The Bible tells us in Matthew 6:1-4 that being seen or recognized should not be the focus when doing a good deed. It should be done to help someone and to be a blessing. To think any differently - especially along the lines of a merit system where we could appear inherently good or altruistic, or where we could possibly earn salvation - is dismissive to the cross and the plan of salvation. In Romans 3:10 (KJV), it reiterates the fact that no one is righteous and therefore, the good deeds that we do are considered to be as filthy rags according to Isaiah 64:6 - KJV. If we were independently capable of being righteous, there would have been no need for Calvary and the plan of salvation.

In any event, God was speaking to me in this faith bootcamp that I found myself in with the setbacks, misfortunes, losses, and overall disappointments I had suffered. He was using these vicissitudes in my life to allow me to see and experience the browner grass that was on the other side of my fence when I was growing up as a child so that I would be able to relate and empathize with individuals in less favorable environments than I was accustomed to as a child. During my upbringing in my immediate family, I wasn't familiar with financial deprivation, divorce, single parenting, or homes without Christ. I was raised in a christian home by both parents and my father was a surgeon. I had no idea that those facts alone were not the norm for a minority family like mine (especially at that time), and especially one that was African american. Furthermore, because of the affluent neighborhood which was predominantly minority that I grew up in, I was led to believe that most people - including minorities - lived the same. I wasn't familiar with the vast ongoing economic and unethical disparities in society that minorities struggled with daily for the most part. Although I had peers from all walks of life, I wasn't always aware of their living arrangements because my family always invited friends and family over our house and my mom was always hosting the dinners because she loved to do this. Consequently, our house was the hotspot after church or after some of the school activities because my parents enjoyed entertaining and mingling socially and we had socials or game nights over our house frequently. I chuckle when I recount some of these socials at our house because I remember times when all of the teenagers would be upstairs knocked out (sleep) when it approached midnight. But our parents, on the other hand, would be just starting to come alive after midnight and we would hear shrieks of laughter as they engaged in their card games of Rook to the wee hours of the morning. It seemed like the roaring of laughter and merriment went on all night long as we teenagers - the youth - were upstairs snoring our lives away. My parents were real party animals with no alcohol or substances involved - just pure christian fun. At any rate, I learned later that my upbringing was considered a "privileged" lifestyle that was not typical for most minorities like myself. And, although this background placed me in an elite category by default, I didn't focus on this because my parents taught me that my value was not based on what I had in my hand or pocket, but what I had in my head and heart instead. They also taught me that my worth is appraised at Calvary where God's inexplicable investment in His treasure (us) was made through the gift of His Son's death. The importance of this relationship with God was emphasized as everlasting while material things were not because of their transient nature - here today and gone tomorrow as we were learning in our setback at the time. Our current situation proved this to be true, and the girls and I were very aware that we only withstood the mind blowing and life changing turbulence in our lives because our foundation was steadfast and solid. This foundation was not in the Rock of Gibraltar, but in the Rock of Ages - Jesus Christ.

Well, as I redirect back to the title of this chapter, I realize that God used this tragedy to allow me to walk in the shoes of others who had experienced some serious life struggles and felt that they were all alone and sometimes abandoned. By doing this, I was able to authentically understand how they felt and what they were going through. These struggles were magnified after my divorce, which resulted in some alienation from some family and friends. And although these struggles vary for different individuals, God allowed me to experience multiple struggles so I would be able to understand diverse situations and circumstances. Consequently, I was confronted with struggles on all levels - professional, spiritual, social, and financial. And, despite my misfortune, I was not to think that it was strange as 1 Peter 4:12-16 emphasizes. Instead, I was to recognize that as a child of God, tribulations and trials come with the territory and I must learn to glorify God in spite of them. Besides teaching me perseverance and spiritual stamina in adversity, God was divinely orchestrating things to equip and qualify me for the ministry He impregnated me with in this struggle. He intentionally had me navigate through this arduous journey in order to discover the ministry He envisioned for me, as well as to help me understand the plight of those financially deprived and destitute so that I could discover the loopholes that are prevalent in the social system in efforts to fill them, which would only then begin to make a difference. This was crucial if I was passionate about advocating for those in need. I couldn't begin to help if I didn't know where help was needed or what needed to be done. It was equally important that I know how to help. Because my ministry's mission targets broken individuals and broken relationships, the focus is broad. With this far-reaching and all-inclusive purview, individuals from all walks of life are included. It doesn't matter what an individual's financial or socioeconomic status is because there are needs that go beyond financial. These needs encompass the emotional, mental, social, and spiritual needs of individuals, which are independent of one's financial status. Therefore, this ministry embraces anyone broken - male or female and privileged or underprivileged.

As I ruminate on my upbringing, I acknowledge that I lived a sheltered life in general which blinded me occasionally from many of the prevalent social burdens in our society. In addition to being oblivious to these societal woes and their pervasiveness, I was also unaware of the challenges and shortcomings in the system to resolve these overwhelming encumbrances of suffering, dysfunction, and hardship. I was clearly in another world or a bubble, and a reality check was mandatory for my God-endorsed assignment. Devoid of these life challenges and experiences, I would not be relatable or half as effective in this calling God had on my life. Nor would I be credible or resourceful in reaching and impacting my targeted future clientele. Realizing this, I knew that the best way for me to be equipped and qualified for the task was to experience some of these disadvantages and conflicts personally. Therefore, God allowed me to suffer identity theft, insurance fraud, dejection, betrayal, financial instability, and residential instability. Along with these misfortunes, I was also subjected to a violent one-time episode of intimate partner violence where I experienced a close call with being history. It was during these struggles and others that I learned to relate to many of the societal issues I sought to relieve. These experiences allowed me to understand and sympathize with individuals in dire circumstances and financial crises, but also helped me to empathize with them because I had suffered similar hardships and setbacks. My ability to empathize with individuals in these situations authenticated me as an advocate in a powerful way and prepared me for my role in the ministry God was soon to birth through me.

Looking back on my perception of pain and suffering during my childhood and adolescence, I realize now that my lifestyle had me detached - for the most part - from the gravity of suffering that was all around me and that plagues the society that we live in today. As mentioned above, I had to become familiar with these social woes if I really wanted to help. Therefore, I had to get a real clue of what was really going on and "walk a mile in someone else's shoes" as Mary T. Lathrap states in her poem. I realized that no one would even listen to someone like me who lived in a bubble essentially all of my life and was out of touch with the real world. It was absolutely necessary for me to undergo this brutally authentic faith bootcamp in my adulthood during this ongoing trial that I was facing at the time. I had to taste the bitter flavor of society's concoction of deprivation, unethical disparities, and overall injustices so that I could at least get a peephole into someone else's life who was socially and financially deprived. As I stated previously, the setbacks and hostilities that the girls and I faced, were part of God's process of equipping and qualifying me for the mission He assigned me. Through this process, I would gain wisdom, understanding, and grace concerning the various walks of life.

The travesties and corruption the girls and I faced eventually caused us to hit rock bottom after experiencing identity theft and being defrauded. Following these experiences, we were not only able to sympathize, but to empathize as well. This ability to empathize with those I desired to help would allow me to transform lives in a remarkable and most impactful way. In essence, God was communicating to me the power of true authentic ministry and transforming my heart into a heart like His where altruism always resides. As a child who was painfully disturbed when I witnessed anyone emotionally hurt, distraught, or suffering from deprivation in the sheltered world I lived in, I was eager to be in a position now as an adult to be able to do something to help. With the vision God gave me, I realize that this can be done on a large scale, which is even more motivating. I emphasize "large scale" because the ministry God was growing in me and about to birth through a nonprofit organization would be expansive and far-reaching. I was already accustomed to routinely engaging in community outreach events and also helping individuals on an independent and personal level, as well as a professional level in my practice of obstetrics and gynecology when I saw a need. However, this would be different because this ministry would be more focused on these social needs and less of the clinical. I would not resign from medicine, but would be passionately involved in this new ministry also. Having this separate ministry with its specific focus, I would now be able to do things on a more broad and universal scale where more lives would be impacted. To say that I was thrilled when I received this vision from

God would be an understatement, and I'm even more excited today as I think about the lives God will impact and forever change in a positive way through this ministry. Similar to a salesperson that has to be familiar with the product being sold to effectively sell it, I had to be familiar with what I was trying to sell in this ministry in order to be credible and compelling at the same time. As I sat back and allowed these thoughts to marinate one morning, several thoughts raced through my mind. How did I navigate successfully through these dark seasons in my life and actually come out stronger? I had a story to tell of God's amazing grace that saw me through it all and not only brought me out as a survivor, but as a conqueror as well. With God as the Captain of my ship, I was able to successfully and victoriously weather the turbulent and fierce storms in my life without sinking; but, on the contrary, to emerge emotionally and spiritually intact. As a matter of fact, I am more spiritually robust today because of these storms. Sharing my story through this authentic ministry that God was soon to birth through me would be life transforming and powerful. And, having this story to share gives my ministry an authentic touch that strengthens its ability to positively transform lives by constructively redirecting one's attitude, restoring hope, revamping purpose and favorably rehabilitating one's character. And just think, my story is not complete even today because the loose ends have yet to be tied up and the ultimate restoration is even at the door.

Chapter 13

INSIGHT GAINED

ONE DAY WHILE quietly reflecting on some of the interesting encounters and disturbing discoveries that confronted me along this journey of turmoil, I found myself repeatedly rehashing the pain and anguish I felt from being mistreated, defrauded, and essentially betrayed. My feelings were still ripe because the fraud was ongoing and sinking the girls and I into a deeper and yet deeper abyss of financial and social distress. The continual shenanigans and fraud we encountered were financially paralyzing and socially distressing for us - to say the least. As I sat there that day and mulled over everything that had taken place thus far during this journey, it became crystal clear that these things didn't happen by coincidence as I concluded earlier on. Instead, things started appearing very intentional and calculated. As aforementioned, this whole ordeal appeared to be a nefarious concoction targeted against me with the motive of selfish gain high on the list too. Why someone would devise this unscrupulous and dishonest sham was painfully disturbing. In any event, during this time of deep thought for me, I allowed God to speak to me and give me inspiration in my moment of heartache and sorrow as new insight was gained. I contemplated the many disappointing times where I was misjudged, misunderstood, ridiculed and abandoned in my time of grief. In these times of grief, there appeared to be literally no one who understood what I was going through. And then there were some friends and family who had some clue of what was going on, but chose to remove themselves from the scene altogether offering no genuine support or help during this hardship. Nevertheless, while sitting there pondering all of these lonely and despondent times, I heard God's voice speak to me reminding me that He was all that I needed and that He would never abandon or forsake me. During this meditative window in time, I allowed God to minister to my spirit and give me a mysterious peace as I redirected my focus from my circumstances and placed it on Him - my Jehovah Shalom (Source of peace) and my Resource Center for every need. I was activating the promise of Isaiah 26:3 and a tranquility came over me that I could not explain as I took my mind off this alarming snafu I was entangled in at the time.

Over the next several days of pondering things more intensely, I began to discern the personal attack involved in this conundrum as I recalled verbal and emotional assaults on my character as a physician, parent, and businesswoman. Whoever was involved was not just interested in monetary gain by fraud, but also fixed on destroying my character and me as a person. Hence, this ongoing and organized corruption involving my PII and BII appeared to be more of a personal attack. The falsifications, fraud, theft, and lies were overwhelming and extremely hurtful and I wondered how anyone could even do such a thing. But then I remembered that this battle wasn't really personal, but spiritual instead. I was engaged in all out spiritual warfare, so there was no need to take anything personally. This had absolutely nothing to do with me, but everything to do with Christ. And, being an advocate for Christ, I knew that I would face much opposition from Satan - Christ's loyal foe. He would not leave one effort unemployed to rain on my spiritual journey with his intent to discourage and defeat me. The Bible exposes his agenda or M.O. in John 10:10 (KJV - King James Version translation), which states that he only seeks to steal, kill and destroy as I mentioned before. This exposure reveals him to be the real culprit or enemy behind the scenes of this corruption. And this was evident when I reminisced about that memorable morning when I witnessed the forces of evil being unleashed in my household firsthand and saw Satan's hand as the source of the violence and toxicity that provoked my husband to almost end my life. The infernal and wicked forces in the noxious milieu that morning took advantage of my husband's momentary vulnerability and manipulated his uncontrolled emotions causing them to escalate, which triggered that life-threatening act. This is a perfect example of the importance of being ever ready and armoured spiritually to prevent being susceptible to demonic manipulation by the enemy with the baleful repercussions involved. This spiritual armor is the word of God, which highlights the importance of one's devotional life. One's daily devotion time can be lifesaving as it was for me that epic morning. Because my spiritual connection was intact and fully charged that morning from my routine morning devotion time, God had an invincible current permeating the atmosphere that served to thwart Satan's attack later that morning and I was spiritually armed and ready to fight.

As I gained more insight, I also realized that more than one person was involved in this financial hanky panky and the suspects were not strangers. This was obvious with some of the personal attacks and also with the perpetual nature of things. The fact that every move I made to acquire more information was mysteriously blocked when I attempted to get more information on the discoveries being made at the time, was highly suspicious and gave me an inkling of concern that some internal and closely related foul play was definitely responsible for this. The alias names associated with my personal and professional identifiable information pointed to someone closely connected to me also and not just some random offender who I didn't even know. Instead, it was someone I knew, and probably knew well, which only served to complicate matters more. However, regardless of what my intuition led me to surmise, I was clear that I would need some concrete evidence to validate my thoughts and views in this matter. So, I was back to my old familiar place along this journey. I was back to square one with exercising patience and just learning to wait on God. This was not the preferred position I desired, nor was it a comfortable position during this difficult time; nevertheless, it was the position God chose for me at this unusual time in my life, so I acquiesced.

It was in this moment of stillness that I gained much insight and understanding that gave me guidance in this puzzling ordeal. As I stated above, I realized that the main culprits were no strangers to me and I almost didn't want to know exactly who they were, or any of the others involved for that matter. My reservations to expose the culprits stemmed from a dreaded feeling of who I might discover. In short, I was thinking along the lines of minimizing the emotional blow from discovering the involvement of someone close to me. This revelation I knew would be devastating and heart breaking. In essence, it would be too close to home.

Besides being hurtful, I knew that the revelations would call for some confrontation, which I was not a fan of secondary to the strife and discord involved. Therefore, I did everything I could to dismiss the divine discernment that began to open my eyes in this enigma. Although this enlightenment was helpful and revealing, I knew that it would warrant some form of confrontation which I dreaded. So, I harbored mixed emotions as I received new insight in this ordeal because although I wanted things to come to an immediate end, I was also reluctant to deal with the individuals that would be exposed and the disappointment and pain I would experience when things finally surfaced. However, from the beginning I had clues and some confirmation as you recall in the various discoveries made that were discussed in previous chapters. God revealed to me that the players in this game of deception were not strangers, but someone I knew instead, and He did this gently. Afterall, this was God's battle - not mine. I also knew over time as the Bible plainly says numerous times throughout its multiple books, what is done in the dark, will come to the light if it is not confessed and forgiven. It's just a matter of time.

Chapter 14

———— ⚬⚬ ————

A Recap With A Snapshot And Charge

UNFORTUNATELY, IN THAT game changing moment when my life took another course as things abruptly shifted that day, the girls and I watched these spiritual powers take control of my husband who was defenseless and powerless in his spiritually unarmored state. My husband's spiritual gas tank was on "empty" that morning and the Devil exploited this vulnerability that was exposed. In my husband's spiritual weakness at that moment, the Devil wielded his infernal influence through him and tried to kill me. Because my husband was not in his right mind considering the circumstances, he became an available puppet or conduit for the Devil to employ that day in a life threatening fashion. He also was without his spiritual armor, and thus, an easy target for the Devil to manipulate. Throughout our marriage, physical abuse was not part of the equation, so I was completely stunned with the domestic incident witnessed that morning. Sure, I had seen him get angry, but he had never attempted to physically harm me before. And although we disagreed with each other on occasion, harsh altercations with physical involvement were not our routine. Nonetheless, that morning he apparently snapped and the atmosphere instantly turned toxic. Consequently, our family unit was destroyed and the girls and I had to move on and start a new life on our own. Even though this was the wisest and safest thing for us to do at the time, it was also the toughest thing to do because I loved my husband and didn't want to just abandon him in his obvious time of need. But, the circumstances dictated this decision to guarantee the safety of the girls and me, which was my utmost priority at the time. Therefore, relocating was not an option for us, but a necessity as we immediately detached from our malignant surroundings to avoid any precarious outcomes. My "fight or flight" response was triggered in that instant and I dauntlessly executed this task to uproot from our current environment and leave in order to ensure that the girls and I were out of harm's way. Nothing but God's grace and abiding presence allowed me to take this bold stand and to execute such a formidable gesture with this sudden shift from our norm. Reflecting on this incident, I see how we were literally on our own at that point. Since family support for us locally was nonexistent because my siblings and mother lived out of town (my father was deceased), it would be a lonely journey for the girls and me. Chicago, where they resided at the time, was no hop, skip and a jump away from Georgia where we resided, and other relatives lived out of town as well. So, this initial phase of our journey would be a lonely one for us, because although family came to visit from out of town on occasion, we had no local family support, and thus, were alone for the most part. However, in the end, we grew closer because of it.

At any rate, as I reflect on how our world was fiercely shaken that day, causing our stability, normality, and security to be thrown up in shambles, I unreservedly acknowledge even to this day that the only reason I was able to stand through all of this was because God planted my feet on solid ground. By yielding to God that morning, my mental, emotional, spiritual, and physical homeostasis were sure and I experienced an inexplicable peace despite Satan's intent to leave me mentally, emotionally, and spiritually bankrupt by this catastrophic event, and eventually nonexistent. What a chilling thought! Totally infernal in nature.

Despite this malignant incident that changed my life, I clung to God's promise in Isaiah 26:3 which kept my mind and spirit in perfect peace from that day forward in spite of all the chaos introduced into my life that day and thereafter. Observing my husband in his inebriated and confused state that morning, I realized that our marriage was in a woebegone state and desperately warranted Christian counseling. Regrettably, it was too late at that point to salvage the bond that had been abruptly severed that morning. It was obvious that constructive coping mechanisms needed to be established and implemented in lieu of the destructive habits being employed to deal with stress - alcohol. It was at these times that I found God to be an ever-present Help in trouble as the promise says in Psalm 46:1.

One particular afternoon, about two years before the domestic incident, I was pondering over the problematic issues in my marriage after having my morning devotion earlier that day and suddenly became mentally and emotionally saturated in despair. Our marriage had become spiritually bankrupt and the estrangement that had taken place over time, along with the apathetic attitude in the marriage was extremely disheartening and frustrating as well. We had literally become like two ships passing in the night, yet acting as if everything was copacetic. I'm still not sure to this day what came over me that triggered what happened next, but I made the decision to just leave. At that point, I concluded that I had enough and had reached my limit of just coexisting in an unequally yoked spiritual relationship. I planned to take the kids and seek another temporary residence until I figured out the next move. While vacillating over these thoughts of leaving, I decided to share my plans with a family member who challenged this idea. This family member suggested that I ask my husband to leave instead of the kids and me. He didn't see the prudence in the kids and me being uprooted from our stable environment instead of my husband as the man of the house, and I agreed. He advised me to explain to my husband that I needed time alone to think and process all that was going on in our marriage at the time. I also had plans to propose that we get christian counseling because of the poor communication I observed in our relationship and the strong indifference I noticed over time.

Along with this family member's advice to ask my husband to leave instead of the kids and me, he went on further to suggest that I discard any alcohol that I came across in the house. Now, this is where I had a problem with the advice. It doesn't take a rocket scientist to deduce that this would have triggered a World War III where absolute mayhem on a domestic platform would have erupted. The Bible clearly speaks against provocation, and this action would have definitely evoked an unpleasant response, to put it mildly. For this reason, I did not comply with the suggestion proposed, but prayed for God's guidance instead realizing how ridiculous this advice was for me in my current situation. I decided to ask God for a sign on what to do at this point because I was reminded that spiritual things are spiritually discerned (1 Corinthians 2:14 KJV) and the advice I received that afternoon was not spiritual. Therefore, I would ask God for a sign if I should follow through with initiating this temporary separation from my husband. If God did not agree with this plan, He would persuade my husband to join me for devotion in our bedroom that afternoon. On the other hand, if he didn't ask to join me in devotion while I was in this valley of decision at the moment, that would be my sign to ask him for space and for a separation. Now, I'll give some context to this specific sign I was asking God for that day. It was midday at this time on the weekend and we had already had our morning devotion much earlier. I just saw the need for another one that day in this dilemma and wanted to see if he would join me realizing the need as well which would have been very unusual for us in the spiritual bankruptcy we were experiencing then in our marriage. So, this would be a definite sign if it turned out positive. Well, as fate had it, he came in the bedroom and sat at the foot of the bed on my side and tearfully looked at me and humbly asked if he could join me in devotion. Tears filled my eyes as I nodded my head in acceptance of his request and we hugged and prayed together once it was over. Mysteriously, I don't recall any of the content of the devotion that day, but I honestly felt that the onset of spiritual healing had taken effect.

From that day forward, I would frequently see him on his knees in prayer in the morning and at bedtime. He even consented to join this support group at the church helping individuals to stop harmful habits (e.g. smoking, drinking, etc.) and I accompanied him there. The facilitator stressed that this group was open to anyone trying to break a bad habit, which made the group more inclusive. At that point, anyone could join because we all have a bad habit or two (or three) that we need to break (Romans 3:23). As far as things were concerned, it looked like we were on the right path now - addressing all of our marital concerns. Where things went wrong, I couldn't tell you - I'm no heart or mind reader. I just remained hopeful and prayerful as his supportive wife until that morning when he snapped. Prior to that occurrence, I resolved to stay put after getting my message from God that I needed to stay - at least for the time being. However, after our domestic setback, God gave me an unequivocal message that I needed to leave without hesitation and move on. I had done all that I could do as a concerned and encouraging spouse with the estrangement that had become glaringly evident at this time in our marriage and the children would see this later on as well. The friction in the atmosphere that morning represented the culmination of several years of indifference. Apathy had raised its ugly head and climaxed with feelings going awry that day. On that account, it behooved me to exercise tough love and move on to allow him to see that he needed to get help. This was one of the most important decisions that I ever had to make, and I realize to this day that this decision was life-saving for the girls and me because we had experienced a life-threatening event. Put simply, I was a victim of attempted murder. I wouldn't say it was premeditated or even intentional (I hope not) because it was enacted under the influence of alcohol. Sounds preposterous, I know, but as the popular saying goes, "It is what it is". I'm not proud or happy about this experience - heavens no! I'm just a believer in being transparent and pragmatic when necessary. So, our choice to disconnect and start anew was timely and prudent. Let us pause for a minute here and emphasize knowing when to leave. When things become life-threatening, it's time to leave for sure, although when signs are revealed earlier on that have potential to lead to a life-threatening event over time, things become imminent to leave then in order to assure a harmless departure by not waiting until things become toxic. Although these thought processes are both on point, I admonish anyone in these circumstances to pray and allow God to navigate you through the process of leaving because I realize transportation, money, family support, or a safe place may be difficult to obtain. Then again, all four of these exigencies could serve as an impediment for someone trying to leave if they all are lacking or unavailable. This is when Divine intervention becomes critical and life-saving because it will help to connect the dots and fill the loopholes. God is just a prayer away.

Another pause is warranted here as I speak to those with religious convictions that support not leaving your spouse for any reason at all. I completely hold the marital bond to be sacred, holy, and blessed by God when He is at the center. When this bond excludes Him, however, trouble tends to set in and the bond is weakened and tainted. This exclusion of God removes His protective hedge, which can leave one in harm's way. At any time one's life becomes threatened (husband or wife), that individual must do the safe thing and leave. Being a martyr for your spouse in a malignant relationship by being complacent with the present hostility gives no glory to God and perpetuates this deplorable social cycle and problem. Hence, the passion I have with fulfilling the vision God gave me where I see myself as an advocate to help alleviate this tragedy for those who have no resources and no one to help so that leaving becomes difficult to nonexistent. By the way, in the vision I see myself as an advocate not only for the victim, but for the perpetrator as well. That's right! As aforementioned in one of the earlier chapters of this book, there is no way to decrease and ultimately remove this grave societal concern without getting to the root of the problem, and the root is the perpetrator for all practical purposes. Sure, the recipient (the victim, survivor, or conqueror) can undergo counseling for self-esteem and decision-making issues, but sometimes these are not issues and yet, the individual can still end up in one of these predicaments. In this case, Christian counseling is helpful to assure the individual that there is an "ever present Help in trouble" as Psalm 46:1 says, and this Help (God Almighty) is always available. I'm told that He never sleeps or slumbers Psalm 121:3,4 and promises to be with us through any adversity. In fact, He admonishes us not to be afraid or dismayed because He promises to be our Strength and Help in these desperate times. Hallelujah! I remember a time earlier on in the beginning of this journey when I hired a personal investigator because of my safety concerns. This was an expensive investment and I learned later to say like David in Psalm 4:8, as I paraphrase, that I will lay down and sleep in perfect peace without an ounce or iota of fear or anxiety because God alone will keep me safe and in perfect peace without a doubt. So when plagued by trepidation and worry, commit Psalm 4:8 to memory and stand on it! I'm not a preacher, but I feel like preaching right about now. In essence, it's like David said in Psalm 23:1 - "The Lord is my Shepherd, I shall not want." (KJV). He is sufficient. In fact, He is more than enough - He is our everything. The message in Hebrews 13:5,6 suggests that because God is always with us, we need not fear what man can do to us. And for anyone who feels that their current status is a no-win situation, look up and let God hear your heartfelt prayer to give you insight, wisdom, and direction. Being a martyr for the gospel or any "worthy" cause is one thing, but being a martyr in a hostile environment without an honorable cause is another thing. If marital counseling has been inefficacious and circumstances are beginning to appear hopeless and worse than usual, then one's marital options have become minimal at this point and it now behooves the individual to leave before a fatal tragedy ensues. Because the body is God's temple, it must be kept free from harm - physical, emotional, mental, and spiritual. That being said, God would not want anyone to stay in a hostile or menacing environment that has potential to lead to a fatal situation. I'll pause and digress for a moment to stress that this is not just relating to physical harm, but to emotional, mental, or spiritual devastation also that may be prevalent in the home environment and can consequently kill the spirit and cripple one's calling in Christ. Nevertheless, I'll focus on timely leaving right now as I share my experience with you. My decision was made right after that nearly fatal incident when my life was almost snuffed out. I made this decision with God's help and stood firm on it claiming Psalm 121 daily. This incident spoke volumes of the lethal state of things at that time, and even though God blocked this potential fatality, it was a very close call. Hence, vacillation has no place in these hostile circumstances. Instead, an undaunted decision has to made as one steps out in faith and leaves. You have to trust that God is going to take care of you and act. As you recall, the girls and I packed up after his arrest that day, and by the next day, we were gone. In some instances, warning signs will be evident and the time to leave will come before toxicity sets in, which is ideal. Nonetheless, although I left and didn't turn back, I made sure that I kept him in our prayers during our family worship. I also asked God to free him from Satan's relentless and merciless manipulation and to give him a change of heart. And over time when the tension settled down after this domestic mishap and the lines of communication normalized somewhat between the two of us again, I told him how the girls and I prayed for his deliverance daily from the time we left because we were genuinely concerned about his well being.

As the weeks and months went by and discoveries were unfolding as mentioned in earlier chapters, I came to the conclusion that this was no random hacker or charlatan as previously stated, but someone I had done business with before or knew personally. At this moment of discovery, I had to stop, breathe, and exhale as I struggled to hold back the tears that began to swell in my eyes. My survival mode kicked in just then and I fought my emotions as I continued perusing through the internet and paperwork to see what else I could find. Finally being able to connect some of the dots in this mystifying puzzle was fulfilling, but troubling as well. Although I was getting some closure on some things, I was also becoming emotionally disturbed and devastated with the facts that were now emerging. I realized that through this misfortune God was teaching me how to unconditionally love - one of His greatest gifts. Consequently, He had given me a forgiving spirit and suffused my heart with His unconditional love for this imposter. However, I knew that for forgiveness to be experienced in toto, this imposter would have to acknowledge his wrong, confess it, and make amends or reconcile. From the time of these discoveries until now, I have been praying to this end.

Chapter 15

***

LIFE'S GREATEST GIFT

WHEN I WAS growing up as a child, I remember singing a hit song during that time titled, "What the World Needs Now is Love" by Jackie DeShannon. This song was so upbeat and positive that it seemed to create a cathartic wave wherever it was played. Listening to this song today in my adulthood, I realize the truth in the lyrics of this profound song. I couldn't agree more that we definitely need more love and that, ironically, it's the one thing that there's just too little of in this world as the lyrics point out. We have way too much violence, hate, jealousy, corruption, and strife while love - the true essential - is lacking. Instead of infiltrating the world with these poisons, we should be intentional and passionate about infusing the world with love. However, if we're honest, there are times we don't feel so lovey dovey, and this is fine because we're not asked to be overly affectionate, just kind. Of course we need our daily devotionals to fuel our empty spiritual tanks with God's unconditional love in order to love others. Therefore at this time in my life with all that was going on, I was even more intentional about maintaining my connection with the power Source and Resource Center of this unconditional love - God.

As a child, I was fond of another song that I sang often in church school and church that spoke about love and its importance in the life of a christian. The name of the song is "They'll know we are christians" by Peter Scholtes. In the lyrics, he writes that others will know we are christians by our love, which is powerful because, in essence, it gets back to what we discussed earlier in 1 Corinthians 13. As a refresher, this chapter in 1 Corinthians reveals what genuine love is and what it is not. In essence, it's not the outward display of benevolence. In other words, as this chapter reveals, an individual can give everything they own to the poor and even be a martyr for the underprivileged of society, but without love, it is not genuine and means nothing. In essence, these benevolent acts alone don't define love because they can be performed without an ounce of love, and instead, just be done for recognition and acclaim or just performed out of a sense of duty. This is when Satan insidiously persuades one to believe in a merit system that promotes good deeds as a way of earning salvation. However, this is obviously a distorted belief because the Bible points out that in our carnal natures we are devoid of unconditional love. Thus, we are totally incapable of doing good deeds that are genuine without God, Who is the sole Source of love and every good deed. The Bible goes on further to expound in Isaiah 64:6, and I reiterate from the previous chapter, that all of our good deeds are as filthy rags anyway because of our sinful natures, so we need God's love in order to really be genuinely loving towards others. It's not something naturally ingrained in us. It comes from God. Furthermore, if there was a merit system that we could easily comply with that would earn us salvation, Calvary would have been pointless as aforementioned. We could have earned our own salvation. But we know this is farcical because the sacrifice offered to pay the penalty for sin had to be unblemished, untainted, and essentially, perfect - all the traits that we lack and that point solely to Christ - our perfect Sacrifice. Therefore, there is no merit system. We just need God - desperately! He alone can infuse us with the love that looks beyond the faults of those who harm and mistreat us so that we can see their needs instead, which is what I needed to do in my current situation. This reminds me of an old familiar song that I'll mention later whose lyrics convey this message. Anyway, I realized that the needs of these individuals who intentionally hurt and misused the girls and me spanned from their brokenness and emptiness that desperately cried for healing and God's love. So, as you can see, there's wisdom in the old adage that says hurt people, hurt people. While digesting this well known proverb one day, a liberating feeling came all over me and immediately freed me from my feelings of grief and despair because of the mistreatment I had suffered. This enlightenment opened my heart and mind to the spiritual eyesight that God was conveying to me in that moment. Instead of feeling sorry for myself or being disappointed and angry with these individuals who were mistreating and exploiting me, I was able to focus on their needs and pray for their deliverance and healing from brokenness. I refused to harbor feelings of hatred, resentment, and strife in my heart towards them when my spiritual eyesight had unveiled their spiritually vulnerable and crippled condition. Seeing them in this state made me more compassionate towards them because I could see their spiritually hopeless condition and how Satan capitalized on this opportunity to entangle them in his deception and woefully use them for his infernal advantage. Thoughts of vengeance were dispelled as I saw their desperate need of healing and their urgent need of a relationship with Christ. Besides, God says vengeance is His (Romans 12:19) and He will take care of your situation in His time. We must wait, be patient, and trust God to do just what He said. Nevertheless, my perspective in this situation completely changed as I began to focus less on how the girls and I were wrongfully treated and more on how miserably manipulated and controlled the culprits in this mess were all because they were unarmored as discussed earlier. Over time, my practice took a huge hit from the ongoing theft and fraud that forced me to temporarily close the doors and take a hiatus in this financial crisis. In addition to this drama, I was still trying to emotionally, mentally, spiritually and physically rebound from the domestic crisis that occurred around this same time as well. I needed a timeout to process and heal from this ongoing chaos and confusion. During the hiatus I spoke about earlier when I transferred my patients to a colleague who covered for me, I allowed God to comfort and speak to me as He gave me direction in this difficult time.

While I patiently waited, my mind was flooded with a myriad of questions and thoughts concerning the reason behind all of this deception which was mentally and emotionally frustrating and upsetting. On the morning of the incident when Satan tried to snatch my life, I thought this situation was purely a domestic problem that stemmed from unresolved marital issues. But I was sadly mistaken as other facts emerged over time showing differently. The revelations were clear that the duplicity exposed started prior to me even meeting my husband. Hence, my marriage and my husband had nothing to do with the origin and intent of this malicious scheme to destroy my character, career, and credibility because, as stated already, it commenced long before I knew my husband. Although my marriage had its issues, this discovery of doubledealing revealed another ball game altogether. Meditating on all of these facts left me bemused and overwhelmingly distraught. I couldn't fathom such a malicious intent that perpetually raised its ugly head and sporadically wreaked havoc from time to time causing this disheartening journey for the girls and me. This wicked scheme was demoralising in nature and knew no boundaries as it went beyond attacking just me, but my baby girls also without any remorse. If you're asking yourself why the devil would do all of this, I'll remind you and emphasize again what John 10:10 reveals. It states that the devil only comes to steal, kill, and destroy, which is his sole M.O. His fate is sealed with doom, so as far as he is concerned, he would prefer to have some company along life's ride leading eventually to his dismal destiny of destruction because after all, misery loves company. Furthermore, the pain of missing out on heaven in the end, hits him right at his very core because he once resided in heaven as a good angel until he and the angels that he convinced to rebel with him against God, were kicked out (Revelation 12:7-9). Consequently, he knows exactly what he is missing out on and is bitter and remorseful. For us, however, we can only read about the peace, love, and happiness that we'll enjoy there and then meditate on the descriptions we've read about that depict heaven because we have never been there. Because of this, the devil uses every distraction that he can possibly concoct to discredit, invalidate, and rule out heaven for us by dismissing it from our purview altogether. He also attempts to distort the idyllic and blissful nature of our heavenly home in attempts to cause us to be disinterested in going there because he is so miserable that he has forfeited this opportunity for himself. He is no longer welcome there.

At any rate, as God slowly revealed things through my new spiritual eyesight, it was a revelatory game changer for me concerning how I viewed what was going on. With this new perception, I was able to mentally and emotionally process the big picture through my spiritual discernment and love those unconditionally who wished me harm. Glancing back at the domestic mishap that shed light on the unsuspected quagmire of ongoing fraudulence that had the girls and me enmeshed in much hardship and confusion, I changed my perspective and view of this drama. I saw it as spiritual warfare and not as a personal attack. Satan was relentlessly executing all his efforts to block God's intention for my life and he was using whatever vulnerable vessel he could find to achieve his diabolical goal. Unfortunately for me, this just happened to be individuals from my inner circle - people who were close and dear to me. And I knew this was not by mistake or happenstance, but a calculated stratagem contrived by the enemy (the devil) as he painstakingly employed every tactic in the book to seal the demise of my God-given purpose. He was aware that using anyone in this case would be hurtful, but by employing individuals I knew, the pain would be all the more excruciating and heart-wrenching. Also, who else but those closest to me would have access to this information that they could use for their malevolent advantage. However, I was connected to the endless and inexhaustible Source of joy, love and peace - my Elohim, my Jehovah Shammah, and my Jehovah Rophe .... Hallelujah! My pain, consequently, was ephemeral in nature and I was able to weather these storms untainted with the bitterness and resentment that encroach upon the hearts of those exploited, defrauded, and heartlessly ridiculed all because of my endless connection to the One Who is altogether lovely.

Thus, as christians we must manifest the same unconditional love that God shows us despite ourselves. The sacrifice of His Son for our sins revealed the epitome of what selfless and sacrificial love looks like. And the way He still looks past our shortcomings and failures and sees our needs reminds me of the song "He looked beyond my faults and saw my needs" by Dottie Rambo referenced a little earlier. The beautiful words of this song depict the way we should be with others - look beyond their imperfections and see their need for God's love that we as christians are commissioned to show them. From the beginning of our mishap to this present day, I have been intentional with the girls that we avoid harboring any bitter feelings, grudges, or hatred despite our circumstances. I emphasize and stress that although we were defrauded, wrongfully ridiculed, and mistreated, we are obligated as Christians to love unconditionally all the more passionately. And we have maintained this attitude in the midst of the ongoing issues that have yet to be resolved. I informed the girls that what they witnessed that morning as they saw their dad in a state of inexplicable rage, were the forces of evil being unleashed through him - an unarmored human conduit this particular morning. What do I mean by "unarmored"? I'm speaking about being devoid of the spiritual armor every Christian should be equipped with on a daily basis. Ephesians 6:11,12 unveils our enemy who we contend with as soon as our eyelids open. This enemy is the devil, a fallen angel with spiritual powers, who we are no match for without our armor and he has a host of other evil angels with him that carry out his biddings as referenced earlier in Revelation 12:7-9.

These other angels that are his allies are those that were banished from heaven with him. For all of you superhero and Avenger fans, notice how you never see these heroes fighting their foes without their unique gear on. Our gear as christians is described in Ephesians 6:11,12. Of course I know that these intrepid warriors are fictional, but the analogy still emphasizes the importance of being armored and prepared for an enemy at any time. And as christians, we should be just as intentional because of the spiritual warfare we encounter daily with our enemy - the devil. Like this chapter in Ephesians says, "we wrestle not against flesh and blood, but against principalities, against powers, against the rulers of the darkness of this world, against spiritual wickedness in high places" (Ephesians 6: 12). Therefore, our weapons of warfare can't be carnal because these physical weapons are no match for the spiritual powers we are bombarded with on a continual basis. Instead, they have to be "mighty through God to the pulling down of strongholds" as 2 Corinthians 10:4 tells us. We have to align ourselves with the One Who possesses all power in heaven and on earth (Matthew 28:18) - the Omnipotent One. Or shall I say, the real Superhero! My Avenger extraordinaire! Only then can we be victorious as conquerors through Christ.

So looking at the big picture once again through my new spiritual eyesight, I was able to love unconditionally despite the unfounded ridicule, mistreatment, betrayal, and overall chicanery I endured. As God cocooned me in His perfect love and filled the void in my heart from the pain and loneliness experienced due to the disloyalty and deception of these individuals I knew, I was able to heal with time. This healing was vital for me in my preparation to advance to the next spiritual level where God was taking me. Harboring negative feelings from this misfortune would have blocked my blessing and prohibited me from moving forward into the greater that God had in store for me concerning the vision He gave me. It also would have blocked my testimony. How could I tell someone about forgiveness if I didn't forgive those who wrongfully treated me?

Reminiscing on the excursions I had with the girls when we were forced to relocate from the onset of this crisis, I laugh about the fun times we ironically had during this tragedy in our lives and how we grew closer together because of it. Reflecting on these times, I see this as a blessing in the midst of disappointment. Due to the circumstances we were thrust into, we learned to lean on each other as we faced our inevitable new norm where our family unit dwindled down to just the three of us. Though awkward at first, we quickly acclimated and decided to just focus on enjoying and loving each other while waiting on God to fix our mess. Little did we know that there was so much more to mentally and emotionally absorb in our dilemma than we realized. Over time with the discoveries that surfaced, we came to the conclusion that this was no overnight quick fix, but we were in this for the long haul. Accepting this fact, I purposed to just live life fully and enjoy each day as we waited on God. I didn't want to be guilty of putting my life on hold and later suffer the repercussions of time lost. We had no clue that the wait would be this long and enervating, but our "patience" muscles were undergoing weight training, or shall I say, "wait" training. By now, one would assume that we were pretty buff in this area of waiting on God because bafflingly, to this date, we're still anticipating God's intervention in bringing this particular chapter in our lives to an end.

The spiritual maturation that I acquired with this personal and professional setback was another blessing during this difficult time. I was able to connect with the unseen or invisible world in a surreal way that I never would have experienced without this adversity. As a result, I saw the hand of God move on my behalf in miraculous ways that went beyond showing up for me the morning of the near fatal incident. I saw Him show up for me in other difficult situations along this journey as well. Now, I do recall a very amazing phenomenon that occurred years before this particular setback in my life as I've had supernatural experiences before this time in my life. This supernatural encounter I'm speaking of was so spine chilling that I still get goosebumps when talking about it. I was in medical school and not yet married when it happened. It will always be an amazingly unforgettable and epic experience for me. However, it is a discussion for another time as my focus is on the miracles that occurred during this specific time in our lives. Witnessing these twenty-first century miracles during this time was no surprise for us after a while, but rather our norm in this crisis. If you recall, I shared some of these miracles in earlier chapters and I'll share some more now. As I think about this sensitive time in my life, I am amazed how God kept me in perfect peace. One of the biggest miracles during this time was not just my sound mental, emotional, spiritual, and physical well-being throughout this nightmare, but the mental, emotional, and spiritual stability evinced by the girls as well. God upheld us through it all (Isaiah 41:10) and was truly the Lifter of our heads (Psalm 3:3) in spite of the shame, disgrace, and embarrassment Satan tried to cause us in our time of conflict. During this time, we endured many disdainful looks when attending church from those who disagreed with my decision to separate and then ultimately divorce my husband. They criticized me even when they had no idea of the danger we were facing in our situation at the time. They also were devoid of the other facts supporting my decision that became apparent later. Oxymoronically, we were treated at times like we were the culprits for the crisis that caused us much anguish and suffering when we were merely the helpless victims. But through all of the ridicule, misunderstandings, falsifications, and strife, God gave me a heart like His where I could still love unconditionally so that I could bless those who mistreated us and pray for those who despitefully used us as Matthew 5:44 encourages us to do as Christians. The other miracle that was significant was God's protective hedge around the girls and me that exonerated me despite the fabrications hurled against me and the fraudulent shenanigans that were strategically pinned on me via identity theft. I didn't dare discount God's favor on my life during these distressful times - not even for one moment. I knew then and I know now Who is in control and has the final say so. And even today I still praise Him for it. Things definitely could have gone awry were it not for God's omnipotence working in my favor and shielding me from the corruption of being wrongfully blamed for this despicable farce because it was my sensitive information being used after all.

I also was privileged during this time to engage with my girls in an up close and personal manner. As our mother-daughter bond grew stronger, they talked to me about everything and felt uninhibited when sharing. Our close-knit situation fostered this openness and this positive bonding. This rapport established opened doors for me to have heart to heart talks with my girls and to instill precious life pearls and spiritual proverbs into their hearts, minds, and souls. It was my aim during our current misfortune to be a walking, talking, and living example of a true Christian in the midst of our adversity that they could emulate. So I made it my goal to act and not "react" when facing conflict in efforts to demonstrate the Christian way to deal with problems and disagreeable situations. With this positive objective, retaliation was never an option, but unconditional love was the recourse instead. I also strove to persuade them that the greatest relationship one can have in life is not with friends and loved ones, but with God. This priceless relationship trumps all others and gives one an everlasting joy uninfluenced by the world, untainted by corruption, and unmoved by circumstances. It also connects one to all knowledge and wisdom because God alone is omniscient, which makes Him the perfect Navigator for our life journey. Because He is the Waymaker, He can make a way out of no way. And because He is God, there is no mountain, situation, or task that is insurmountable when He is our Ally, Coach and Captain. With this connection, success is inevitable. But even with all of these valuable perks just mentioned from this enviable relationship, the perk yet to be mentioned that surpasses them all in importance is His "everlasting" presence. His omnipresence is promised in Hebrews 13:5,6 which makes this relationship unending - a concept rarely experienced with the separation, divorce, and death that is ubiquitous in this imperfect world. But His relationship transcends this world into our eternal home if we accept Him and His gift of salvation. What a promise and a blessing! The girls were able to directly observe this promise in action along our journey because through it all, God was there for us when we called on Him. And even when we were too despondent at times to initiate or utter a plea for help, He responded to our heartfelt plea for help and provided for us and instilled an inexplicable peace inside of us that defied all logic when considering the chaos, peril, and distress we faced along our journey. In addition to giving us this peace that surpassed all understanding as the Bible describes in Philippians 4:7, He chose to deliver us from troubling situations in some instances and then at other times, He simply encircled us in the midst of the crisis with His protective hedge in lieu of delivering us. This hedge of protection served as our fortified spiritual wall that the enemy could not scale as God sheltered us under His wings. It also served as our lighthouse in our current turbulent storm. Then there were times He would reverse the unfavorable circumstances to favorable ones instead. And even though He didn't always respond when or how we wanted Him to, we trusted that He knew what was best and chose to be satisfied with His way because we knew that He was working things out in the end for our good.

So after digesting everything we were up against in this trial, we came to the conclusion that our greatest weapons to possess in circumstances such as ours include faith, hope, and love - the greatest of these three being love. Sounds familiar? This last line is paraphrased from 1 Corinthians 13:13 (KJV). When we look at the attribute of faith, we are reminded of its indispensable quality in the life of a Christian. No power can be manifested without this vital factor. When recounting the miracles of Jesus, we see how the recipients had to possess this confidence or belief in Jesus in order to receive their miracle or blessing. God stresses that He can't do anything for us when our faith is lacking (James 1:6,7). Delving a little deeper into the significance of this conviction for the believer, the Bible tells us that Jesus informed the disciples that the same power they were privileged to be eyewitnesses of in His life on earth was the very same power available to them. Put another way, He was enlightening them that they could perform the same miracles they saw Him do and cast out demons as well if they had faith. Faith is the prerequisite for the Christian who desires to tap into the supernatural power that God offers every Christian through the gift of the Holy Spirit. Because we exhibited an unshakeable and unmovable faith in God from the onset of this trial and throughout its journey, God sustained us in these tough times and allowed us to weather this fierce 5-tier storm that wrecked our household that memorable morning. And we're still standing today because we utilized this valuable weapon of faith in the spiritual warfare we were engaged in as we described earlier on and we're still using it. Believing that God would see us through this storm as He promised in His word (Psalm 34:19) gave us hope to hold on in spite of how ominous things appeared. In essence, it was our faith that birthed hope. So, here is where the weapon of hope was used to keep us encouraged and to keep us holding on. Devoid of hope, one has nothing. Hope is facing challenging and troubling circumstances optimistically because a brighter and more favorable outcome is anticipated. This is seen with the dutiful father's proclivity for hard work to provide for his indigent family aspiring to be poverty-free consequently some day. It is also witnessed in a single parent's ambition to compensate for the deficiency in the family unit by supplying for all of the children's needs while also raising them to be successful young adults in society. It is that glimmer of expectancy in the eye of a homeless person as pedestrians pass by with inquiring looks, or that spark in an orphan's eye when consideration for adoption is being entertained. One might even observe it in the resilience of a cancer patient that has been given a good prognosis with the treatment plan implemented. Or it can be seen in a response of gratitude on social media from a person acknowledging another person's life line offered in a despairing situation. No matter how it's perceived, hope is essential in life with the strife and woe that is ubiquitous in our world. As a Christian, our undying hope is in a better place - heaven.

Recapitulating on the details of this storm, I'll now explain the 5 areas of attack as I categorized it as a 5-tier storm earlier. Afterwards, I'll expound on the last and greatest weapon - love. These multiple attacks targeted five areas of my life: the personal, professional, financial, social and spiritual areas. As far as the personal attack goes, my identity was stolen and tainted with fraudulent accounts established in my name that created a delinquent history over time. Consequently, my personal credit profile, history, and score were negatively impacted. On a professional level, my medical credentials were compromised and used fraudulently as my insurance reimbursements were stolen causing my practice to sink into a precarious financial abyss that ultimately led to my temporary clinical hiatus. In addition to this, my business identity was attacked by falsifications employed to mar its name and reputation, and my professional name underwent attack from nefarious efforts by these culprits who aimed to tarnish my name and ultimately destroy my career. Surprisingly, these perpetrators were not some random cyber predators, scammers, or con artists as realized earlier in this book. No, unfortunately, these charlatans were those from my inner circle. Recapitulating on the details of the personal and professional attacks of this storm, it becomes clear how these specific attacks contributed to the financial scandal that left me monetarily in shambles. Also, the fact that the perpetrators were individuals in my inner circle, explains the social attack in this storm. It was most upsetting for me when things became clear that individuals I knew were involved and, therefore, could not be supportive, but God never left my side. So, we have the personal, professional, financial, and social attacks. We now will expound on the spiritual attack. From the beginning, I came to recognize the spiritual warfare involved in this five-tier storm; hence, the spiritual attack. But I will take time to expound further on the attack from this angle of the storm - the spiritual aspect. Besides witnessing what felt and looked like a demonic mayhem that morning of the attack, I was also spiritually attacked mentally and emotionally by numerous questions bombarding my psyche concerning the event. The devil tried to tempt me to be angry with God for the hellish tumult that flooded my apartment that morning. As time elapsed, the devil also tried to burden me with despondency and hopelessness from the indifference, ridicule, misunderstanding, and lack of support from my inner circle. It was an all out spiritual attack on my relationship with God and the temptation to blame Him for allowing this severe misfortune. But thank God that I was introduced to Him as a young child, and over the years through my childhood, adolescence, and adulthood, I had come to know Him as my personal Friend and Savior. In fact, He had become my BFF (Best friend forever) - there was no one I could trust more and no one who could love me more even when I constantly fell short on my end of the relationship. I'm talking about Someone who loves me with all of my foibles and deficiencies. This is agape love and God is the sole Source of this authentic love. The special thing about this acknowledgment is that I had a viable and authentic relationship with God throughout my childhood, adolescence and adulthood that allowed me to experience these attributes of God firsthand. Throughout my life when I was teased or misunderstood about any idiosyncrasy of mine, He was the Strong Tower I could run to and be safe (Proverbs 18:10). When I felt disappointed by a friend or betrayed by someone close, I fell into the comforting arms of my heavenly Daddy - the Comforter extraordinaire (2 Corinthians 1-3,4). This reminds me of a song by the songbird CeCe Winans - "Comforter". Better still, when I found myself on the ground getting back up from my blunders, I could attest to the song by Donnie McClurkin "We Fall Down But We Get Up". In this song, we're reminded that a saint is just a sinner who falls down, but repeatedly gets up. What a beautiful song! This message of hope is powerful. So, because of my relationship with God, I knew that when I couldn't trace His hand, I could always trust His heart as the song "Trust His Heart" by Babbie Mason (another songbird) says (the lyrics to this song are amazing). As Satan tried to instigate spiritual disharmony by assailing my spirit with multiple questions directed against God concerning my near-death experience

SILENT TOO LONG

and the lack of optimal and consistent support from my three secular strongholds (my inner circle; my church; and the law enforcement), I responded that my Stronghold par excellence - God - was supporting me and sustaining me through it all and never left my side. I went on to gently remind him that this impregnable and invincible Divine Stronghold was the same One that stood between that tumultuous storm and me that morning and calmed it in an instant when I cried to Him so that I could tell my story today. As I dialogued with him mentally that day, I invited him to follow me emotionally and mentally to Golgotha where I proposed to paint a picture for him of the world's greatest love story. I could only imagine the devil being hesitant and speechless in that moment as he didn't anticipate this curveball that I was throwing his way. This is when I took this conversation by its reins and changed its trajectory as my interrogation now began. The questions the devil hurled at me that attempted to discredit God's love for me, motivated me to redirect some questions back at him and demand answers. I asked him to explain Calvary since he claimed that God is selfish, apathetic, indifferent, and unmerciful towards humankind. When looking at Calvary, these assertions lose their weight and credibility and appear absurd. My next question, while he appeared stumped with the first question, was for him to explain to me the response of humankind for such a selfless and loving sacrifice paid for their sins by their Creator Who was faultless. I kept the questions coming while I addressed Christ's lonely and unappreciated life of sacrifice that culminated in being put to death by the very ones He came to save - mankind. I then took things to a more personal level and asked where he (the devil) was when I was almost killed by a carjacker driving recklessly behind me who was fleeing from the cops on BW (Baltimore-Washington) Parkway in Maryland on an icy winter's night. On this particular night (many years prior to this current incident), I was coming home from a full day in the hospital during my residency training when my car suddenly hydroplaned after being hit by this carjacker and I found myself up in the air momentarily before landing in the median of the highway. My question for the devil was where was he because I knew where God was. He was right there beside me with His protective hedge surrounding me throughout this entire fiasco. Before being hit, I recall being less than a car length from the car in front of me and adjacent to another car in the lane beside me on the left with the shoulder on my right covered in ice and snow at the time from the inclement weather. With nowhere to safely go on this two lane highway as I saw this convoy of speeding vehicles approaching me from behind, I whispered up a prayer because I was completely trapped in. I later discovered that this convoy of vehicles included twelve cop cars chasing a carjacker on this two lane highway very late that winter night with blind ice spots on the road from the weather condition at the time. Looking in my rearview mirror that night, I saw multiple blue flashing lights speeding at top speed towards me with another vehicle directly behind me speeding at a distance ahead of them. Apparently this was the carjacker who was gaining ground on me by now and all I could do was pray as I anticipated a multiple car collision with the assumed inevitable fatalities .... but God! This wasn't an accident that I should have survived with nearly twelve cop cars chasing this carjacker on an icy winter night on this two lane highway at top speed with two other cars involved - one in front of me and the other on the side of me leaving me nowhere to go, but to be sandwiched in after the anticipated impact. However, after being hit, all that I can recall is my car being safely settled in the median with me inside of it unscathed. The median just happened to be a wide strip of land that had a slope, and I landed at the bottom of this slope. Hallelujah!!! I got out of my car and saw the twelve cop cars with dogs barking as they looked down the slope of this median in the center of BW Parkway where my car had landed. They asked me if I was okay and I reassured them that I was and then proceeded to call a friend. The carjacker had been severely injured yet he still attempted to run in the woods that were along the shoulder on the right of this highway in efforts to flee from the scene. His car was completely totaled. The other two cars that were in front of me and on my left in the express lane on the highway just before the accident were mysteriously nowhere to be found after the accident. It was definitely an aha moment for me as I realized that I had just witnessed a miracle with these two cars not even being involved in this accident because God had airlifted my car from this "highway sandwich" I was trapped in at the time of this chase, and safely landed my vehicle in the median of this highway. I remember just closing my eyes when I realized I was about to be hit and essentially "letting go and letting God have His way" (another inspiring song by the artist DeWayne Woods - "Let Go Let God"). I don't know what it is about me and closing my eyes in life-threatening moments (as in my domestic hiccup), but I still can't believe the complete trust I had in Him as I whispered up my one-second "go-to" desperate prayer - "Lord, help me". Not once did I try to manipulate things by turning my wheel, applying brakes, redirecting my vehicle to the icy shoulder on the right, or anything other than completely trusting God. This was definitely an astonishing and captivating supernatural moment I will never forget and will always evoke strong emotions. This was yet another fiendish attempt by the devil to end my life and eradicate God's calling on my life, but God blocked it! Checkmate infernal one. God was intentional about preserving me for His divine agenda concerning my life which is currently being expressed in my ministry that is even now blooming.

My next inquiry for the devil focused on lonely times I faced in adolescence with peer pressure and disappointment from so-called friends. During these times, I pointed out that God had always been there for me as a positive Force and Source of comfort. But, on the contrary, I found him (the devil) to be nothing but a thorn in my side that deposited negativity. At this point in my discussion with the devil, things were crystal clear who my advocate was - God. And God proved to be more than just an advocate for me when He became my substitute at calvary sacrificing His life in order to pay the penalty for my sins - my Savior. So, facing all of these different levels of attack in this storm - the personal, professional, financial, social and spiritual - I realized that exercising the last weapon yet to be elaborated on was of utmost importance. This weapon is love, which the Bible refers to as the greatest of the three (1 Corinthians 13:13) as mentioned previously.

Love is liberating and empowering in action and, as mentioned earlier, it is the defining character trait of a Christian. Particularly in the face of adversity and mistreatment, this is when love shines its brightest. Love is not noteworthy or impressive when it is solely shown to those who love us because Luke 6:32 points out that even sinners love those who love them. So, this is no monumental milestone for a christian. However, when love extends to our enemies, this demonstrates agape love - God's love. It is this kind of love that distinguishes a true christian - it is the litmus test for christianity. In this journey, it became evident as things progressed that God was sharpening our agape love skills and fine tuning us for the kingdom with this trial. We were learning to be naturally forgiving of others even when the wrong was repeatedly done with no remorse. And this became more complex and uncomfortable when we realized that we were dealing with mistreatment and wrong from individuals we considered to be our village. Yet, in spite of this, we knew that as christians, we were still committed to love them unconditionally as God loves us.

As I consider this ongoing trial that has yet to be resolved even to date, I can honestly say that because of the unconditional love God has instilled in us, the girls and I harbor no bitterness or hostility towards those responsible for the unnecessary strife we have suffered. We are committed to loving them just the same. In fact, they probably are totally oblivious to the true extent of our discernment and awareness of what is really going on in this saga because the girls and I don't wear any feelings of resentment, anger, or emotional pain. Quite frankly, it's because we don't harbor those feelings. God's love has completely eclipsed any negative feelings or thoughts, and we have made a concerted effort to focus only on those things that are edifying as Philippians 4:8 encourages us to do. Negative feelings cannot coexist with a forgiving and unconditionally loving spirit that God admonishes us to have toward those who wrong us as Matthew 5:44 - 48 points out. We have made it our business to be forgiving and unconditionally loving as God is with us and to leave all of the unresolved and unreconciled issues in His hands trusting Him to rectify things in His perfect timing. My prayer is that they would acknowledge their wrong and reconcile with God and us before God does it for them, which will be the less desirable way. We have already committed to forgiving everyone that we know to be involved. Therefore, no one has to be fearful of not being forgiven and treated harshly because we are waiting with open arms to love and embrace those involved just as Christ does for us every time we fall short in our relationship with Him. As a result, we anticipate that chains, cycles, and curses will be broken as captives are liberated, and lives are forever transformed into His likeness. Hallelujah!

In the meantime, look for the sequel because God will undoubtedly turn this story around for His glory. It's all about Him. And prayerfully, the power consequently unleashed will initiate a mighty move of God, along with a contagious shift in the atmosphere of love, peace, joy, forgiveness, and reconciliation as hearts open the door to God's permanent residence. From the beginning of this fiasco and even still today, my prayer has been and will always be that those involved in this deception will join me on the platform God has established for us as they transparently tell the entire story of what really happened. Spiritual breakthrough will emerge as a result and lives will be empowered, transformed, and delivered from the brutal bondage of Satan's controlling grip and walk in the joy of their freedom in Christ. The unconditional love and forgiveness God allowed the girls and me to show to those who were closest to us that caused us so much suffering, hurt, loss, and grief, will be a compelling and persuasive testimony of what God's love can do to transform and save lives. We're claiming spiritual deliverance for those involved in this scandal as chains are broken, demonic influences destroyed, and lives saved through the powerful tools of forgiveness, unconditional love, and transparency - the mission of *Three Women and A Vision* - the nonprofit organization that God gave me the vision for during this arduous journey. The three women are my daughters and me and we seek to uplift, strengthen and empower all those who are broken, underprivileged, and despondent from whatever circumstances they are in as God transforms lives through the ministry of this nonprofit. As social service advocates for the despondent, broken, downtrodden, aggrieved, and underprivileged individuals, as well as those struggling with addictions, we plan to make a powerful impact in our society. God has allowed me to collaborate with colleagues and friends as we partner in this effort to help others. And, as we (*Three Women and A Vision*) do this, the most compelling tool will be our powerful testimony revealing that my daughters and I suffered many of the same injustices through this journey of tribulations and trials that God allowed us to experience in our faith bootcamp, yet He saw us through them all. We will be able to empathize and share with others that God makes all the difference and that what was meant to destroy us, God turned around in our favor to work out for our good. Now, as overcomers, we can be authentic advocates because we've traversed some of the same paths of those we desire to help.

Ultimately, I see the girls and me, along with the major culprits in this scandal, on stage sharing this mind blowing testimony because the anecdotes shared so far in this book are just *the tip of the iceberg* of all the amazing and unspeakable things that occurred along this journey. Although we were devoid of all earthly strongholds (our village; the church; and the legal system) at some of our lowest times, we three women weathered this vicious and destructive storm because we were anchored in our stronghold extraordinaire - El Elyon! This fact cannot be underscored enough. God makes all the difference. He is all that you need. No matter how broken you are and no matter what your circumstances, let this fact resonate. In spite of our shattered family structure, our trauma from an attempted homicide, our betrayal from some of those in our village, our identity theft causing us financial paralysis, and the wrongful judgment by some of our church family who were clueless concerning our trial, we survived by the grace of God and came through victoriously. Through all of our pain, brokenness, and hopelessness, we cried out to God and trusted that He would help us and He did. We didn't lose our minds! He kept us mentally, emotionally, spiritually, and physically. God is truly our Stronghold par excellence. Let Him be yours and don't forget to look for the sequel as this scandal is still ongoing and this chapter has not yet closed.

Lastly, I'll share that I delayed publishing this book because I wanted everything to be resolved first. I felt the book would be more helpful and inspiring when everything was over. Therefore, I delayed publishing this book until now when it was written over five years ago. I planned to just add the additional chapter on reconciliation when appropriate and then publish it. I believed that this would allow all those involved to share their testimonies and also allow the girls and me to share the amazing and powerful testimony of our deliverance by our sole Source of help - God - despite our seemingly insurmountable adversity. At any rate, that was not God's plan and things are still unresolved even after waiting until now to publish this book. But, I'm encouraged not to be dismayed because I realize now that this book was meant to be the catalyst to effect change and initiate the long-awaited breakthrough with those involved even though I've been "silent too long". So, be on the lookout for the mighty move of God that's going on even now through this testimony as you await the sequel because restoration has already begun and its completion is even now knocking at the door. God has made it clear that the comeback from this severe attack and set back will be overflowing.